Austrian Studies Today

Günter Bischof,
Ferdinand Karlhofer (Eds.)

CONTEMPORARY AUSTRIAN STUDIES | VOLUME 25

UNO PRESS

innsbruck university press

Printed in the United States of America

Book design by Allison Reu and Alex Dimeff

Published in the United States by
University of New Orleans Press
ISBN: 9781608011278

UNO PRESS

Published and distributed in Europe
by Innsbruck University Press
ISBN: 9783902936691

iup

Publication of this volume has been made possible through generous grants from the the Federal Ministry for Europe, Integration and Foreign Affairs in Vienna through the Austrian Cultural Forum in New York, as well as the Federal Ministry of Economics, Science and Research through the Austrian Academic Exchange Service (ÖAAD). The Austrian Marshall Plan Anniversary Foundation in Vienna has been very generous in supporting Center Austria: The Austrian Marshall Plan Center for European Studies at the University of New Orleans and its publications series. The College of Liberal Arts at the University of New Orleans, as well as the Vice Rectorate for Research and the International Relations Office of the University of Innsbruck provided additional financial support.

Contemporary Austrian Studies

Sponsored by the University of New Orleans and Universität Innsbruck

Table of Contents

Austrian Studies Today

Introduction

Günter Bischof

"Austrian Studies" is not a very well defined field, because "Austria" as a territorial entity has changed its size dramatically over the course of a thousand-plus year history. Historians grapple with these changing concepts of "Austria" over time. Among many reinventions, there are the ancient "Duchy of Austria" – quasi core-Austria along the Danube; the medieval/early modern "Austria" of the Habsburg territories of the "House Austria"; the "Austrian Empire," proclaimed in 1806 after the collapse of the Holy Roman Empire; "Cisleithanian" Austria of the Dual Monarchy (1867–1918); and there is the state of "Austria," formed in 1918 after the collapse of the Habsburg Monarchy—today's "Austria." In other words, the territorial expanse of Austria has changed greatly over time and needs to be seen in its respective historical contexts.[1] Cultural, literary, music, architecture and art historians relate the extraordinary artistic production that has come out of the historical territories that have been Austria as "Austrian Studies." Also, the lack of a well-developed Austrian identity until the second half of the twentieth century has not furthered the genesis of a field called "Austrian Studies" that is well-defined.[2]

The attempt to circumscribe what constitutes "Austrian Studies" might be helped by looking to the better-defined field of "American Studies." When the United States developed into the world's most powerful state after World War II, it also made the study of America (interdisciplinary "American Studies") into an imperial project signaling the widespread American presence in the world. The American Studies Association defines American Studies as "a locus of interdisciplinary inquiry into the national

1 There is considerable historical literature grappling with this problem, see Martin Scheutz and Arno Strohmeyer, eds., *Was heißt "österreichische" Geschichte? Probleme, Perspektiven und Räume der Neutzeitforschung* (Innsbruck: StudienVerlag, 2008); Richard G. Plaschka, Gerald Stourzh, and Jan Paul Niederkorn, eds., *Was heißt Österreich? Inhalt und Umfang des Österreichbegriffes vom 10. Jahrhundert bis heute* (Archiv für österreichische Geschichte, vol. 136) (Vienna: VÖAW, 1995).

2 Among many books on Austrian identity, see Ernst Bruckmüller, *The Austrian Nation: Cultural Consciousness and Socio-Political Processes*, transl. Lowell A Bangerter (Riverside, CA: Ariadne, 2003); Peter Thaler, *The Ambivalence of Identity: The Austrian Experience of Nation-Building in a Modern Society* (Lafayette, IN: Purdue University Press, 2000); Lutz Musner, Gotthart Wunberg, and Eva Cescutti, eds., *Gestörte Identitäten: Ein Zwischenbilanz der Zweiten Republik* (Innsbruck: StudienVerlag, 2002).

cultures of the United States."[3] The *interdisciplinarity* certainly is part and parcel of "Austrian Studies" too.

But what would be the "national cultures" of Austria? In the late Habsburg Monarchy, it may have been German Studies, Jewish Studies, Hungarian Studies, Czech Studies, etc. But "inquiry into its national cultures"? Given Austrian identity today, in Austria it would mean "German Studies," yet Austrian Studies self-consciously sees itself separate from German Studies. Whereas most political camps saw the First Austrian Republic as a "German state," the Second Republic reconstituted after the disasters of World War II quickly distanced itself from Hitler's Third Reich and saw itself as the "Austrian nation," far removed from Germany. In 1955, the conclusion of the State Treaty and the Austrian Parliament's declaration of "permanent neutrality" came to enhance Austrian identity.[4] As Harold James has reminded us, identity is indeed a notoriously "fuzzy" concept.[5] In the Anglo-American academic tradition and practice, Austrian Studies is usually subsumed within German Studies.[6] But how much does "Austrian Studies" cover today's minorities and their cultures? Slovenian and Croatian Studies? Romani Studies? Today, one might also have to add the study of Muslims in Austria. Are these separate fields, or along the definition of "American Studies," part and parcel of Austrian Studies? Going back to the interwar period (1918–1938), most Austrians may have considered the study of Habsburg Austria and its glorious past as defining "Austrian Studies." That changed after World War II when, as a result of the wartime experiences, Austrians began to distance themselves from all things related to Germany.

In the initial mission statement of *Contemporary Austrian Studies*, this serial publication was conceived of as pursuing the study of "contemporary Austria in its Central European context" (after 1918) from an interdisciplinary perspective, but particularly from the purview of the

3 See the White Paper "What Is American Studies," in *American Studies Association*, April 2015 <http://www.theasa.net/images/uploads/What_is_American_Studies.pdf> (18 Feb. 2016).

4 Dieter A. Binder and Ernst Bruckmüller, *Essay über Österreich: Grundfragen von Identität und Geschichte 1918–2000* (Vienna: Verlag für Geschichte und Politik, 2005), 101–110; Gerald Stourzh, "Erschütterung und Konsolidierung des Österreichbewusstseins – vom Zusammenbruch der Monarchie zur Zweiten Republik," in *Was heißt Österreich?*, ed. Plaschka/Stourzh/Niederkorn, 289–311.

5 Harold James in a special issue on German Identity in the *German Studies Review*, see "Reflections on German Identity: Introduction," *German Studies Review* (Winter 1992): 1.

6 See the mission statement of the German Studies Association in the U.S.: "The German Studies Association is the multi- and interdisciplinary association of scholars in German, Austrian, and Swiss history, literature, culture studies, political science, and economics." *German Studies Association* <https://www.thegsa.org/index.html> (19 Feb. 2016).

social sciences (history, political science, economics). We chose not to include the humanities then (literature, music, fine arts); in the 1980s and early 1990s, there was a flowering of studies on *fin de siècle* Vienna (at the time not yet called "cultural studies"). Part of the CAS mission as defined in the preface to the first volume has been to assert "Austrian Studies" in the global arena as a field separate from "German Studies," "devoted to a self-confident assertion and promotion of a separate Austrian identity vis-à-vis Germany," adding that "after the unification of Germany, such a program seems even more important."[7] With the unification of Germany in 1990, some Austrians became anxious about new dangers of "Anschluss."[8] That anxiety has dissipated since Austria has been moving more closely to Germany, especially economically, within the European Union. Moreover, Germans have been the largest immigrant group in Austria lately.

* * *

This volume celebrates the study of Austria in the twentieth century by historians, political scientists and social scientists produced in the previous 24 volumes of *Contemporary Austrian Studies*. One contributor from each of the previous volumes has been asked to update the state of scholarship in the field addressed in the respective volume. The title *Austrian Studies Today*, then, attempts to reflect the state of the art of historical and social science related studies of Austria over the past century, without claiming to be comprehensive. The volume thus covers many important themes of Austrian contemporary history and politics following the collapse of the Habsburg Monarchy in 1918: from World War I and its legacies, to the rise of authoritarian regimes in the 1930s and 1940s, to the reconstruction of republican Austria after World War II, the years of Grand Coalition governments and the Kreisky era, all the way to Austria joining the European Union in 1995 and its impact on Austria's international status and domestic politics. It does not claim to include the cultural studies approach to Austria.

The essays presented here are not in any chronological order, but reflect the respective volumes as they were published. Next to essays with a more traditional biographical ("great man") approach to distinct political eras and their contexts (Dollfuss/Schuschnigg, Kreisky, Vranitzky, Schüssel), there are topical essays on specific socio-cultural phenomena (religion, sexuality,

7 Günter Bischof and Anton Pelinka, Introduction, in *Austria in the New Europe*, ed. idem (Contemporary Austrian Studies, vol. 1 [hereinafter cited as CAS 1]) (New Brunswick, NJ: Transaction, 1993), 2–3.
8 Oliver Rathkolb, Georg Schmidt, and Gernot Heiss, eds., Österreich und Deutschlands Grösse: Ein schlampiges Verhältnis (Salzburg: Otto Müller Verlag, 1990).

memory & identity, biographical studies), political/economic topics (political culture, social partnership, voting behavior), regional studies (federalism) as well as Austria's position in the international arena (foreign policy, neutrality, Americanization, Austria and the European Union). An introductory essay on representations of Austria in the museum (a hotly debated topic in Austria today) and a concluding essay on the state of the art of "*fin de siècle* Vienna studies" complete the Volume. Some of these later topics would fit the purview of a more culturally oriented approach to "Austrian Studies." Since CAS has claimed since its first volume that it would try to cover "the social and economic sciences" since 1918, we have never pretended to adhere to a more broad-minded inclusive approach to "Austrian Studies" that includes cultural studies. In fact, the highly fashionable field of "cultural studies" has only come into existence and full fruition after the genesis of this journal/yearbook.

Both in Volume 10 and Volume 20 of *Contemporary Austrian Studies* we have provided rough statistics of what fields and which time periods we have been covering in our pages.[9] Given that this is our 25th anniversary volume, we thought this was a good point in time to update this statistical analysis.

	History									Political Science			Reviews					Total
	Political/Social	Diplomatic/International	Economic	Intellectual	Memory	Culture/Identity	Religion	Gender	Intelligence	Domestic/Political Culture	Foreign Relations/International	European Union	Roundtables/Forums	Review Essays	Book Reviews	Annual Review	Introductions	
CAS 1-10																		
1918-1938	2			1				1										
1938-1945	5					2		3	2		2							
1945-1983	5	11	11			1		3	3	11								
1984-2000		2	2		1					17	9	6	3	12	51	10	21	190
CAS 11-20																		
pre-1914	2	1		1				1										
1918-1938	11	5	8	2	2	2		1										
1938-1945	8		1										3					
1945-1983	8	8	4	1	2	6	3	7		3			2					
1984-2000		2								3								
2000-2010	2	2	4	2	1		5	2		10	3	2	3	15	51	10	9	218
CAS 21-24																		
pre-1914	3				2	1				1								
1914-1918					2	1												
1918-1938	5																	
1938-1945	2				1	2												
1945-1989	3	2			4	2				1								
1990-2015		2			2	1				5	2	4	2		30	4	3	87

9 CAS 10, 3; CAS 20, 9.

CAS has always closely followed what related journals in Austrian and Central European Studies have been doing. Next to reading these quarterly or annual publications, one way of surveying their work is to look at their mission statements and see what they claim to be doing. What follows is a quick survey of these Austrian Studies organizations and their journals (in their own words):

The Austrian Studies Association (ASA, formerly the Modern Austrian Literature and Culture Association, MALCA) continues traditions started in 1961, as the only North American association devoted to scholarship on all aspects of Austrian, Austro-Hungarian, and Habsburg territory cultural life and history from the eighteenth century until today. These changes acknowledge what has long been the Association's identity: an interdisciplinary organization that welcomes all eras and disciplines of Austrian studies at its conferences and in its journal, including scholarship on the cultures of Austria's earlier political forms (the Holy Roman Empire, the Austrian Empire, and Austria-Hungary) and scholarship that acknowledges this region's historical multiethnic, multilingual, and transcultural identities and their legacies in the present.[10] ASA publishes *The Journal of Austrian Studies,* an interdisciplinary quarterly that publishes scholarly articles on all aspects of the history and culture of Austria, Austro-Hungary, and the Habsburg territory. The journal highlights scholarly work that draws on innovative methodologies and new ways of viewing Austrian history and culture. Although the journal was renamed in 2012 to reflect the increasing scope and diversity of its scholarship, it has a long lineage dating back over a half century as *Modern Austrian Literature* and, prior to that, *The Journal of the International Arthur Schnitzler Research Association.*[11]

Founded in 1965 by R. John Rath, the *Austrian History Yearbook* remains the only English-language journal devoted to the history of the territories in Central Europe that were formerly under Habsburg rule and now comprise the modern states of Austria, the Czech Republic, Slovakia, Hungary, Slovenia, Croatia, Bosnia-Herzegovina and parts of Italy, Poland, Ukraine, Romania and Serbia. The collapse of the Soviet Union and the search for stability in the former East bloc has brought an upsurge of interest in the region's Habsburg heritage.[12]

10 *Austrian Studies Association* <http://www.austrian-studies.org/associationinfo.html/>(18 Feb. 2016).

11 *The Journal of Austrian Studies* <http://www.journal-of-austrian-studies.org/> (18 Feb. 2016).

12 "Austrian History Yearbook," in *University of Minnesota* <http://cas.umn.edu/publications/AHY.HTML> (18 Feb. 2016).

Austrian Studies, published through the Modern Humanities Research Association in the United Kingdom, is a yearbook devoted to reflecting sustained interest in the distinctive cultural traditions of the Habsburg Empire, the Austrian Republics and the period of German annexation. Its focus is Austrian culture from 1750 to the present. Contributions are also encouraged on the culture of former areas of the Habsburg Empire and on the work of people of Austrian origin living abroad.[13] It has been published since 1992 and will have its 25th volume published in 2017.

The Central European History Society publishes the *Journal of Central European History*, which publishes articles, review articles, book reviews, and conference reports dealing with the history of German-speaking Central Europe, using all approaches to history and dealing with all historical periods.[14] In fact, while AHY and the JCEH concentrate on history, the JAS and AS are more literature and cultural studies oriented.

Of course, since the publication of the first volume of CAS in 1993, the Internet with its many digital platforms has added enormously to discourses of "Austrian Studies." In fact, Habsburg was the first H-Net platform and has provided a steady stream of information, data, and book reviews related to Habsburg Studies.[15] H-German[16] and H-SozKult[17] are similar digital platforms that also cover Austrian issues. There are many more with more specific content. All of them have added vibrancy and immediacy to the study of Austria. In other words, Austrian Studies in the Anglo-American world today has many platforms for scholars to engage in—it can be seen as a field separate from "German Studies."

* * *

Contemporary Austrian Studies and its relative longevity is a testimony to the extraordinary university partnership between the Universities of

13 Modern Humanities Research Association <http://www.mhra.org.uk/Publications/Journals/Austrian.html> (18 Feb. 2016).

14 Central European History Society <http://www.centraleuropeanhistory.org/central-european-history> (18 Feb. 2016).

15 "HABSBURG is devoted to the history and culture of the former Habsburg lands and their peoples from 1500 to the present. Founded in October 1991, it was the first Internet discussion group dedicated to an historical theme," see "HABSBURG—A H-Net Discussion Network," in *H-Net: Humanities & Social Sciences Online* <https://networks.h-net.org/habsburg> (18 Feb. 2016).

16 "H-German is a daily Internet discussion forum focused on scholarly topics in German history. There are no chronological limits," see "H-German," in *H-Net: Humanities & Social Sciences Online* <https://networks.h-net.org/node/35008/pages/39070/what-h-german> (18 Feb. 2016).

17 *H-SozKult – Kommunikation und Fachinformation für* die Geschichtswissenschaften <http://www.hsozkult.de/> (18 Feb. 2016).

New Orleans (UNO) and Innsbruck, often called a "model transatlantic university partnership." In 1976, Gordon "Nick" Mueller initiated the UNO International Summer School in Innsbruck, which in its 41st year is still going strong and has brought some 10,000 young Americans to study in Central Europe for six weeks in the summer. Formerly the University of Florida, now the University of Georgia, have been principal partners of the UNO Summer School. In 1983, the rectors/chancellors of the two universities signed a partnership treaty. This treaty has led to regular student and faculty exchanges, academic conferences and symposia, publication series, among them since 1993 *Contemporary Austrian Studies*. In 1997, CenterAustria was founded at UNO, now called "Center Austria: The Austrian Marshall Plan Center for European Studies," to coordinate all these activities between the two universities (apart from the UNO Summer School). Center Austria has brought dozens of Innsbruck faculty and over 1,000 students to spend a semester or longer at UNO. Probably few university partnerships exist with more intense cross-fertilization across the Atlantic.

Contemporary Austrian Studies has become the flagship publication series of this university partnership. On the UNO side, Günter Bischof has served as editor from the beginning, (even before the initiation of CenterAustria), to this day. The Department of Political Science of the University of Innsbruck has been the institutional partner on the Austrian side. Anton Pelinka (1993–2008), Fritz Plasser (2009–2012), and Ferdinand Karlhofer (2013–2016) have served as editors on the Innsbruck side. While the first 17 volumes were published by Transaction Publishers of New Brunswick, NJ, volumes 18 to 25 have been published by UNO Press in conjunction with *innsbruck* university press. We are grateful to Irving Louis Horowitz and Mary Curtis at Transaction for their cooperation, and to Bill Lavender, Abram Himelstein, and G.K. Darby for theirs at UNO Press. At *innsbruck* university press, Birgit Holzner has been instrumental in making this unique publishing project work, where UNO Press cover the North American/global market, while *i*up takes care of the European market. Gordon "Nick" Mueller, Robert L. Dupont, Susan Krantz, and Kevin Graves served as Executive Editors on the UNO side, Erich Thöni, Franz Mathis, Klaus Frantz, and Christina Antenhofer/Gerhard Rampl on the Innsbruck side. UNO chancellors/presidents Gregory O'Brien, Timothy Ryan, Peter Fos, and Innsbruck *Rektors*, especially Manfried Gantner, Karlheiz Töchterle, and Tilman Märk, have been very supportive as well in keeping the project alive. Dozens of editorial board members and hundreds of contributors have helped fill CAS with content and have kept it going (see the table above).

A number of people have been instrumental in making the completion of this anniversary volume possible. The Innsbruck co-editor Ferdinand Karlhofer—with former editors Anton Pelinka and Fritz Plasser—have helped conceptualize the volume. We are sincerely thankful to all the contributing authors for submitting their essays on time, responding favorably to all editing suggestions from our production team. Vera Kropf, the 2015/16 Austrian Ministry of Science, Research and Economy Research Dissertation Fellow at UNO and PhD student in film studies at the Vienna Academy of Fine Arts, has done a superb job in tracking every manuscript through both the copy-editing and proof-reading processes and towards final publication. She has also corrected footnotes and humored authors towards completion of their manuscripts. Daniel McCoy and Moritz Hackl helped with putting the statistics and the table together for this introduction. Hans Petschar, the 2015/16 Marshall Plan Chair at UNO, was very helpful with the illustration of the volume. We thank him and his team at the Picture Archives and Graphics Department of the Austrian National Library, as well as the Austria Press Agency, for providing us with pictures. Ella Pfalzgraff at UNO Press put her customary enthusiasm into the final round of copy-editing the individual manuscripts; Alex Dimeff skillfully type-set the final pdf of the volume and designed the cover. G.K. Darby and Abram Himelstein, the leadership team at UNO Press, have been hugely supportive to spirit this volume through to final publication. At Center Austria: The Austrian Marshall Plan Center for European Studies, Gertraud Griessner and Moritz Hackl conducted the Center's daily business with superb efficiency thereby allowing the co-editor to work on managing the completion of this volume. Without the dedicated teams at Center Austria and UNO Press there would be no CAS series. At *innsbruck* university press, Birgit Holzner was helpful with the production of the cover and the final round of proof-reading and then producing the volume for the European market. Cooperating with her has become a big bonus in the production of these volumes.

As always, we are happy in acknowledging our sponsors and supporters for making the publication of the *Contemporary Austrian Studies* series possible at all—not a small matter in the age of diminishing budgets for higher education in general and the social sciences and humanities in particular. At the University of Innsbruck, our thanks go to Matthias Schennach of the International Relations Office, as well as Barbara Tasser, Gerhard Rampl, Christina Antenhofer, Marion Wieser, and Eva-Maria Fink in the New Orleans Office. At UNO Kevin Graves, the Interim Dean of the College of Liberal Arts, and Robert Dupont, the chair of the History

Department, have given us greens lights and much support whenever needed. We are also grateful to *Rektor* Tilmann Märk and Provost John Nicklow, for their support of the entire UNO/University of Innsbruck partnership agenda, including its publication series. At the Austrian Cultural Forum in New York, Christine Moser and Christian Ebner have supported our work as has their "boss" Ambassador Wolfgang Waldner, the chief of the Cultural Division of the Federal Ministry for Europe, Integration and Foreign Affairs in Vienna (now the Austrian ambassador to the United States). In the Federal Ministry of Science, Research and Economy and its student exchange office Österreichischer Austauschdienst (ÖAD), we are grateful to Barbara Weitgruber, Christoph Ramoser, Felix Wilcek, Josef Leidenfrost and Florian Gerhardus. Markus Schweiger, the executive secretary, Ambassador Wolfgang Petritsch, the chairman of the board, as well as the board members of the Austrian Marshall Plan Foundation have been our strongest supporters for more than a decade now. It is a great pleasure and privilege to work with them all and acknowledge their unwavering support of Center Austria: The Austrian Marshall Plan Center of European Studies at UNO and its activities and publications.

New Orleans, February 2016

Essays

Heldenplatz. A prominent place for the Austrian House of History.
Vienna, Ledermann 1958
Credit: Austrian National Library

Volume 1: Günter Bischof/Anton Pelinka. *Austria in the New Europe*. New Brunswick, NJ: Transaction 1993

In the Museum of Austrian History

Charles Maier

The House of Austrian History, Haus der Geschichte Österreich (Austria shorn of a genitive) and officially translated as the House of History Austria, is the name for the new museum that has been long in the planning and has now received official legislative approval, with its completion envisioned in time for the centennial of the First Austrian Republic in 2018. Fair warning: This author has been one of the non-Austrian members of the preliminary planning committee, assiduously chaired by Professor Oliver Rathkolb, and the reflections that follow are informed by my participation in that effort. Needless to say, they are personal ones. The project is a daunting challenge, but has the potential to make a significant cultural contribution certainly to the city and, one can hope, to Austria's awareness of its national past and to its role in Europe more broadly.

The public now knows where the House of Austrian History will be—in the Neue Burg, the nineteenth-century addition to the Hofburg—more a grandiose representational palace than a functional structure—distinguished by its concave white-columned façade facing on the monumental Heldenplatz. The interior physical space provides a challenging site, although its location is absolutely central, across the Ring from the *Kunsthistorisches* and *Naturhistorisches* museums. The Museum will also be "related" to the neighboring Äußeres Burgtor, the commemorative neoclassical temple that fronts on the *Ringstraße* and houses monuments to the soldiers who perished in World War I fighting for the Habsburg Empire, the soldiers fighting in World War II for the *Grossdeutsches Reich*, and to the combatants in the Resistance against that same Reich. This coexistence—easier for the dead than it was for the living—suggests that there is more than one Austrian history. Which history or combinations of history ought to be in the House of History Austria?

This is hardly just an issue for Austria's museum: every national historical museum must integrate many different experiences—personal, class, ethnic, gendered, and regional—into one encompassing set of exhibits. In an era that celebrates the diversity of identities, it is not easy to integrate them into unitary sites labeled history museums. But the particular challenges for Austria's House of History merit reflection. Much of the country's modernity has required "overcoming," and even—if not until late in the day—"working through" a troubled past. To present the formative role of that past will require a delicate curatorial hand.

These issues of content have hardly been broached, except with the formulae that historical debate and controversy will be incorporated in the enterprise. Long and intermittent discussions about a historical project have preceded the current initiative, and the common premise has necessarily been that constructing an Austrian Republic represents a significant achievement. President Karl Renner hoped in 1946 to establish a "Museum of the First and Second Republic" that would present its leaders "with no consideration for their party affiliation or other contentious and uncontentious factors."[1] Probably the "*aufklärerischer*" highpoint of such plans was reached in the mid-1900s with the idea for a "House of Tolerance" that would integrate assertions of Jewish contributions, EU anti-racist concerns, and the history of the Austrian resistance. Stefan Karner offered a plan in 1998. Hannes Androsch and Chancellor Wolfgang Schüssel suggested creating a national museum based on the Belvedere's 50th anniversary exhibit that commemorated the State Treaty of 2005. An earlier director of Vienna's large Military History Museum proposed that his institution should house a general history museum.

Discussions in Rathkolb's committee have focused on such basic issues of what space the museum might claim, and what relationship the new museum would have with other institutes—museums in the *Bundesländer*, the Jewish museum; perhaps the large Museum of Technology, which has also featured notable historical exhibits. A plus for the museum is its location below the Austrian National Library, which will remain the official institution that incorporates the museum. The existing collection of musical instruments must be downsized. The ethnographic museum at the *Ringstraße* end of the Neue Hofburg must likewise be compressed or moved. The issue of adequate storage facilities also came up, since it was envisaged that collection material would certainly overflow what might be exhibited at any one point. Artifacts now slumbering in many Austrian attics and basements, it is expected, will be offered to the history museum.

1 The history of the museum project as well as the current proposals that have now been given the legislative go-ahead are contained in the extensive report: "Umsetzungsstrategie für das Haus der Geschichte Österreich: Ideen und Entwürfe des Internationalen Wissenschaftlichen Beirates (Stand 4. September 2015)" and its English version: "Implementation Strategy for House of History Austria: Ideas and Outlines of the International Scholarly Advisory Board."

The questions of spatial arrangements seemed particularly challenging. The galleries must curve along a broad corridor that runs the length of the concave façade overlooking the Heldenplatz. The overall feel is one of pompous late imperial—although such milieus are compatible with other major museums, notably the Louvre. From the central entrance staircase, two ramps ascend slowly from the façade to reach the exhibition galleries on the main floor. The architecture suggests a central memory. Along the windowed façade, at the halfway point on the curved linking corridor, the visitor can step on to the terrace where Hitler greeted his jubilant new subjects on March 15, 1938.

Despite the splendid *mis-en-scène*, visual and architectural elements may thus remain in some tension with the declared mission of the institution. The current project has built upon a 2008 study that the Chancellor's Office and various ministries entrusted to a professional museum advisory service. Their report, prepared by the *Arbeitsgemeinschaft* Claudia Hass and *Lordeurop* (Lord Cultural Resources) included a polling of the potential audience for a house of Austrian history. As might be expected, a majority of respondents endorsed the concept positively or at least partially, especially among the cohorts with higher education (and living closer to Vienna). But the question posed as to the purpose of the museum suggested that respondents thought it should focus on contemporary history (years not defined) and contribute to Austrian identity. Few wanted the museum to serve as a discussion center for controversies, but perhaps respondents had little sense of how a museum might serve as the site for debate. Few wanted the museum to be a memory site, in the sense of a Holocaust memorial. My sense is that the expectation was that a house of history should let visitors emerge with a coherent view of the national society they were living in. Is this a demand for history-lite? How do such expectations mesh with the mission that museum directors feel? Do they allow the grappling with either a contentious past or an increasingly contentious European present? Even leaving aside the polarized struggles of the 1930s and the National Socialist era, can the museum contribute to the increasingly contested issues swirling issues of identity today?

Historians know that the argument of a narrative, implicit or explicit, depends in large part upon where the story starts. The issue of content was broached in an early lively exchange regarding where the history to be presented should begin. Early discussion in the consulting committee took for granted that the new museum was never intended to include the history of the Habsburg Empire as a whole. It was to be a pedagogic project that would cover the period from the mid-nineteenth century on, with special emphasis on the history of the Austrian Republics (and to an undetermined extent the interim years of annexation within the Third Reich). Rathkolb defended the idea that even as a museum designed to focus on the Republican experience (and consequently about German Austria), the exhibits must cover the modernizing trends in the last decades of Cisleithania, whether the music and art, scientific and academic culture, or the mass movements—Socialist, Luegerite-"populist"—of the era. The "classical modern" was a major legacy for the new Republic. The museum, it was agreed, must certainly show the ethnic diversity that transformed the Danubian-based geographical unit into a vibrant culture. It must also do justice to the passionate political commitments that culminated in the late 1920s, through the conflicts of 1934, and into the Anschluss era. The prose of the report (as of the earlier project that had been prepared by the professional consultants, Haas and *Lordeurop*) suggested that all these conflicts of the past should be presented as openly as they had been expressed at the time: "At the institution's core is the examination of the social, political, economic and cultural lifeworlds in Austria from the middle of the nineteenth century to the present. It will encourage historical examination. The House of History Austria will be an active and open forum for discussion of historical questions and present-day topics." How all this will be achieved must still to be discussed and determined. History has winners and losers, but history museums, so agreement seemed to reign (so far!), must provide a rerun of the game and not just a final score.

Formidable problems lie ahead, not insurmountable but not easy either. Some pertain to the way any history museum functions; others to the divisions within Austria. Let me discuss the former first. There is an implicit foundational question: what should a history museum do? At one level, the experts who assembled to consider the museum's plans considered the issue in terms of pedagogy: the museum is intended to host discussions, to link up with *Länder* and local museums, to involve ongoing groups of amateurs as an animated center for consideration of timely issues as well as those of the past. In this spirit, the name of "History Forum" was weighed, although finally rejected as excessively diffusing the purpose of the institution. But there remains another central issue. Does a history museum provide diverse scenes and episodes, or thematic collections, from the past to permit a tourism through time, as an anthropological museum allows a visit to diverse cultural habitats? Or does it impose, or at least suggest, a developmental sequence for a certain political or cultural unit? And if so, which sequence?

I am not a museum curator. I followed the debates in the late 1980s that attended Chancellor Kohl's proposal to construct a new German historical museum history in West Berlin, before the dissolution of the GDR in1989/90 made East Germany's historical museum in the baroque Zeughaus available for a reunited country. I have visited with interest diverse history museums in Austria and Germany: the museum at the Buchenwald concentration site, the Jewish museums in Berlin and Vienna (and the Holocaust Museum in Washington, as well as the memorial in Berlin), military museums in Vienna, Budapest, Brussels, London, and Paris. I was one of the U.S. members on the large original committee summoned to endorse a museum for the history of the European Union, which was later disbanded, to be replaced by a group (in which I played no role) to propose a more modest enterprise. I have had misgivings about some of the exhibits, including the much-praised Jewish museum in Berlin, which I felt imposed a teleology of the Holocaust architecturally on the story of German Jews. (In this respect, the more modest Jewish museum in Vienna appeals to me far more.) Of course, these are all intensely personal reactions, stemming from the prejudices that I bring as much as the exhibit itself. That will be likely true for every museum visitor. No one enters a museum as *tabula rasa*. But the curators have a great advantage. Like the narrator of a text, they get to impose a privileged order on historical material.

Historians bring their professional biases to planning committees. They tend to communicate through articles and books, and they organize their knowledge most frequently in narrative form. This is logical enough; historians generally like causal stories in which later events follow causally, or are believed to follow causally, from earlier ones. The temptation for the historian is to plan the museum as a sort of text, enlivened by artifacts. In any case, the historians' past encompasses some sort of coherence and even cohesion. But history museums can overload their exhibits with printed details. Their exhibits can depend too heavily on long texts. They are not alone. Art museums increasingly succumb to interpretive texts that patronizingly explain to presumably less tutored visitors how they should understand the visual object.

Control of the narrative was a major theme in 1986/87, when Chancellor Helmut Kohl summoned a committee of advisers drawn from academia and some of the press to plan a German historical museum in West Berlin. The West German intellectual world was still preoccupied by the *Historikerstreit* that had brewed in the preceding years. On the one side—associated with such historians as Michael Stürmer, Andreas Hillgruber, and Joachim Fest, biographer of Hitler and editor of the *Frankfurter*

Allgemeine Zeitung, not to mention the most problematic exponent Ernst Nolte—were the historians who argued that the museum must present a German national narrative. Generally they associated this with a linear presentation of exhibits in chronological order, touching down on familiar epochal divisions: Reformation, early modern Germany, unification and the First World War, Weimar and the Third Reich. (A special museum devoted to the history of the Federal Republic was already planned for Bonn and has since been constructed.) The project aroused criticism from "critical" historians, such as Hans Mommsen and Hans-Ulrich Wehler, and social thinkers such as Jürgen Habermas, who feared it would serve those who wanted to insist that what was past was past. By containing an established version of German history within a linear structure, a neo-nationalist narrative would recover legitimacy. The museum's reification would cease to call citizens to debate with the past and would deprive the museum of any pedagogical challenge. The past would pass away, and history would be merely history.[2]

Not all in the critical camp agreed: Jürgen Kocka defended the project as a member of the committee. He believed it compatible with an "Enlightenment" set of critical values. But each of the linear displays had to be complemented by a *Vertiefungsraum*, which imposed questions on the material. Indeed much of the debate took place in terms of proposed architectural projects. The historian of antiquity, Christian Meier, wanted the museum to radiate outward from a central space devoted to the Holocaust (which in effect was how the Jewish Museum was shortly to be designed). The planned museum faced a particular challenge as to what counted as German: without seeming to harbor a "revanchist" agenda, how could one include the German-speaking communities that, until 1945, had lived in Eastern Europe, whether on the Baltic, in Pomerania, or in the Sudetenland? One plan was to have an elevated walkway cross a great floor map that showed where Germans had lived through the centuries. As it turned out, all these museological reveries came to naught when the East German historical museum fell into Bonn's possession. Its exhibits, although they were to be purged of their Marxist interpretation, followed a conventional narrative structure and have formed the basic linear construct of today's permanent collection in Johann Nering and Andreas Schlüter's elegant baroque Zeughaus, which has been augmented by the austere modernist addition designed by I. M. Pei. For the nearby Neue Wache,

2 For an account of the debate, see Charles S. Maier, *The Unmasterable Past: History, Holocaust, and German National Identity* (Cambridge, MA: Harvard University Press, 1988), 121–159.

Berlin's equivalent of the Äußere Burgtor, Chancellor Kohl installed a Käthe Kollwitz Pietà to offset the fact that millions of the dead soldiers honored fought for what recent generations regret as dubious causes.

Historians want to control the narrative; museum curators prize the artifact: Franz Ferdinand's automobile and bloodstained uniform are a centerpiece at the Vienna military history museum. Exhibit designers wager that the object will "grab" visitors, and can transcend the different ages and educational levels with which visitors arrive. But what the visitor does with the sensational artifact remains obscure. Does viewing the Archduke Franz Ferdinand's tunic help the visitor understand the causes and impact of World War I? Yes, if, but only if, appropriately contextualized. Film clips can produce emotional impacts: among the exhibits on the centennial of World War I that I visited two years ago, the newsreels of the German army marching through a silent Brussels (part of the exhibit in the Brussels military museum) made a powerful impression and forced the question as to why they were there. Certainly not to overcome the mortal threat from Belgium. Does the visual material help the visitor get a sense of the past as formative on the present? Perhaps. I often wonder what a busload of ten-year olds take away from these exhibits, besides a welcome chance to escape the classroom. Today, interactivity is the mantra for exhibits, and it is also conjured up as a strategy for the Austrian museum description. Perhaps, as in the Washington Holocaust Museum, the House of History Austria assigns the visitor a supposed avatar whose life experience is followed through the course of the exhibits. Probably virtual-reality headsets will soon be available. And yet experiential immediacy should be only be one goal of what is sought; without analytical clarity, the history museum serves as a theme park.

Austria's museum faces some similar challenges to the German museum. Its designers have not fretted over the geographical scope of the museum—it is about the history of the area that became the First and Second Republic, not the earlier empire—but a fundamental challenge, in terms of history, will be to decide how to deal with Austria's National Socialist and Austro-fascist past. To date, the problems are confronted with generalities about using the exhibits to provoke debate. Does Arthur Seyss-Inquart get a place after Victor Adler? Kurt Waldheim and Jörg Haider along with Franz Vranitzky?

From the viewpoint of the historian, the greater problem will be how to present the contentious issues of Austrian history. How does one do justice to Red and Black when it comes to the 1930s? How will the role of Austrians in the Third Reich be presented? How will the voices of

Karl Kraus, and later Thomas Bernhard, be presented? Similar problems arise for all countries. In the U.S., the search for a historical synthesis is often presented with a rather unreflective melancholy, as if there really might be such a synthesis. But our national histories are really exercises in counterpoint, not nineteenth century harmonic cadences, and a national history museum must suggest the plurality of ideas that were held.

Twenty years ago, Austria was still engaged in the great memory wars that Nazism and fascism had left in the West, and Communism had left in the East. The memory wars of West and East were different: the painful legacies that afflicted post-Communist societies involved less that of widespread enlistment in the Stalinist project than collaboration with the secret police. But the memories of fascism in Austria involved less secrecy (though denunciation was rampant in all fascist societies) than acquiescence and enthusiasm. In 1995 Anton Pelinka could still write, "The Austrian Republic is built on a one-sided and therefore distorted view of historical reality." He attributed these to "opportunist foreign-policy considerations."[3] In his scathing verdict, Austrians competed to deny responsibility. "History was recounted, written, recorded, and made by the political camps" by which he meant the SPÖ and ÖVP.

To have built a history museum on that earlier conspiracy of silence would have been a travesty. At best it would have been a museum of lies and dedicated to what Pelinka saw as the founding falsehood: Austria as victim of Nazism. Yet in 1995, Pelinka also testified to signs of change both among professional historians and the political class, primarily because of generational transition. He conceded, moreover, that the mendacity of the founding moments in 1945 and 1955 had been necessary: "If the standards used by critical historiography and social sciences to evaluate Kurt Waldheim in 1986 had determined or even only codetermined thinking in 1945, who could have survived? Too many were compromised, too many were anti-Semitic. The political culture of the postwar period was characterized by the fact that instead of a political market a permanent power monopoly was created. Instead of the willingness to take risks, securing and stabilizing existing conditions became Austria's goal....Now in the post-postwar period it has become possible to be outspoken and to take risks. Exposing lies is the order of the day....[Still] just as no society can do without taboos, the post-postwar period will not be an exception."

Pelinka himself urged a historical museum in 1995. Now that it is coming into existence, its greatest challenge may be less to present the open

3 The citations from Anton Pelinka come from his essay, "Taboos and Self-Deception: The Second Republic's Reconstruction of History," in CAS 5, 95–102.

conflicts and violence of the interwar period, or even the initial enthusiasm for the Anschluss than to convey the silences of the postwar years. The 1930s saw a state that embodied a frozen civil war, finally dissolving into the Third Reich. The Second Republic saw a state that had to conceal the currents of opinion that had led to that disastrous outcome. Doing justice to the ambiguities of national rebuilding in the first half century of the Second Republic will be at least as great a challenge as openly presenting the conflicting political commitments of the First Republic. Can a museum overcome the concealment of the past on which so much of the consociationalism and *Proporz* of the postwar republic rested?

Of course politics is not the only dimension for the future museum. Visitors, including the tourists visiting the capital, will not visit in order to don a historical hair shirt. Social life, material misery and progress, the record of brilliant cultural innovation, popular activities—whether sports, local festivals, the Opera Ball, the vigorous loyalties of Austria's regions (stressed by committee member Heidemarie Uhl)—all deserve to be exhibited and reflected on. Austria's branding—whether by the Trapp family singers or the Prater Ferris wheel in *The Third Man*—should find a place. The café should serve folkloric foods. Still, at the core of the last century of Austrian national existence as a unique national framework within a larger Europe, is the story of political institutions—those that ripped the First Republic out of the larger empire, that perched it uneasily between the ideological and geopolitical European and even global camps, that re-established the country in 1955 and allowed it autonomy. And likewise at the center of this history is a series of political choices—disastrous ones as in 1938, and hopeful and mature ones, as in the vote for Europe in 1995.

I suggested at the beginning that there was more than one Austrian history. Starting with the twentieth century, Austria has had several narratives, and to attempt to synthesize or simplify them prematurely would distort reality. Nonetheless, international society imposes some common responsibilities, and the Austrian state is a formal component of international society. As a nation, it has had to fill out the legal shell that treaties from 1919, 1955, 1995 and even 2009 have endowed it with. The role of the Austrian museum should be not only to celebrate that transformation, but to further it. Ultimately a history museum has to posit a protagonist—a people in time. According to the 2008 inquiry, most Austrians thought that the history museum would be a good idea. Just recently, so did the large majority of the Parliament. They were not refusing to acknowledge a history; perhaps they wanted to learn about that history. For Robert Musil a century ago, Kakania had a negative identity—an identity created by what it was not. What the House of History Austria may demonstrate is that the negative identity of Austria—its survival between the powerful ideological currents and large states of Europe—allowed a national community to function, sometimes maddeningly provincial and parsimonious and self-absorbed, but mature enough to scrutinize as well as celebrate its achievement.

National Election Campaign 1975.
"Heave-ho! Towards a good future."
Photographic template for the SPÖ election poster. Bruno Kreisky with members of the Young Generation. The official poster was finally realized without Bruno Kreisky.
Margret Wenzel Jelinek 1975
Credit: Margret Wenzel Jelinek, Austrian National Library

Volume 2: Günter Bischof/Anton Pelinka. *The Kreisky Era in Austria*. New Brunswick, NJ: Transaction 1994

A New Historiography of Bruno Kreisky

Oliver Rathkolb

It is most likely a fact that the biographical examination of a politician who shaped an era reflects the transformation of historical perceptions in a society. Bruno Kreisky played an early formative role in the Republic of Austria as Under Secretary of State for Foreign Affairs, from 1953 to 1958, and as Foreign Minister from 1959 to 1966. He subsequently initiated a series of reforms in Austrian society as Chancellor, from 1970 to 1983, and dominated the international position of the small neutral republic.

In his contribution to the Contemporary Austria Studies[1] in 1994, Peter Malina therefore stated that a biographical examination of Kreisky serves as a mirror of Austrian society, i.e. of one's own perception of history.

This reflection increases the difficulty of examining such a dominant and fascinating figure both critically and reflexively, as does the fact that he himself played the dominant role in shaping both his early biographies[2] and, thanks to three volumes of memoirs (one of which was released posthumously), the later historical work on his impact on politics and society. These factors play a role in the critical examination. Former colleagues also primarily shaped analysis and contents of the first overview publications. At this point, I would like to point out, for example, the 1983 collection of articles on *Die Ära Kreisky. Schwerpunkte der österreichischen Außenpolitik*[3] (*The Era Kreisky: Focal Points of Austrian Foreign Policy*), and a biographical essay by his former press aide Wolfgang Petritsch[4] from the year 2000.

1 Peter Malina, "'Imagination is more than Knowledge.' Bruno Kreisky's Life as Biography," in CAS 2, 205–221.
2 Viktor Reimann, *Bruno Kreisky. Das Porträt eines Staatsmannes* (Vienna: Molden, 1972); Paul Lendvai and Karl Heinz Ritschel, *Kreisky. Porträt eines Staatsmannes* (Düsseldorf: Econ, 1974).
3 Erich Bielka, Peter Jankowitsch, and Hans Thalberg, eds., *Die Ära Kreisky. Schwerpunkte der österreichischen Außenpolitik* (Vienna: Europa Verlag, 1983).
4 Wolfgang Petritsch, *Bruno Kreisky. Ein biographischer Essay* (Vienna: Kremayr&Scheriau, 2000).

The political scientist H. Pierre Secher[5] in the United States produced the first critical biographical study in the 1990s, with special emphasis on Kreisky's Jewish roots and influences. In doing so, he attempted to take a fresh look at Kreisky, who never concealed his Jewish heritage, but clearly subordinated it to the mainstream of Austrian society's victim's doctrine after 1945, stressing the perception of the Austrians being primarily a subject of Nazi German aggression. Secher used both primary and secondary sources, as well as interviews with the then-retired chancellor, whom he saw as an "alienated Jew"[6] very much formed by the anti-Semitic environment after his return from exile in Sweden in 1950. He too referred to the continuity of his Anti-Zionist views from the 1920s, which were not changed by his repression during the Nazi regime, and his exile in Sweden, perceptions that erupted in aggressive attacks against Israeli politicians and policies vis-à-vis the Palestinians.

The US historian Jacqueline Vansant[7] raised a similar argument, though a bit clearer, in her examination of Kreisky's construction of an Austrian identity in his autobiographical texts. Kreisky was one of the creators of Austria's small state—with a strong international focus—identity. In 1965, the federal government, following a failed project intended to create an Austrian identity, accepted Foreign Minister Kreisky's proposed course of action to use the Declaration of Neutrality and Parliament's Neutrality Law of October 26, 1955, as the focal point of their differentiation from Germany.[8] The federal government had originally intended to use research projects to prove in the 1960s that Austrians were, per capita, superior resistance fighters to Germans. In spite of the high degree of individual resistance, which was only occasionally militarily significant, it could not be attributed to either one of the large political parties—ÖVP (Austrian People's Party) and SPÖ (Social Democratic Party of Austria). The project was therefore historicized, and Kreisky's neutrality suggestion was adopted. One could also argue that neutrality served as the central counterpoint to the Moscow Declaration of November 1, 1943 and therefore the second central staple of the Austrian victim doctrine and identity reflection.

---

5 H. Pierre Secher, *Bruno Kreisky: Chancellor of Austria* (Pittsburgh: Dorrance Pub Co, 1994).

6 Ibid., 202.

7 Jacqueline Vansant, "Challenging Austria's Victim Status: National Socialism and Austrian Personal Narratives," *The German Quarterly* 67, no. 1 (Winter 1994): 38–57.

8 Maria Wirth, *Christian Broda. Eine politische Biographie* (Göttingen: V&R unipress, 2011).

After 2000, first critical editions of Kreisky's memoirs were published, for instance by Matthew Paul Berg, Jill Lewis and Oliver Rathkolb.[9] This development saw an intensification of efforts to critically analyze the context of the memoirs' content via annotations and commentaries. Internationally, this publication was discussed positively in the *New York Times Book Review*,[10] along with a biographical study of Jörg Haider by Christa Zöchling, as the two counterpoints of Austrian politics in the Second Republic—Kreisky in the 1970s and Haider in the 1980s—were juxtaposed. Even in 2000, the international relevance of Kreisky was still evident in a positive way, despite his frequently highly negative comments regarding Israeli politics in regards to Palestine and his excessive attacks on Simon Wiesenthal and his politics of the past regarding National Socialism and the Holocaust. Nonetheless, an international acceptance is evident in these cases. The same cannot be said of Jörg Haider's rightwing populist politics.

Subsequently, the occasion of Kreisky's 100th birthday saw the release of a series of publications. Among them, Wolfgang Petritsch's biography[11] deserves particular attention—a comprehensive examination of the extent of secondary literature, Kreisky's memoirs, and Petritsch's personal recollections of his time in Kreisky's cabinet (1977–1983) as press spokesman, combined with a series of critical approaches, in particular regarding the examination of National Socialism, which saw Kreisky defend the Austrian mainstream and follow a new approach with partly heavy international criticism of Israel.

Kreisky's foreign policy produced what might be the densest mix of scholarly literature, first among them the study by Elisabeth Röhrlich,[12] which grew out of a dissertation that presented a critical view of the foreign policy process with new analyses of primary sources, along with new facets and contours. It pays particular attention to Kreisky's time as foreign minister in the 1960s and to individual periods in the 1970s and is based on very thorough research of Austrian and international archival material. The foreign policy aspect is further illuminated by recollections of former Austrian diplomats and historians in various countries, gathered in

9 Matthew Paul Berg, Jill Lewis, and Oliver Rathkolb, eds., *The Struggle for a Democratic Austria. Bruno Kreisky on Peace and Social Justice* (New York/Oxford: Berghahn, 2000).

10 J. S. Marcus, "Shadows on the Danube," *The New York Review of Books* 48, no. 6 (12 April 2001): 60–65.

11 Wolfgang Petritsch, *Bruno Kreisky. Die Biografie* (St. Pölten: Residenz, 2010).

12 Elisabeth Röhrlich, *Kreiskys Außenpolitik. Zwischen österreichischer Identität und internationalem Programm* (= Zeitgeschichte im Kontext, Vol. 2) (Göttingen: V&R unipress, 2009).

the form of country examinations in the collection "Von außen gesehen"[13] ("Viewed from the Outside").

Nonetheless, an international academic study on the international impact of his Middle East policies is still lacking. The author of this article tried to develop a pattern of future comparative research by focusing on Willy Brandt, Bruno Kreisky and Olof Palme as "policy entrepreneurs" towards the Middle East: "With regards to Middle East policy, it was Kreisky and Brandt who prepared the ground for the PLO to be accepted as a partner in the peace talks by making skillful use of the media, by supplying relevant actors with an endless stream of information and by exploiting personal contacts."[14]

A negative polemic example concerning the Middle East issue is the chapter on Kreisky in a book of Joshua Muravchik, a neoconservative author and fellow of the Foreign Policy Institute of the Johns Hopkins University School for Advanced International Studies[15]. As in previous studies, Kreisky's frequent confrontations with Simon Wiesenthal over former Nazi members and Nazi War criminals dominate the interpretation of his Middle Eastern policies, excluding thereby the real issues and presenting Kreisky as a disloyal pro-Nazi and anti-Semitic Socialist. No question Kreisky's reaction against Wiesenthal was extreme and disproportionate, particularly when he indirectly accused Wiesenthal of collaboration with the Nazi regime in 1975. Bruno Kreisky did not want to be played off as a Jew against that stable bloc in society that advocated the reintegration of ex-members of the NSDAP and of former soldiers of the Wehrmacht in the 1970s. It was quite simply a gut reaction. As early as 1970, Wiesenthal attacked Kreisky because of four former NSDAP members in his minority government (one of them even being an SS member, who soon resigned). At the time of the ÖVP-led grand coalition, Wiesenthal had abstained from criticizing members of the government for their former NSDAP membership, as is evidenced by the case of Reinhard Kamitz, an important ÖVP finance minister whose Nazi past was an open secret. This political bias of Wiesenthal was just briefly mentioned by Tom

13 "Von außen gesehen," in *Mit anderen Augen gesehen. Internationale Perzeptionen Österreich 1955–1990*, ed. Oliver Rathkolb, Otto M. Maschke, and Stefan August Lütgenau (Vienna/Cologne/Weimar: Böhlau, 2002).

14 Oliver Rathkolb, "Brandt, Kreisky and Palme as Policy Entrepreneurs: Social Democratic Networks in Europe's Policy Towards the Middle East," in *Transnational Networks in Regional Integration. Governing Europe 1945–83*, ed. Wolfram Kaiser, Brigitte Leucht, and Michael Gehler (Hampshire: Palgrave Macmillan, 2010), 169.

15 Joshua Muravchik, *Making David Into Goliath: How the World Turned Against Israel* (New York: Encounter Books, 2014), 85–98.

Segev in his compassionate biography on Wiesenthal,[16] although he sees Wiesenthal's extended backing of the former UN Secretary General and Austrian President Kurt Waldheim as another tragic chapter in his life. He interprets it as explicable and excuses Waldheim's lies about his real wartime knowledge and record.

An important point that became evident as of the mid-1990s was the media aspect of Kreisky: initially accentuated by Gabriele Bernadette Waldner in a communication studies analysis of the "media star Kreisky"[17] and, in his centennial year, continued through a film and tome by Helene Maimann, which included evaluations by former colleagues, international politicians, and journalists. It illustrates a few new aspects of Kreisky's political longevity and tension points.[18]

The first general survey of the Kreisky years also comes from a former colleague of Kreisky's, Heinz Fischer, who penned the book "The Kreisky Years 1967–1983."[19] Political science analyses by Gerhard Schmid[20] and a collection of several recollections of the Kreisky era[21] also fit into this survey category. The author of this article published an overview article on the Kreisky years in English and has several chapters on Kreisky's political activities in his book on the Paradoxical Republic of Austria, 1945–2005.[22]

The political scientist Christian Dickinger delivered a further critical component.[23] It did not address the conflict surrounding his politics of the past, but instead revolved around the tension between Kreisky and his potential successor Hannes Androsch, which Dickinger examined. Androsch was a highly gifted economic expert and politician as Austrian minister of finance from 1970 to 1981, and as vice chancellor from 1976 to 1981. When the Austrian Federal President Franz Jonas died on 24 April 1974, Androsch and others tried to push Kreisky into the Presidency—away from

16 Tom Segev, *Simon Wiesenthal: The Life and Legends* (New York: Schocken, 2012).

17 Gabriele Bernadette Waldner, "Bruno Kreisky, Medienstar: Zur Bedeutung von Kalkül und Intuition in der politischen Kommunikation," Thesis, University of Vienna, 1995.

18 Helene Maimann, ed., *Über Kreisky: Gespräche aus Distanz und Nähe* (Vienna: Falter Verlag, 2011).

19 Heinz Fischer, *Die Kreisky-Jahre 1967-1983* (Vienna: Löcker, 1993).

20 Gerhard Schmid, "Die Ära Kreisky 1970–1983; ihre Auswirkungen auf das politische System Österreichs," PhD. diss., University of Vienna, 1996.

21 Werner Gatty, Gerhard Schmid, Maria Steiner, and Doris Wiesinger, eds., *Die Ära Kreisky. Österreich im Wandel 1970–1983* (Vienna: StudienVerlag, 1997).

22 Oliver Rathkolb, "The Kreisky-Era 1970–1983," in *Austria in the Twentieth Century*, ed. Rolf Steininger, Günter Bischof, and Michael Gehler (New Brunswick, NJ: Transaction, 2002), 263–293; Oliver Rathkolb, *The Paradoxical Republic: Austria 1945–2005* (New York/Cambridge: Berghahn, 2014).

23 Christian Dickinger, *Der Kreisky-Androsch-Konflikt. Versuch einer Annäherung* (Saarbrücken: Südwestdeutscher Verlag für Hochschulschriften, 2010).

real power. Since then, Kreisky began to observe his closest collaborator in government and was subsequently accused of misusing his political power for personal interests. Over the course of several years, Kreisky, in the face of opposition from the Trade Union's President Anton Benya and other strong cabinet members like the Minister of Justice, Christian Broda, and Minister of Research and Science, Hertha Firnberg, tried to force Androsch out of government. Ultimately, Androsch moved on to become governor of the state-owned Creditanstalt-Bankverein, Austria's largest bank. Barbara Liegl and Anton Pelinka deliver a psychological examination of the Kreisky-Androsch conflict.[24] Substantively, it does not offer up any new insights, but it does examine the topic from a psychological vantage point, thereby blurring the political background of the conflict.

Additional new analysis and information on the Kreisky governments can be primarily derived from the outstanding monography on Christian Broda and his impact on deep-reaching judicial and penal reforms in Austria by Maria Wirth[25] and collective studies on Johanna Dohnal, the Undersecretary in the Chancellery, in charge of Women's Affairs.[26] Unfortunately the existing biography[27] on Minister Hertha Firnberg, who completely changed the University systems to develop innovative and flat hierarchies and established a strong research agenda, is rather meagre.

Internationally, Heinz Niederleitner[28] analyzes the media aspect through the first terrorist confrontation on the refusal to let Russian Jews emigrate via Vienna. After 2004, the ÖVP perspective on Kreisky received increased attention, for instance in a study by Robert Kriechbaumer, reconstructing the public debate and conducting interviews with political opponents.[29] Kriechbaumer concludes that despite the profound positive effects on the

---

24 Barbara Liegl and Anton Pelinka, *Chronos und Ödipus. Der Kreisky-Androsch-Konflikt* (Vienna: new academic press, 2004).

25 Wirth, *Christian Broda. Eine politische Biographie.*

26 Erika Thurner and Alexandra Weiss, eds., *Johanna Dohnal – Innensichten österreichischer Frauenpolitiken: Innsbrucker Vorlesungen* (Innsbruck: StudienVerlag, 2008); Maria Mesner and Heidi Niederkofler, eds., *Johanna Dohnal: Ein politisches Lesebuch* (Vienna: Mandelbaum, 2013).

27 Marlen Schachinger, *Hertha Firnberg: Eine Biographie* (Vienna: Mandelbaum, 2009). See as a starter for future academic research Hubert C. Ehalt and Oliver Rathkolb, eds., *Wissens- und Universitätsstadt Wien: Eine Entwicklungsgeschichte seit* 1945 (Vienna: V&R unipress, 2015), 107-194.

28 Heinz Niederleitner, *"Vergatterung der Patrioten": Das Medienereignis Schönau-Krise 1973 – eine kommunikationsgeschichtliche Analyse* (Berlin: VWF, 2002).

29 Robert Kriechbaumer, *Die Ära Kreisky. Österreich 1970–1983 in der historischen Analyse, im Urteil der politischen Kontrahenten und in Karikaturen von Ironimus* (Vienna/Cologne/Weimar: Böhlau, 2006).

modernization of Austrian society, the expansion of the state's influence increased, ultimately resulting in high budget deficits and corruption.

It is important to note that the most primary source-oriented examination of Kreisky comes from the age of dictatorship under the Christian Social Chancellors Dollfuß/Schuschnigg, with Ulrike Felber publishing the prison diaries.[30] The young revolutionary Bruno Kreisky was imprisoned for one and a half years and convicted of high treason. It took until late 2012 for Kreisky to be officially pardoned.

It is interesting that Kreisky's 100th birthday in 2011 not only engendered new literature, but even led to Kreisky becoming an interesting projection surface for the arts. Gerhard Szyszkowitz and the Freie Bühne Wien,[31] as well as the Kosmos Theatre in Vienna, play an important part in this context.[32] The play by Tanja Witzmann represents an attempt to question Kreisky's work and the myth that surrounds him using artistic means and to re-analyze and re-evaluate them for a younger generation[33]—with a decidedly positive overall impression: Kreisky as an autocratic but also democratically-minded politician with leadership qualities and extraordinary personal traits. Future studies will deepen the knowledge of the effects of his governments on society, political culture and economy[34] as well as in the internal arena.

30 Ulrike Felber, ed., *Auch schon eine Vergangenheit. Gefängnistagebuch und Korrespondenzen von Bruno Kreisky* (Vienna: Mandelbaum 2009).

31 Gerhard Szyszkowitz, *Kreisky,* Direktion Freie Bühne Wieden, 2009.

32 Tanja Witzmann, *Die Quadratur des Kreisky,* Kosmos Theater Wien, 2011.

33 Kreisky still is attractive for young academics and researchers, too: See the excellent, but unpublished MA-Thesis of Daniel Aschheim, "Bruno Kreisky's Premature Role as Peacemaker in the Middle East: The Paradoxes of Jewishness, Socialism and the Middle Eastern Conflict," MA-Thesis submitted to the European Forum, Hebrew University of Jerusalem, Dec 2015, and Claudia Aurednik's outstanding analysis of the minutes of Kreisky's first Fact Finding Missions to the Middle East: Claudia Aurednik, "Die 'Fact-Finding Mission to the Middle East' der Sozialistischen Internationale," Thesis, University of Vienna, 2013 (download available: <http://othes.univie.ac.at/26712/1/2013-02-01_0340493.pdf>).

34 Here the forthcoming published version of a Ph.D. thesis by Maximilian Graf on Austria and the GDR (Maximilian Graf, "Österreich und die DDR 1949–1989/90. Beziehungen – Kontakte – Wahrnehmungen," Ph.D. thesis, University of Vienna, 2012) will present new insights on the export of the nationalized industries into the Eastern bloc and highlight the role of Kreisky in the Ostpolitik (compare: Maximilian Graf, "Ein verdrängtes bilaterales Verhältnis: Österreich und die DDR 1949–1989/90," *Zeitgeschichte* 39, no. 2 (2012): 75–97).

Austrian State Treaty. Leopold Figl, Austrian Minister of Foreign Affairs presents the signed Treaty at the Balcony of Belvedere Palace to the people.
Vienna, Erich Lessing, 05 15 1955
Credit: Erich Lessing / Austrian National Library

Volume 3: Günter Bischof/Anton Pelinka. *Austria in the Nineteen Fifties.* New Brunswick, NJ: Transaction 1995

Austria in the 1950s[1]

Peter Ruggenthaler

In Volume 3 of *Contemporary Austrian Studies* (1995), *Austria in the Nineteen Fifties*, the dominant theme was the Austrian State Treaty in the context of international politics. Stephen E. Ambrose dealt with U.S. foreign policy in the 1950s, and Oliver Rathkolb analyzed foreign relations between the United States and Austria in the late 1950s. In the volume's most closely argued article, Michael Gehler raised the question whether the solution that had been found for Austria in 1955 was seen as a template for Germany. He concluded that "there are many reasons to believe that the Kremlin's efforts to ease the political tensions in spring 1955 not only included the wish to overcome the formation of the blocs. [The Soviets] also saw the Austrian solution as a model for a neutral or neutralized Germany" (64). Gehler undergirded this thesis with (Western) analyses of Soviet policies and with statements made by Soviet politicians during the negotiations of the Austrian State Treaty. In the 1990s, historians did not have full access to Soviet archives, even though they were beginning to open.

1998 saw the publication of a new and substantially enlarged edition of Gerald Stourzh's history of the Austrian State Treaty entitled *Um Einheit und Freiheit*. It contained detailed analyses of the Soviets' negotiating position, for which Stourzh was able to draw for the first time on newly available Soviet Foreign Ministry documents, and on reams of documents published by the Woodrow Wilson Center dealing with the power struggle in the Kremlin and the differences in the views held by the Soviet leaders. Stourzh sought to dislodge the view advanced by Gehler and others on the basis of a key document he had discovered. Molotov's position on Germany had been fixed in advance down to the last detail. The remit given to him included proposing a four-power meeting without a previously agreed agenda. This was deemed necessary as the Soviets anticipated an attempt on the part of the Western powers to turn the German question into a key issue; in all probability they would try "to reach some sort of agreement in that respect" in Vienna. In addition, the Soviets maintained that "in regard

1 Translated from German into English by Otmar Binder, Vienna.

to the German question it was obvious that no rapprochement between the Soviet Union and the Western powers was going to possible in the near future." In case the Western powers insisted on convening a four-power conference on the German question, Molotov was to state categorically "that the situation in Europe had been profoundly affected by the ratification of the Paris Treaties and that the time had therefore not yet come when a debate of the German question was going to be fruitful" (478). In short, the signing of the Austrian State Treaty in Vienna's Belvedere Palace on 15 May 1955 had no impact whatsoever on the Soviet readiness to solve the German question.

The documents discovered by Stourzh left Michael Gehler, Rolf Steininger, and others largely unimpressed. They continued to assert that there had been a window of opportunity in the immediate aftermath of the signing of the State Treaty that could have been exploited. In their eyes, the culprit was none other than Konrad Adenauer, who considered the State Treaty to have been "a huge Austrian mess" ("*österreichische Schweinerei*").

The documents on the conclusion of the State Treaty that were released as part of the bilateral Austro-Russian research project "Die Rote Armee in Österreich 1945 bis 1955" ("The Red Army in Austria 1945–1955"), carried out at the Ludwig Boltzmann Institute for Research on Consequences of War, bear out Stourzh's thesis: there is not a single document that makes even a passing reference to the State Treaty being eyed as a model for Germany. Wolfgang Mueller followed in Stourzh's footsteps both in his 2005 PhD dissertation and in his 2011 *Good Example of Peaceful Coexistence*. I myself have used all opportunities I was offered to come out in favor of this assessment (2005, 2007, 2015). It is not only the case that there is no reference of any kind in any of the available Soviet sources to the leadership under Khrushchev ever toying with the idea of using the State Treaty for Austria and the country's neutralization as a template for Germany. The Kremlin's motivation, on the contrary, was entirely different: its aim was to resolve the "German question" in Central Europe in accordance with Moscow's top priority of keeping the "German threat" under control. Indistinguishable from Germans proper in the reading of the Soviet leadership, the Austrians were to live in a state of their own; a state, moreover, which was to be kept permanently separate from Germany. What had to be safeguarded by all means was Austria's ability to continue to exist with its traditional borders intact to prevent the annexation of any of its western parts by Germany, in case the country was partitioned. By 1955 the Soviets had achieved the maximum in the economic exploitation of Austria, especially as far as the country's oil and gas reserves were concerned. Continued economic involvement would have called for high investments, which was the reason why Foreign Trade Minister Anastas Mikoyan vetoed it. This is a point Walter Iber has made quite clear in his excellent PhD thesis: Foreign Minister Molotov was vehemently opposed to the withdrawal of Soviet troops from Austria, presumably on account of his rigid stance toward Yugoslavia. While the frequently cited "wedge" in NATO's flank—Austria and Switzerland formed a solid barrier in the routes connecting Germany and Italy—was a "welcome by-product" (Vojtech Mastny), it was certainly not the main reason why Moscow gave its consent to the State Treaty.

What all this ultimately boils down to is this: historians whose work is based on Soviet sources come to the conclusion that the Austrian Treaty cannot possibly have been intended as a template for Germany, while those who rely exclusively on Western sources and ignore the more recent results of international mainstream research on the Soviet Union predicated on Soviet sources insist that this was nevertheless the case.

CAS Volume 3 does not contain any explicit reference to the 1952 Stalin Note, the significant repercussions of which made themselves felt in the negotiations on the Austrian Treaty. In the meantime, the Stalin Note has given rise to a flood of specialized literature. Here, too, the same two camps are to be found: Gehler, Steininger and others still believe that a unique historical opportunity was left unused in 1952. If the Western powers had entered into talks on Austria, the conclusion of a State Treaty would have been the result. This would have made it easier for Stalin to consent to Germany's neutralization. Soviet documents, however, clearly point another way: Stalin's 1952 "offer" of neutrality for Germany was not genuine; it was in truth a ploy to enable the USSR to seal off the GDR and to facilitate its integration into the Eastern Bloc. The Western powers were to be saddled with the blame for Germany's division. Negotiations about Austria were at this stage out of the question. Creating a precedent by allowing Austria to attain neutral status was in itself a worst-case scenario for Moscow.

Michael Gehler's 2015 *Modellfall für Deutschland?* is a weighty 1,400-page tome. Based on the author's decades of research, it is saturated with meticulously presented knowledge of the sources in Western archives. This is no mean achievement. There is, however, a downside to Gehler's exhaustive treatment of Western sources, in that he ignores almost completely the recent literature on Soviet foreign policy predicated on Russian source material. Even the work of top experts such as Vladislav Zubok and Vladimir Pechatnov is relegated to the status of one footnote each; Mark Kramer appears only in the bibliography—and with only one article—and the same is true of the standard reference work by Aleksandr Fursenko and Tim Naftali. Jochen Laufer, who can look back on more than two decades' work on the German question in Russian archives, has failed to attract Gehler's attention both with his monumental source editions and with his numerous other publications. The list of highly relevant work that is disregarded in *Modellfall für Deutschland?* is far from complete. As in many of his previous publications, Gehler seems inclined to believe that the Soviet Union—even under Stalin—would have been more cooperative if only the "West" had held out its hand. A case in point is his critique of the claims I have been putting forward: findings whose merit has been accepted by scores of other scholars are not even acknowledged in Gehler's discourse. For example, the author raises the question why the Soviet Union came up with the offer of all-German elections in the Second Stalin Note, a fact that would seem to underscore the seriousness of the Soviet offer. It would surely not have been amiss here to mention that, as I have shown, the passage offering free all-German elections was deleted from the draft of the First Note at the last moment. This goes to show that Moscow was being very careful in the formulation of the First Note not to push its luck. How would the West have reacted if the Kremlin had offered free elections for all of Germany right at the start of the Battle of Notes? The West would have had no alternative than to accept Stalin's offer.

Gehler's assertion that "in its policy vis-à-vis Germany, Moscow was late both in 1952 and in 1955" (115) is highly revealing. What does this mean? The claim casts a telling light on Gehler's approach to Soviet policy. Stalin had both maximum and minimum goals. In the celebratory mood sparked by victory in the "Great Patriotic War," Stalin may well have originally conceived the maximum objective of integrating, on a socialist basis, all of Germany into the Soviet sphere of influence. Integrating only the part occupied by the Red Army into the Soviet empire was the minimum goal, where Stalin kept both the precise manner how this was to be done and the name under which this new entity was to be known open until the decision to create a new state, the GDR, was taken. I am by no means the only one to advocate the thesis that Stalin concluded in 1952 that the time was ripe to seal off the GDR and to enforce its closer integration into the Eastern Bloc. This is borne out by all Soviet documents that have come to light. There are no internal Soviet documents capable of supporting a different interpretation. And within this frame of reference, the same is true of 1955; Khrushchev was not late. He had temporarily achieved the goal he had set himself for his foreign policy in 1955 before maneuvering himself into a corner in the Berlin Crisis of 1958.

Gehler's unwillingness to take into account the theses of scholars who fail to give Stalin credit for a more flexible approach reduces the potential of the book under review to a significant extent. It deprives the author of insight into the international research literature based on Soviet sources. While Gehler is of course perfectly free to reject any thesis advanced in that body of literature, his work would gain from an awareness of it. Instead, Gehler opts for a shortcut by joining the chorus of voices asserting that, in view of the paucity of reliable sources, we shall never know Stalin's true intentions. The fact that Stalin did not keep a diary enhances the importance of Molotov's documents, as they shed an indirect light on Stalin's reasoning. While ostensibly in charge of the USSR's foreign policy, Molotov needed Stalin's approval for every one of his moves. The exchange of notes between Molotov on one hand and Stalin, members of the Politburo, and the Foreign Ministry on the other make it possible to discern Stalin's "handwriting."

Having said all this, it would nevertheless be a great mistake to reduce Gehler's monumental work to its assessment of Soviet policies. Having spent decades sifting and analyzing in detail huge archival resources in Western Europe and in the United States, Gehler shows, for instance, that a great number of Western diplomats were in fact convinced that Stalin was acting *bona fide* in 1952. Going far beyond the question whether the Austrian Treaty was meant to serve as a template for Germany, he emphasizes the multitrack nature and the multidimensionality of international diplomacy that enabled the Austrian State Treaty to come into being (1232).

A certain amount of partisanship on the part of historians in support of their most dearly held contentions is not only inevitable; it is even salutary. If there were no hotly contested issues, monumental works such as *Modellfall für Deutschland?* would probably not be forthcoming. And in any case, the differences in opinion are not that great after all. Gehler reaches the following conclusion: "Austria as a template for Germany failed, not so much because of the alleged lack of Soviet will between 1952 and 1955, but because of its categorical rejection by the European West, which was playing for time in order to shore up the integration of the Federal Republic and make it permanent" (1240). For the first part of his conclusion, Gehler is indebted to his disregard for a large body of relevant literature on Soviet foreign policy and to his excessive dependence on analyses of Soviet intentions and goals put forward by Western analysts at the time. The second part, in which Gehler sums up the results of his decades of research, is hardly likely to arouse contradiction.

Austrian historiography has also dealt in detail with the second half of the 1950s in terms of the history of diplomacy. A cooperative project of the Ludwig Boltzmann Institute for Research into the Consequences of War, the Center Austria of the UN, Harvard University and the Russian Academy of Sciences resulted in an edited 1,000-plus-page volume on the 1961 Vienna Summit and the developments leading up to it, which was published in German, Russian and English. The Soviet files that we are aware of today make it quite clear what hopes the Soviet leadership pinned on a neutral Austria after 1955, what fears and anxieties proved well-founded and what measures were taken to make the "bogeyman on the Socialist horizon" that Austria had given rise to disappear again, and to cast the country in the light of a model of peaceful coexistence. An analysis of the post-1955 era reaffirms the conclusion that Moscow never intended to use neutral Austria as a template for Germany.

Select Bibliography

Bischof, Günter. *Austria in the First Cold War, 1945–1955. The Leverage of the Weak*. New York: St. Martin's Press, 1999.

-------, Stefan Karner, and Barbara Stelzl-Marx, eds. *The Vienna Summit and its Importance in International History* (The Harvard Cold War Studies Book Series). Lanham: Lexington, 2014.

Gehler, Michael. *Modellfall für Deutschland? Die Österreichlösung mit Staatsvertrag und Neutralität 1945-1955*. Innsbruck: StudienVerlag, 2015.

Graf, Maximilian. *Österreich und die DDR 1949–1990. Politik und Wirtschaft im Schatten der deutschen Teilung*. Vienna: VÖAW, 2016.

Iber, Walter M. *Die Sowjetische Mineralölverwaltung in Österreich. Zur Vorgeschichte der OMV 1945–1955* (Veröffentlichungen des Ludwig Boltzmann-Instituts für Kriegsfolgen-Forschung, Vol. 15). Innsbruck: StudienVerlag, 2011.

---- and Peter Ruggenthaler, eds. *Stalins Wirtschaftspolitik an der sowjetischen Peripherie: Ein Überblick auf der Basis sowjetischer und osteuropäischer Quellen* (Veröffentlichungen des Ludwig Boltzmann-Instituts für Kriegsfolgen-Forschung, Vol. 19). Innsbruck: StudienVerlag, 2012.

Karner, Stefan, and Barbara Stelzl-Marx, eds. *Die Rote Armee in Österreich: Sowjetische Besatzung 1945–1955*, vol. 2: *Dokumente*. Graz: Oldenbourg, 2005.

Mastny, Vojtech, and Gustav Schmidt, eds. *Konfrontationsmuster des Kalten Krieges 1946 bis 1956: Entstehen und Probleme des Atlantischen Bündnisses bis 1956*, Vol. 3. Munich: Oldenbourg, 2003.

Mueller, Wolfgang. *A Good Example of Peaceful Coexistence? The Soviet Union, Austria and Neutrality, 1955–1991.* Vienna: VÖAW, 2011.

Rauchensteiner, Manfried, ed. *Zwischen den Blöcken. NATO, Warschauer Pakt und Österreich.* Vienna: Böhlau, 2010.

--------------- and Robert Kriechbaumer, eds. *Die Gunst des Augenblicks: Neuere Forschungen zu Staatsvertrag und Neutralität.* Vienna: Böhlau, 2005.

Ruggenthaler, Peter. "On the Significance of Austrian Neutrality for Soviet Foreign Policy under Nikita S. Khrushchev," in *The Vienna Summit*, ed. Bischof et al., 329–348.

------------. *Stalins großer Bluff. Die Geschichte der Stalin-Note in Dokumenten der sowjetischen Führung.* Munich: Oldenbourg, 2007.

------------. *The Concept of Neutrality in Stalin's Foreign Policy, 1945–53* (Harvard Cold War Studies Book Series). Lanham: Lexington, 2015.

------------. "Warum Österreich nicht sowjetisiert wurde: Sowjetische Österreich-Politik 1945 bis 1953/55," in *Die Rote Armee in Österreich*, ed. Karner and Stelzl-Marx, 649–726.

Steininger, Rolf. *Der Staatsvertrag: Österreich im Schatten von deutscher Frage und Kaltem Krieg 1938–1955.* Innsbruck: StudienVerlag, 2005.

Stourzh, Gerald. *Um Einheit und Freiheit: Staatsvertrag, Neutralität und das Ende der Ost-West-Besetzung Österreichs 1945–1955* (Studien zu Politik und Verwaltung, Vol. 62). Graz: Böhlau, 1998.

Suppan, Arnold, Gerald Stourzh, and Wolfgang Mueller, eds. *Der österreichische Staatsvertrag 1955: Internationale Strategie, rechtliche Relevanz, nationale Identität/The Austrian Treaty 1955: International Strategy, Legal Relevance, National Identity* (Archiv für österreichische Geschichte, Vol. 140). Vienna: VÖAW, 2005.

Social Partners. Minister of Social Affairs Rudolf Hundstorfer at the parliamentary enquête "Social Partnership in the 21st Century."
Vienna, Helmut Fohringer, 04 29 2009
Credit: APA PictureDesk

Volume 4: Günter Bischof/Anton Pelinka. *Austro-Corporatism: Past, Present, Future*. New Brunswick, NJ: Transaction 1996

There's Still Life in the Old Dog Yet: Reflections on Change and Continuity of Austro-Corporatism

Ferdinand Karlhofer

As outlined in my contribution to CAS 4, written some twenty years ago, the 1980s and early 1990s had not been the heyday of corporatism, neither in Austria nor elsewhere in Europe. Essential constituents of macro-economic steering were severely challenged, above all central coordination of collective bargaining, which had become the object of the deregulation and flexibilization that came along with the international neoliberal drive. At closer look, though, it soon became apparent that a good deal of the diagnoses and projections that expected an irreversible trend toward disorganized capitalism were plausible but possibly premature. Indeed, in-depth studies concluded that countries with particularly long corporatist traditions (such as Austria) successfully managed to adapt to a rapidly changing environment without abandoning the well-tuned modus operandi. Rather, as a scholar put it, "what happened was that the forces at work changed the output of the system without necessitating systemic change."[1]

Regarding the development in Austria, domestic as well as international impacts have prompted the corporatist actors to readjust organizational structures and pursue a more pronounced member orientation in order to represent associational interests more effectively. The following update deals with change and continuity of the system of social partnership in the period from Austria's entry into the European Union in 1995 up to the present day. Particular attention is given to the integration effects emanating from "going Brussels," the associations' loss of influence in connection with domestic challenges, and finally the recalibration of corporatist structures and politics in most recent years.

1 Oliver Clarke, "Towards a Synthesis of International and Comparative Experiences of Nine Countries," in *International and Comparative Industrial Relations*, ed. Greg J. Bamber and Russell D. Landsbury (London: Routledge, 1993), 273.

Profile and function of Austro-Corporatism

For good reason Austria, ex aequo with Sweden and Norway, ranks first on Siaroff's much-noticed scale for "integrated economies"—integrated economy defined as "a long-term co-operative pattern of shared economic management involving the social partners and existing at various levels such as plant-level management, sectoral wage bargaining, and joint shaping of national policies in competitiveness-related matters (education, social policy, etc.)."[2]

What is exceptional about "Austro-Corporatism"? Basically, it has been the interplay of three features keeping the system stable and ensuring successful outcome: (1) legal framework for shop floor representation of employees, (2) extensive system of chambers for business and labor based on mandatory membership, and (3) interpenetration of associations and political parties. As for the chambers, they have far-reaching competences, including control over the social security system, involvement in social and economic legislation, and participation in public administration. All things considered, it is the—party-governed—chamber system that provides the basis for cooperative relations between the actors involved in socio-economic affairs.

From its establishment in the late 1940s through to the turn of the century, *Sozialpartnerschaft* enjoyed a high reputation in Austria's political system. This was clearly the case until the 1980s, and even, albeit with certain qualifications, in the 1990s, when the chamber system—traditionally the main pillar of social partnership—faced a severe crisis. Social partnership owed its prestige in the public to its role as a reliable and calculable mechanism for interest intermediation, thus decisively contributing to the country's economic development. Although there have always been close ties between chambers respectively trade union federation on the one side and political parties on the other, the functioning of corporatist policy-making remained untouched from government changes. Called into being under the Grand Coalition of ÖVP and SPÖ (1945–66), social partnership had its golden age right under the single party government of the ÖVP (1966–70) followed by the SPÖ (1970–83). Even when the FPÖ, a party critical of corporatism all along, joined a coalition with the SPÖ (1983–86), this had no effect on the interest system.

Party-based political influence on labor market organizations, both on the chambers and on voluntary associations, has been and continues to be

2 Alan Siaroff, "Corporatism in 24 industrial democracies: meaning and measurement," *European Journal of Political Research* 36 (1999): 175–205.

substantial. The three big chambers are governed by political factions on the basis of periodical elections: the ÖVP holds the majority in the Chamber of Commerce and the Chamber of Agriculture, while the SPÖ is dominant in the Chamber of Labor. Alike, the Austrian Federation of Trade Unions (Österreichischer Gewerkschaftsbund, ÖGB) is composed of political factions, with the SPÖ holding the majority and the ÖVP as the strongest minority.

The interpenetration of associations and political parties, as described above, has found its expression in the composition of legislative bodies at a national as well as at a sub-national level. Over decades, regardless of the party composition of government, the ministry of social affairs was held by union leaders. In the late 1970s, more than fifty percent of the members of the National Council were at the same time high-ranking functionaries, including the presidents of the big labor market organizations. Since then, however, the number has decreased significantly (to around ten percent in 2015). The presidents of the three big chambers waived their seats in the late 1990s, the president of the ÖGB followed in 2006.[3]

To sum up, interpenetration of associations and political parties is certainly not an exclusively Austrian property. It is rather the comprehensiveness of the chamber system and the scope and intensity of the parties' influence that have given rise to attribute the Austrian political system with the terms *Kammerstaat* (respectively *Verbändestaat*) and *Parteienstaat*.

EU-integration: privileged involvement in government politics

With Austria becoming a member of the EU, the year 1995 marked a historical turning point for the social partnership. No doubt, when it came to support the government's effort for joining the EU, the labor market parties were well aware of the loss of influence to be expected for corporatist policy-making coming along with entering the common market. Thus, in the run-up to accession, the associations' debates—particularly internally between the elites and their respective ranks and files—predominantly revolved around integration effects on the autonomy of domestic politics. Eventually, the social partners unanimously argued in favor of the entry, the more so as they were in return granted close involvement in the government's EU policy. In April 1994, two months before the referendum, the then-coalition parties SPÖ and ÖVP entered into an agreement concerning the formal

3 Ferdinand Karlhofer, "The Long Shadow of Corporatism: Scope and Limits of Think Tank Activities in Austria," *German Policy Studies* 2 (2006): 359.

incorporation of the social partners into Austria's permanent representation in Brussels.

Up to the present day, the Austrian mission in Brussels is the only representation of an EU member state accommodating both government officials and interest organizations in one house. According to the official website of Austria's Permanent Representation to the EU, "the Permanent Representation of Austria to the European Union is Austria's 'embassy' at the EU so to speak; and it is the largest of all Austrian diplomatic missions worldwide. Some 110 people represent Austria's interests here, including foreign ministry staff and experts from each of the federal ministries, the Liaison Office of the Federal Provinces as well as representatives of the social partners, the Federation of Austrian Industry, the Austrian National Bank, the Association of Municipalities and the Association of Cities and Towns."[4]

From the very beginning, social partners and officials have cooperated closely (surprisingly, even after the political turn of 2000, when domestic corporatist relations severely worsened—see below). Expressed in a weekly jour fixe covering all groups, the Austrian Mission has, in a sense, extended the domestic corporatist pattern to the European level.

Domestic challenge and political turn

While the social partners had come to grips with "going Brussels" quite successfully, it was just the domestic arena where corporatism soon got into dire straits. What happened at the turn of the century came as a surprise since, due to its excellent performance throughout the Second Republic, Austro-Corporatism had always enjoyed a high reputation. Taking this into account, every previous government had explicitly committed itself to the principle of social partnership when taking office.

In sharp contrast, the government change in 2000 marked a spectacular break in the relations between associations and the state. At least in the very first years after the political turn, the climate for negotiations had little in common with the traditional understanding of cooperative relations. When the center-right coalition, composed of ÖVP and FPÖ, took office in February 2000, the "reform of social partnership" was declared a priority objective of the new government. Effectively, its policy

4 "Austria's Permanent Representation to the EU and its tasks," in *Federal Ministry for Europe, Integration and Foreign Affairs* <www.bmeia.gv.at/en/european-foreign-policy/european-policy/austria-in-the-eu/austrias-permanent-representation-to-the-eu/> (15 Feb. 2016).

aimed at reducing the social partners' influence; contrary to the past, their expertise was now less demanded,[5] and repeatedly the chambers' formal right to give an opinion on a draft law was bypassed. In general, legislative action tended to override the principle of parity at the expense of labor, thereby making the latter into a fierce opponent of the government. In 2003, the conflict culminated in a wave of strike activities, the number of which hit a post-war peak by far.

Formally, the coalition pact had held out its plan of "reforming" social partnership with regard to several issues (labor market service, reform of the pension system, gender equality), and thereby explicitly providing for the involvement of the social partners. In practice, however, the tension between government and social partners escalated immediately after the coalition took office, resulting in an abrupt suspension of corporatist practices. There was obviously a tendency to ignore the principle of parity in the treatment of business and labor interests from the very beginning—in a threefold way:

Social bias: Most of the relevant government bills for labor and employment law changes aimed at a cutback of employment rights, thus severely challenging trade union and Chamber of Labor. Most provocative was certainly a passage in the coalition contract which read, "change of all provisions disproportionally burdening business".

Break with the rules of the game: Social policy, of all things, had always been a field where the corporatist actors were used to negotiate a consensual solution, which generally was adopted by government and Parliament. In doing so, they secured social peace and contributed to the economic upturn over half a century. With the new government leaving no scope for negotiation, this function could no longer be performed.

Inclusion and exclusion: The coalition was obviously strongly influenced by business interests. In contrast to previous practices, the business associations—Economic Chamber and Federation of Industry—still enjoyed privileged access to policy makers, while labor organizations increasingly were excluded.

The rationale of social partnership had always been that none of the partners exploits his current position at the cost of his counterpart, but rather seeks to come to a compromise—ideally a win-win situation for all actors involved. Now, by contrast, the trend seemed to go in the direction

5 "Some commentators suggest that such consultation may have been offered by the government for the sole reason of appeasing the social partners, and, in the case of the unions, to prevent further industrial action." (cf. European Industrial Relations Observatory, "2003 Annual Review for Austria," in *EuroFound*, 12 May 2004 <http://www.eurofound.europa.eu/observatories/eurwork/articles/2003-annual-review-for-austria> (3 Feb. 2016).

of redistribution, resulting in a zero-sum game in which only one side wins. As a result, tripartite relations got changed for the worse. During the period of office of the ÖVP-FPÖ coalition (2000–2006), the ÖGB and the Chamber of Labor were no longer accepted as equal partners in the game.

The broader context of change

Aside from the political turn as outlined above, there were other forces at work responsible for the declining demand for corporatist policy advice:

To begin with, in the 1990s, the Austrian chamber system suffered from a severe loss of legitimacy, which, in the end, even challenged its future existence. Basically, the chambers, as organizations with compulsory membership, are—other than free associations—not faced with density problems, since there is no exit option for members. Thus it is not associability, but rather the turnout in elections, that must serve as an indicator for organizational stability. It was the turnout, of all things, that decreased in all chamber elections, most dramatically in the Chamber of Labor which, between 1984 and 1994, registered a decline from 64 to 30 percent. In order to cope with the crisis, all chambers started extensive reform processes which, all things considered, put the focus on the improvement of services for members. By the late 1990s, the crisis was overcome, the members' confidence could be regained, turnout increased again. One consequence, however, was a gradual shift from a "logic of influence" towards a "logic of membership,"[6] eventually making the chambers less reliable actors in terms of cooperative relations.

Further on, given the international drive of continuing decentralization with the center of gravity of industrial relations shifting from the macro- to the meso- and the micro-level, the foundations of corporatist policy-making have eroded thoroughly. Quite obviously, with some time lag, the "winds of change" have been blowing in Austria, too. During the 1990s, social partnership came increasingly under stress. The process of interest concertation and problem solving was more and more complicated through divergent interests and goals of the parties involved. It became clear that Austro-Corporatism, in a historical sense, had already passed its zenith. Notably, the Parity Commission on Prices and Wages, formerly the core of social partnership, does not exist anymore. At least, it has not been convened since 1998.

6 Here following the terminology introduced by Philippe C. Schmitter and Wolfgang Streeck, *The Organization of Business Interests: Studying the Associative Action of Business in Advanced Industrial Societies* (Cologne: Max Planck Institute for the Study of Societies, 1999).

Constitutional entrenchment of chamber system and social partnership

The so-called Austrian Convention, inspired by the European Convention, which had been called into being shortly before in order to elaborate an EU constitution, offered an opportunity to regain terrain for corporatism. Composed of a broad variety of delegates representing political parties, interest groups, federal states, NGOs etc., the convention took up its work in 2003 and delivered its final report in 2005. To cut the matter short: The convention's proposals for constitutional reform, while comprehensive and ambitious, failed miserably. The report presented to the Austrian Parliament was immediately rejected, mainly due to divergent party positions. Most parts of the draft constitution were picked to pieces, and only a small number were assigned to parliamentary committees for further processing. Down to the present day, only a few points of the report have been subject to constitutional politics. The most burning questions, such as civil rights, federal power sharing, electoral reform, and so on, have so far not been considered in constitutional legislation.

Against this background, it is simply astonishing that it was just the corporatist actors who managed to achieve their goals while others were doomed to failure: the social partners—in particular the trade union federation and the chambers of commerce and of labor—were by good reason strongly interested in participating actively in the convention's proceedings. Bearing in mind that the then-center right-wing coalition immediately after its ascension to power had started taking action against corporatist policy-making, the associations were eager to take advantage of the window of opportunity opened up in connection with the Convention. The main goal they pursued was the constitutional entrenchment of the chamber system. With some delay, in 2008, a respective proposal of the convention was adopted by the Austrian Parliament with two-thirds majority; at the same time, the commitment to the social partnership was incorporated as a "state goal." The amendment has far-reaching consequences, since from now on the legal architecture of the corporatist system is protected against changing simple majorities in Parliament.

Recalibration of social partnership with the employers taking the lead

Notwithstanding domestic counter measures, such as entrenching the chamber system in the constitution, the impacts of globalization, which can be noticed in all industrialized countries, have not reprieved Austria either. During the 1990s, social partnership came increasingly under stress, mainly due to the limited scope for action coming along with Europeanization and economic structural change. The capacity of interest concertation and problem solving was more and more complicated through divergent interests and orientations of the actors involved. It became clear that Austro-Corporatism, in a historical sense, had already passed its zenith.

To sum up, the associations, while far from withdrawing from the negotiating system as such, have set out to extend their strategic repertoire. Namely, the employers' attitudes have become ambivalent: while the Economic Chamber has still an interest to cooperate with labor organizations, the Federation of Industry regards itself meanwhile as a lobby organization rather than a social partner.[7]

Corporatism appears to be no longer the one and only way of interest representation; instead, a parallelism of both corporatist and lobbyist practices has become the rule. The trend in Austria seems to confirm the change of paradigm mirrored in recent comparative research on interest groups: the increasing differentiation of societal interest intermediation pluralizes corporatist arrangements, thereby confronting the actors with an increased diversity of preferences, interest representation, collective action, and political strategies.[8] As a matter of fact, there is no longer a continuous pattern of interest intermediation in Austria; rather, the boundaries between "corporatist" and "pluralist" forms of interest representation have become indistinct.[9]

Noteworthy, though, is the fact that the social partners in September 2006 concluded an agreement (Bad Ischl Declaration)[10] about a reform of the *modus operandi* for future cooperation. Since then, the social partners have agreed upon a considerable number of position papers and opinions delivered to the (new) government.[11] Mostly the expertise comes from the Austrian Institute of Economic Research (Wirtschaftsforschungsinstitut—

7 Karlhofer, "The Long Shadow," 371–72.

8 Cf. Thomas von Winter, "Lobbyismus: Forschungsstand und Realität," Paper presented at the conference "Lobbyismus in Deutschland. Fünfte Gewalt – unkontrolliert oder einflussreich?" University of Leipzig, 2003.

9 Emmerich Tálos and Bernhard Kittel, *Gesetzgebung in Österreich: Netzwerke, Akteure und Interaktionen in politischen Entscheidungsprozessen* (Vienna: Wiener Universitätsverlag, 2001), 231.

10 "Deklaration der Österreichischen Sozialpartner," in *Die Sozialpartnerschaft Österreich*, September 2006 <http://www.sozialpartner.at/wp-content/uploads/2015/08/BadIschlDeklaration_2006_09_05.pdf> (4 Feb. 2016).

11 See the overview given in the official website <www.sozialpartner.at>. The record includes, among others, a proposal on "Growth and Full Employment."

WIFO), a non-profit think tank for economic and socio-political advice. For good reason, the WIFO board is chaired by the president of the Federal Economic Chamber, thereby indicating that the former symmetry between the actors involved has, in a sense, become asymmetrical, with the employers taking the lead to the disfavor of labor.

Select Bibliography

Afonso, Alexandre. *Social Concertation in Times of Austerity: European Integration and the Politics of Labour Market Reforms in Austria and Switzerland.* Amsterdam: Amsterdam University Press, 2013.

Karlhofer, Ferdinand. "Filling the Gap? Korporatismus und neue Akteure in der Politikgestaltung," *Österreichische Zeitschrift für Politikwissenschaft* 36, no. 4 (2007), 389–403.

---------. "Österreich. Zwischen Korporatismus und Zivilgesellschaft," in *Verbände und Verbandssysteme in Europa*, ed. Werner Reutter. Opladen: Leske und Budrich, 2012, 521–550.

---------/Emmerich Tálos, eds. *Sozialpartnerschaft – Österreichische und Europäische Perspektiven.* Vienna: LIT Verlag, 2005.

Pernicka, Susanne, and Günter Hefler. "Austrian Corporatism – erosion or resilience?" *Austrian Journal of Political Science* 44 (2015), 40–56.

Tálos, Emmerich. *Sozialpartnerschaft. Ein zentraler Gestaltungsfaktor in der Zweiten Republik.* Innsbruck: StudienVerlag, 2008.

Traxler, Franz. "Austria," in *Handbook of Business Interest Associations, Firm Size and Governance: A Comparative Analytical Approach*, ed. Franz Traxler and Gerhard Huemer. London: Routledge, 2007, 39–63.

Franz Vranitzy in Israel.
In June 1993, Vranitzky was the first Austrian chancellor to visit Israel. Teddy Kollek, mayor of Jerusalem, showing the city to the Austrian Statesman.
Jerusalem, Barbara Gindl, 06 09 1993
Credit: APA PictureDesk

Volume 7: Günter Bischof/Anton Pelinka/Ferdinand Karlhofer. *The Vranitzky Era in Austria*. New Brunswick, NJ: Transaction 1999

An Assessment of the Vranitzky Era Today

Anton Pelinka

In the Austrian debates—among journalists, among social scientists, as well as among historians—there has always been a consensus that there was a Kreisky Era. It is less self-evident to name the years of Austrian politics an era when Franz Vranitzky was Federal Chancellor (1986–1997) and chairman of the SPÖ, the Social Democratic Party (1988–1997). The Vranitzky years seem to be overshadowed by the Kreisky years and by the decline of the SPÖ from the heights of a still-dominant party, starting in 1999.

This assessment argues that there was a Vranitzky era due to the impact that Vranitzky had on Austrian politics. Vranitzky had three significant imprints as chief of government and as party chairman. These three justify calling the years between 1986 and 1997 an era:

—Austria's successful application for EU membership
—Official Austria's acceptance of a "co-responsibility" for the Nazi crimes
—The shifting of the SPÖ towards a more centric orientation

Vranitzky was the dominant figure in Austrian politics during the years after Kreisky. According to the biography broadly accepted as the definitive book on Kreisky, the relationship between Bruno Kreisky and Franz Vranitzky is defined by Kreisky's long lasting suspicion that Vranitzky was a kind of "agent" of Kreisky's lost (better: disowned) political son, Hannes Androsch. But in the last year of Kreisky's life, Kreisky and Vranitzky reconciled. In the end, Kreisky accepted Vranitzky as his political heir (Petritsch 2010, 396).

The European Integration

From the very beginning of the European integration process, as expressed by the Rome treatises in 1957, there was a broad consensus among the mainstream political parties in Austria that Austria should not join the European Economic Community (designed to become the European Communities and then the European Union). The reason for Austria's abstention was linked to Austria's neutrality. The Austrian government from 1957 onwards always argued it would be legally possible but politically inadvisable to join a community which, during the years of the Cold War, was seen as part of a Western bloc system.

This perspective started to change in the 1980s. The East-West conflict began to mellow, due to the dramatic changes within the Soviet Union and the signals Mikhael Gorbachev was sending to the global community in general and to the United States in particular. As a consequence, Austrian politicians—reacting also to the articulation of specific economic interests, especially of the export oriented industry—started to perceive the new international atmosphere as a possible "window of opportunity," a potential chance to redefine Austria's European attitude.

It had been the Austrian People's Party (ÖVP) and its leader, Alois Mock, who had been in the vanguard of this tendency, seeing neutrality as no longer an obstacle for Austria to join the European Community. And it had been the SPÖ, since 1986, again in a coalition with the ÖVP, that hesitated. The SPÖ-leadership had always argued that Austria's neutrality—declared "permanent" in a constitutional amendment 1955—was a value in itself and would be endangered by an application for membership in the Community.

It had been Vranitzky who succeeded in changing the SPÖ's position. He convinced his party that all Austrian interests—economic, social, cultural—pointed towards membership. And as soon as the global East-West-relations did not prevent anymore a membership bit, Austria should send the famous "letter to Brussels" applying for membership. The formula of the new consensus between SPÖ and ÖVP was "joining the EU as a neutral country." That Sweden and Finland had redefined their neutrality in a similar way helped to formulate such a policy.

Franz Vranitzky did not invent this new interpretation. But he was decisive in making it possible within his own party to see membership in a not only democratic but also capitalist "club" in a positive way. The new position the SPÖ acquired under Vranitzky was the necessary domestic precondition for the shift in Austria's policy towards the EU (Pelinka, Schaller, Luif 1994).

Austria and the Nazi Past

Until 1986, the Austrian discourse was dominated by a certain interpretation of the Moscow Declaration of 1943 which put all the emphasis on the first paragraph of this policy document of the Allied powers—the paragraph declaring Austria as the first victim of Nazi Germany's aggressive expansionism. The second paragraph, giving Austria a co-responsibility for the war (and other) crimes of "Greater Germany," tended to be neglected or even forgotten.

This changed in 1986, when Kurt Waldheim was elected Federal President. In the presidential campaign, the SPÖ used some publicly unknown documents in the presidential campaign against Waldheim, who was nominated by the ÖVP, showing Waldheim not only as an officer of the German Wehrmacht (which was known) but also as a Nazi hanger-on (*Mitläufer*) with a dubious record concerning his membership in different Nazi organizations.

This forced a change of the political discourse after the academic discourse, now dominated by a new generation of historians and social scientists, who had already shifted the debate from neglecting and ignoring significant aspects (like the high percentage of Austrians joining the Nazi Party) of Austrian Nazism to critical research into these elements. But Waldheim was elected, and in the same year Vranitzky became chancellor. He successfully defended his party's pole position and was now, at the end of the year, chancellor of an SPÖ-ÖVP coalition, under the constitutional supervision of Waldheim.

As Waldheim was politically boycotted by the Western world, especially by the United States, Vranitzky acted not only as head of government (as chancellor), but also as surrogate head of state, representing Austria in the US, in Western Europe, and in Israel. In that capacity he de facto took over the president's role. And Vranitzky, helped by his excellent English and his sovereign media presence in the US, became the "good Austrian"—while Waldheim was seen representing Austria's darker side. Even Hannes Androsch, not at all a Vranitzky friend within the Social Democratic Party, concedes: Vranitzky "*hatte … Österreich im Zuge der Waldheim Affäre gut repräsentiert*" (Androsch 2015, 194).

Vranitzky played significant role in redefining official Austria's role in the years when Austria as a state did not exist. In Israel and in the Austrian Parliament, speaking on behalf of the Austrian government, he made the formula of Austria's co-responsibility the official position of Austria. Vranitzky had ended, in his formal capacity, the unbalanced, one-sided, opportunistic interpretation of the Moscow Declaration. During the Waldheim presidency, and with it years of Austria's international isolation, Vranitzky signalled "hope" and "opportunity" in grey times—opportunity and hope for an open reinterpretation of Austria's role in Hitler's Germany (Rauscher 1987).

The Vranitzky-SPÖ—a kind of Austrian "New Labor"

When Vranitzky became chancellor and two years later party chairman, the dominant segments of Austria's industries and Austria's banking system were still owned, directly or indirectly, by the state. When Vranitzky left office in 1997, most of the nationalized economic sector had been privatized. This has not been the result of Vranitzky's programmatic intention. But he had realized that in a globalizing economy Austria's financial and economic policy had to adapt.

Vranitzky took care of a shift of the globalization discourse, especially in his own party. The nationalization of industries and banks, a pragmatic product of the specific situation of the years 1945 and 1946 and not of a strict socialist program, had to respond, again pragmatically, to a new economic environment. And as this environment could be less and less shaped by a national government, by the state, privatization became the rule of the game in the 1980s and 1990s.

In that respect, Vranitzky represented a renewed understanding of democratic socialism. And in that respect, he was Austria's Tony Blair; both realized that to be able to have an impact on the markets, you have to accept the logic of the markets. The Tony Blair role would have been also the potential role of Hannes Androsch. But Androsch fell victim to Kreisky's wrath, and what Androsch probably would have done, Vranitzky successfully implemented. This may be the psychological reason behind the enmity between Androsch and Vranitzky: in their policy outlook, they are too similar.

When the socialism of Lenin imploded in the Soviet Union, the SPÖ—the party which had always kept its distance from Communism—decided to change its name: from Socialist to Social Democratic Party. This symbolic renaming during the Vranitzky years must also be seen as Vranitzky's willingness to define his party as a center-left party.

The Lasting Consequences

During Vranitzky's chancellorship, Austria was governed by a grand coalition again. After twenty years of one party governments (four years of ÖVP, thirteen years of SPÖ, three years of the SPÖ-FPÖ coalition), Austria experienced the revival of the coalition between the two parties which had dominated the foundation of the Second Republic and the first three decades. The renaissance of the system of power sharing between center-left and center-right created the background for a rather stable consensus, necessary for the shift of Austria's European policy and for the official reassessment of Austria's Nazi past.

At the beginning of this period, in 1986, the two major parties had lost some of their electoral strength. But they were still in command of a stable two-third majority. When Vranitzky resigned, in 1997, this situation was still the same: SPÖ and ÖVP together were in command. The Vranitzky Era was an era of relative stabilization of the party system and of the dominance of the two governing parties. The two parties' dramatic electoral decline happened in 1999, after Vranitzky had already left the government and the leadership of his party.

This does not imply that Vranitzky's retreat was the decisive factor for the significant weakening of both the SPÖ and ÖVP. The reason for this dealignment had to do with structural changes in the society and the now visible lack of the power of government to guarantee the standards the Austrian society was used to, like full employment. The younger generation had begun to see political parties not as surrogate churches, but as functions which were less able to deliver than in the past. The result was the rise of third parties—first and foremost the FPÖ, but also the Greens and the new liberal parties (like the Liberal Forum in the 1990s and the Neos, beginning with 2013).

The Vranitzky years are to be seen as the last period of preventing the deep fall of the two parties responsible for the successes of post-1945 Austria. However, Vranitzky may have postponed the end of two-party-dominance, but he could not prevent it. The Vranitzky Era was not only responsible for postponing significant changes in the Austria party system; it also was responsible for significant and lasting innovations: the Vranitzky formula of Austria's co-responsibility will stay to define Austria's history in the 1930s and 1940s. And Austria's EU membership will be a (better: the decisive) parameter for Austria's political fate in the foreseeable future.

Select Bibliography

Androsch, Hannes. *Niemals aufgeben. Lebensbilanz und Ausblick, Aufgezeichnet von Peter Pelinka*. Vienna: Ecowin, 2015.

Pelinka, Anton, Christian Schaller, and Paul Luif. *Ausweg EG? Innenpolitische Motive einer außenpolitischen Umorientierung*. Vienna: Braumüller, 1994.

Petritsch, Wolfgang. *Bruno Kreisky. Die Biografie*. St. Pölten/Salzburg: Residenz, 2010.

Rauscher, Hans. *Vranitzky. Eine Chance*. Vienna: Ueberreuter, 1987.

Powerplant Kaprun.
Transport of a turbine housing for the Limberg dam with the Lärchwand inclined lift.
View of the Kaprun Valley.
US Information Services, 11 16 1953
Credit: Austrian National Library

Volume 8: Günter Bischof/Anton Pelinka/Dieter Stiefel. *The Marshall Plan in Austria*. New Brunswick, NJ: Transaction 2000

The Marshall Plan in Austria

Günter Bischof

The Marshall Plan in Austria, Volume 8 in the *Contemporary Austrian Studies* series, with its almost 600 pages, was the weightiest CAS volume we published. It was based on a conference we put together in New Orleans in the spring of 1998 on the occasion of the 50th anniversary of the European Recovery Program (ERP)—the official name of the "Marshall Plan"—beginning to operate in Austria.[1] In 1997/1998 many of the 16 European countries receiving ERP-aid between 1948 and 1952 commemorated the American largesse of the Marshall Plan with conferences and public occasions. Apart from Austrian national radio channel Ö1 of ORF, no public authorities in the SPÖ-ÖVP coalition government of Viktor Klima found it incumbent upon themselves to attempt a historical assessment of the Marshall Plan's contribution to postwar Austrian recovery. The New Orleans conference did exactly that. As we are nearing the 70th anniversary of the Marshall Plan what is the state of "Marshall Plan studies" in Austria? What kind of progress has been achieved in the past 15 years since the publication of *The Marshall Plan in Austria*? This essay tries to assess the progress in Marshall Plan scholarship in five fields: 1) the Marshall Plan and its genesis; 2) Austrian economic recovery; 3) Western integration; 4) public diplomacy; 5) memory.

The Genesis of the Marshall Plan

Every few years, a new book appears in the American publishing world celebrating the Marshall Plan as the United States' great contribution to European economic recovery after World War II. Greg Behrman recently produced such a narrative history of the Marshall Plan, which paid equal attention to the genesis of Marshall's program and the actual execution of the plan. Behrman particularly stresses the contributions of Will Clayton,

1 A German version of the conference volume was published too, see Günter Bischof and Dieter Stiefel, eds., *80 Dollar: 50 Jahre ERP Fonds und Marshall-Plan in Österreich 1948–1998* (Vienna: Ueberreuter, 1999).

Dean Acheson, George Kennan, and Robert Lovett, Marshall's chief aides in the State Department, as well as Senator Arthur Vandenberg, who helped shepherd the program through Congress. He also values the role the principal Marshall Plan administrators such as Paul Hoffman, Averell Harriman, Richard Bissel and Milton Katz played in executing the plan. Behrman also credits Marshall's principal European partners Ernest Bevin and Georges Bidault, the British and French foreign ministers respectively, for their role in shaping the European response to Marshall's offer. Part of this literature of admiration is also an assessment of General George C. Marshall's great act of American statesmanship. Ever since Michael Hogan's work,[2] the recent literature also stresses the corporatist New Deal nature of the ERP (Mills). It is a common characteristic of books on the Marshall Plan such as Behrman's and Mills' that they concentrate on the large European nations (France, Great Britain, West Germany, Italy) and ignore the smaller participant nations such as Austria. More recently, the Marshall Plan has also been interpreted as a tool of American "nation building" after wars.[3]

With the publication of the splendid Volume 6 of the official *Papers of George Catlett Marshall*, namely the period of his incumbency as Secretary of State (1947–1949), we have a much better picture of Marshall's crucial role in the genesis of the "plan" that was named after him. Rarely in history did a leading diplomat have to confront so many major crises concurrently (Chinese Civil War, Palestine and birth of Israel, division of Germany and Berlin airlift, etc.)—with the prospect of nuclear war looming large in the background. In a letter to retired Secretary of War Henry L. Stimson, Marshall wrote on July 27, 1948: "As you know the situation has been one crisis after another" (509). In a speech in Richmond (in his native state of Virginia) on February 23, 1948, Marshall noted: "Nothing approximating the present world turbulence has ever been known before." He reminded his audience that the U.S. could not abdicate its leadership role in the world and stay aloof (382f). In spite of Chinese and Latin American pushback (500), he lifted European economic recovery to the top of his agenda, arguing that Europe back on its feet again would benefit the entire world. The extraordinary story of the genesis of the "Marshall Plan" is well known and can be relived in this volume.

2 Michael J. Hogan, *The Marshall Plan: America, Britain, and the Reconstruction of Western Europe, 1947–1952* (Cambridge, UK: Cambridge University Press, 1987).

3 In his chapter on the post-World War II occupation of Germany, Jeremy Suri sees the Marshall Plan as the principal tool of American "nation building," see: *Liberty's Surest Guardian: Rebuilding Nations after War from the Founders to Obama* (New York: Free Press, 2011), 124–164.

Marshall's epic effort to get this program passed in Congress is less known.[4] The editors of the volume have wisely selected a number of speeches Marshall eloquently delivered around the country in the second half of 1947. Marshall impressed on the American public again and again the importance of European recovery. He warned Americans and the Congress about the U.S. being at the "crossroads" (358). During the spring of 1948, nothing less than the survival of Western European democracy was at stake. Marshall liked to end his speeches and testimonies to Congress by appealing to American political leadership in the world (446). Not launching the program would be "a world tragedy" (361). In early 1948, Marshall testified regularly before congressional committees and pressed Congress to make this historic decision and break "the vicious cycles" that were inhibiting recovery in Europe (327). Marshall had to assuage senators' and congressmen's notion that his recovery plan would create shortages of goods in the United States and stimulate inflation (323). He did not hesitate to impress on the Senate what was at stake: if the U.S failed to assist in the reconstruction of Europe, "we must accept the consequences of its collapse into the dictatorship of police states" (319). Marshall's testimonies before Congress, more than anything else, made the passing of the ERP possible.

In a gloomy letter to Bernard Baruch late in 1947, Marshall estimated the chances of Congressional funding for ERP being only fifty-fifty (267). Marshall was very guarded in his public speaking (preferring to be off the record). He was keenly aware of the importance of an informed citizenry in a democratic polity. Keeping the American people informed was a challenge: "Our international responsibilities have increased much faster than the public understanding of the many complex factors involved" (546n2). Battling Congress in daily appropriation battles, he noted tongue-in-cheek: "God bless Democracy! I approve of it highly but suffer from it extremely" (484). Marshall, with the help of an extremely talented staff, managed to get the European Recovery Program, amounting to more than thirteen billion dollars in economic aid over four years, through Congress. The detailed record of his role as Secretary of State leaves the reader in awe of the enormous burdens this man carried and the enormous achievements of his long career. One can only agree with Winston's Churchill's praise: "It

4 "Selling the Marshall Plan" to the American public to create the pressure in Congress to pass the program has received attention from scholars, see George Fujii, "Selling the Marshall Plan in the United States," in *Images of the Marshall Plan in Europe: Films, Photographs, Exhibits, Posters* (TRANSATLANTICA 3), ed. Günter Bischof and Dieter Stiefel with Hannes Richter (digital editor), (Innsbruck: StudienVerlag 2009), 39–57; Michael Wala, "Selling the Marshall Plan," *Diplomatic History* 10 (Summer 1986): 247–265; Greg Behrman, *The Most Noble Adventure: The Marshall Plan and the Time When America Helped Europe* (New York: Free Press, 2007), 114–140.

gives me confidence in these days of anxiety—in some ways more painful than wartime ordeals—to know that you are at the helm of the most powerful of nations, and to feel myself in such complete accord with what you say and do" (223n2).

The Marshall Plan's Role in Austrian Economic Recovery

The Marshall Plan in Austria looked both at the macro- and micro-economic picture of the ERP's role in Austrian economic recovery. While Hans Seidel looked at the larger contribution of the Marshall Plan to Austria's economic and financial recovery, other essays analyzed the ERP's role in the recovery of individual sectors of the Austrian economy like iron and steel (Kurt Tweraser), electricity (Georg Rigele), and tourism (Günter Bischof). Both Seidel and Tweraser have in the meantime published full-length book studies on their subject matters and greatly improved our understanding of the complex political process Austrian macro- and micro-economic recovery (Seidel and Tweraser).

Seidel analyzed the roots of the Austrian postwar economic miracle and credits American Marshall Planners for not forcing the American model of market capitalism down the throats of postwar Austrian leaders. The Americans accepted the unique model of "traditional Austrian capitalism", where the "invisible hand" of market forces was replaced by the "visible hand of both private and public regulation of markets" (71–75). The unique Austrian corporate model of "*Sozialpartnerschaft*" (social partnership) incorporated a political economy where the state, labor, and industry regularly negotiated wages and prices and thereby secured the social peace. The American Marshall Planners—often socialized in 1930s New Deal policies—accepted the Austrian and other models of European political economy (like the German "social market economy") with more or less state interference. As Charles S. Maier has shrewdly observed: "The young economists who staffed ERP agencies had learned the new Keynesian doctrines just before the war. They appreciated huge and integrated markets, but *understood that sometimes government spending was required to help markets function*" (my emphasis).[5] Such non-doctrinaire American experts helped the Marshall Plan succeed in various national contexts.

The representatives of the European Cooperation Administration (ECA) in Paris and Vienna also often accepted the Austrians' pleas for being

5 Charles S. Maier, "From Plan to Practice: The context and consequences of the Marshall Plan," *Harvard Magazine* (May-June 1997): 40–43, here 43.

a “special case” (*Sonderfall*) in Western European recovery.[6] Austria was a poor country, and its urban population could not be fed from indigenous sources due to postwar bottlenecks. Austria was occupied by four powers and the national government did not enjoy full sovereignty. Given its crucial geopolitical position, Austria was particularly threatened by Communist subversive activity and takeover. And still, the Austrian people (and particularly its workers) were fiercely anti-Communist and had opted to stay in the Western camp (299). Given its special status, Austria received some $130 of Marshall aid per capita and ranked amongst the highest ERP-aid recipients. Unlike other ERP recipient countries, the lion’s share of American aid in the first two years of the Marshall Plan (1948–1950) came in the form of food and coal (i.e., “relief, not rehabilitation”). American pre-Marshall Plan aid allowed Austria to cover its trade deficit (“trade gap” producing the “dollar gap”) and continued to do so throughout the Marshall Plan.

Seidel also is the first one to give adequate attention to the final years of the Marshall Plan in Austria (1951–1953), when ERP aid was running out and the U.S. began to help Western Europeans with rearmament during the scary days of the Korean War, rather than economic rehabilitation. Officials of the European Payments Union criticized Austria for not doing enough to achieve internal and external stability (Austria still ran a sizable deficit in intra-European trade financed by the EPU). In Austria, the ECA officials forced a “stabilization program” on the Austrian government. American Marshall Planners wanted the Figl and Raab governments to reduce regulations in the Austrian economy and stop credit expansion to reduce high inflation rates and balance the federal budget. The ECA in Vienna used the “stick” of withholding the release of counterpart funds to stabilize the economy (Seidel, 483–563).[7] In these difficult years of adjustment, the Austrian “special case” argument no longer did the trick of continuing an unabated flow of ERP-aid. Austria had to learn to live within its own means after the progress made due to American aid in its economic recovery.

American Marshall Planners also accepted the Austrian “special case” of harboring and oversized state-owned industrial sector (due to the nationalization of “German assets” after the war). Both Tweraser and Seidel dwell extensively on ERP-generated counterpart funds being invested in

6 Austria’s “special case” status is regularly addressed in scholarship, see Hans Seidel, “Austria’s Economic Policy and the Marshall Plan,” in CAS 8, 273-75; Michael Gehler, *Vom Marshall Plan zur EU: Österreich und die europäische Integration von 1945 bis zur Gegenwart* (Innsbruck: StudienVerlag 2006), 31f; Günter Bischof, “Der Marshall-Plan in Österreich/ The Marshall Plan in Austria,” in *Österreich Baut Auf/Rebuilding Austria*, ed. Helmut Lackner and Georg Rigele (Vienna: Technical Museum, 2005), 12–66, here 51f.

7 See also Seidel, “Austria’s Economic Policy and the Marshall Plan,” in CAS 8, 279–282.

this ECA officials in Vienna hesitated to favor the iron and steel sector, as well as funding infrastructure projects in electricity (like the massive hydroelectric power plant project in Kaprun) and mining, when their long-term goals were to benefit consumer industries that one day might export again and earn dollars for the Austrian balance of payments (Seidel, 212–322). Tweraser shows in great detail the often nasty bureaucratic battles and negotiations in Vienna between American ECA and high-level Austrian officials. The Austrian economic experts themselves disagreed between favoring the iron and steel works in Linz (in the American sector), or Donawitz (in the British sector), or investing the precious counterpart funds in consumer goods industries (Tweraser, 225–362).

Increasing industrial productivity was another one of the major goals of the ERP. In the state sector as well as in the private sector, American Marshall Planners insisted on increasing productivity, as higher productivity would benefit all segments of Austrian society, including workers.[8] However, Austrian labor unionists resisted the American cult of productivity in cases where it threatened tested mechanisms of Austrian corporate governance (*Sozialpartnerschaft*).[9]

While the iron and steel sector and the electricity industry benefitting from ERP-generated counterpart investments are well-researched, other sectors such as the paper and textile industry, the building of public housing, as well as the modernization through Marshall Plan funds in Austrian agriculture still need to find historians. The contribution of the Marshall Plan in the modernization of the Austrian tourist industry has recently been addressed by Simone Telser's Innsbruck dissertation. The tourist industry benefitted, above all in Western Austria, from counterpart investments by way of modernizing hotels and building skiing facilities to enable the launching of a "second" winter season. By the mid-1950s, Marshall Plan investments allowed Austrian tourism to return to its traditional role of earning foreign currency to balance the Austrian budget.

Marshall Plan and Austria's Western Integration

Austria's participation in the Marshall Plan set her on a long-term path of Western European integration (Bischof, 2006). Since Austria's path to European integration was one of fits and starts, it is better to speak of a

8 Charles S. Maier "The Politics of Productivity: Foundations of American International Economic Policy after World War II," *International Organization* 31 (1977): 607–633.

9 Kurt Tweraser, "The Politics of Productivity and Corporatism: The Late Marshall Plan in Austria, 1950-54," in CAS 3, 91–115.

European "integration dynamic" as Michael Gehler suggests.[10] Given the Soviet Union being one of the occupation powers in the land and Moscow's fundamental opposition to the Marshall Plan, Austria from the beginning had to "tread very gingerly" ("*auf leisen Sohlen gehen*").[11] The ERP allowed Austria to participate in Western European institutions, namely the Paris-based joint institutions of the Marshall Plan organization (Organization of European Economic Cooperation=OEEEC; European Cooperation Administration=ECA; European Payments Union=EPU). Here Austria had to cooperate with the fifteen other ERP recipient countries. These institutions were also a basic school of training and socializing young officials and economists to think "European," as Hans Seidel has stressed (Seidel, 90; Bischof, 2005, 56–58). Richard Bissel, a high level ECA economist, has aptly observed: "With a year of two they [the national delegates to the OEEC meetings in Paris] became in spirit less an assemblage of national representatives that a group of Europeans."[12] Michael Gehler has provided us with the basic history of Austrian integration into Western Europe. Austria during the four-power occupation period (1945–1955) carefully had to balance between its national "integrity" (e.g. regaining its national sovereignty) and "integration" (e.g. choosing its pace of European integration carefully given the Soviet presence in the land) (Gehler, 39–45). Given that the Soviets denounced the Schumann organization as a "NATO arsenal," Austria did not join the European Coal and Steel Community but tried to achieve some form of "association" status; with no success, Austria's closer integration into the Western framework was arrested (Gehler, 46–51).

In 1955 the Austrian State Treaty was finally signed and Austria regained her full sovereignty for the price of "permanent neutrality." Austrian neutrality was the Soviet condition for the withdrawal of occupation forces from the country. Until the end of the Cold War, when it came to further Austrian steps towards Western European integration, the Soviet Union guarded Austria's neutral position very carefully. Moscow allowed Austria to join the United Nations in 1955 and the Council of Europe in 1956, but did not permit joining the European Economic Communities in 1957, thus stymieing Austria's further participation in the tightening process of Western European integration. Austria applied for EC membership in 1989, only when the Cold War ended and the Soviet Union imploded, and became a full member of the European Union in 1995 (Gehler).

10 Michael Gehler, *Europa: Ideen – Institutionen –Vereinigung* (Munich: Olzog, 2005), 139.
11 See document # 7 in Michael Gehler, *Der Lange Weg nach Europa:* Österreich *von Paneuropa bis zum EU-Beitritt*, vol. 2: *Dokumente* (Innsbruck: StudienVerlag, 2002), 137.
12 Richard M. Bissel, Jr., *Reflections of a Cold Warrior: From Yalta to the Bay of Pigs* (New Haven: Yale University Press, 1996), 48f.

Scholars have been debating whether Western European integration was the ultimate goal of American Marshall Planners. Roy Jenkins has argued that "The Marshall Plan undoubtedly provided a major impetus toward European unity, and that was one of the great attractions for the United States."[13] Alan Milward has suggested that economic integration was the ultimate vision of the Marshall Plan.[14] Curiously, British observers seem to focus on the Marshall Plan's role towards European integration while contemporary British officials slowed down the European integration process every step of the way (Bischof, 2006, 37–41). While members of Congress often admonished the Europeans to work towards unification, the goal of the Marshall Planners was only closer European cooperation and self-help. Greg Behrman stresses that there was no such "cogent American vision" of a future "United States of Europe." Senator Vandenberg and the American Marshall Planners did not want to infringe on the sovereignty of European nation states. It was up to the Europeans to "find a path forward" towards more integration (Behrman, 409fn336). Scholars have to be careful in not projecting a teleological line from the Marshall Plan ultimately leading to EEC-EU integration.

Marshall Plan and Public Diplomacy

"Today, no serious discussion of the Marshall Plan, unless it's focused on hardcore economics, would dream of overlooking the propaganda/information/education/psychological warfare dimension of the effort. This emphasis is new," argues David Ellwood, a pioneer in Marshall Plan film studies. He adds: "the myth of the Marshall Plan was born under the Plan itself and represents the greatest, most enduring triumph of the European Recovery program information/propaganda effort. I am convinced that the film program was the heart of the effort" (Ellwood in Bischof/Stiefel/Richter, 61). The Marshall Plan film program was conceived to educate and ultimately convert the European publics towards accepting the goals of the ERP—closer European cooperation, increase of productivity towards greater affluence, the superiority of American

13 Roy Jenkins, "Special Relationship: The Postwar Bequest," *Foreign Affairs* 76, no. 3 (1997): 203; the crucial role of the United States in the European integration process has been addressed by John Lamberton Harper, *American Visions of Europe: Franklin D. Roosevelt, George F. Kennan, Dean G. Acheson* (Cambridge, UK: Cambridge University Press, 1996), and Geir Lundestad, *"Empire" by Integration: The United States and European Integration, 1945–1997* (Oxford, UK: Oxford University Press, 1998).

14 Alan Milward, *The Reconstruction of Western Europe, 1945–1951* (Berkeley: The University of California Press, 1984), 123.

consumer democracy over Soviet communism. Each of the sixteen ECA country outfits included an information division, directed towards the masses to see and understand the benefits of the American-sponsored Marshall Plan. They targeted specific groups, such as trade unionists, and executives in business, industry and the government, as well as agricultural workers and housewives (who managed the economies of the household) (Ellwood in Bischof/Stiefel/Richter, 63).

Paul Hoffman, the ECA chief administrator in Washington, had made his mark as a car salesman, marketing specialist, and eventually CEO of the Studebaker car company. He made sure that the Marshall Plan came with "a strong information arm"—information about the ERP programs sold in "nonideological language" (De Grazia, 348). Five percent of Marshall Plan funding was dedicated towards overt and covert Marshall Plan information/propaganda. This amounted to a whopping $200 million spent every year of the Marshall Plan on public diplomacy programs, including film, radio, press, photography, and travelling exhibits. In Austria the United States Information Service became the United States Information Agency (USIA) in 1953. The Pictorial Section led by the gifted photographer Yoichi R. Okamoto trained dozens of young Austrian photographers to document the blessings of the Marshall Plan across the country in every phase (Friedlmeier/Petschar/Pfunder in Bischof/Stiefel/Richter, 169–201).[15] In Germany Marshall Plan propaganda also reeducated the Germans after Adolf Hitler with new visual languages sold through every tested film media—newsreels, documentaries, re-orientation films, feature films, cartoons and productivity films (Schröder in Bischof/Stiefel, 69–86). Next to these well-staffed country units, the Office of the Special Representative in Paris, the chief ECA administrator in Europe Averell Harriman, employed some 180 people to generate the propaganda to sell the benefits of the Marshall Plan to Europeans. Among them were first-rate Hollywood producers, journalists and advertisement agents to design programs suiting the respective national contexts and cultures. The Marshall Plan's extensive propaganda effort turned "American myth into American model" and fed "the revolution of rising expectations" in Europe (Ellwood in Bischof/Stiefel/Richter, 67). The message to Europeans was: "YOU TOO CAN BE LIKE US."

15 On Okamoto, see also Marion Krammer and Margarethe Szeless, "Yoichi Okamoto and the 'Pictorial Section': Austrian-American Relations in Press Photography 1945–1955," in CAS 23, 275–292.

Marshall Plan Memory

Given the intense interests of scholars in the memory of World War II and the Holocaust, it was only matter of time before historians would get interested in Cold War memories.[16] Public and cultural remembrance of Cold War events can be reconstructed through museums, exhibits, monuments, memorials, commemorative parks, as well as historical anniversaries. Of course, contemporary eyewitnesses carry personal and private memories of Cold War events such as the Cuban Missile Crisis or the fall of the Berlin Wall. No historians have tried to summarize and analyze the memory(ics) of the Marshall Plan. One way of tracing Marshall Plan memory in the various European recipient states of Marshall aid would be studying their public anniversary commemorations, which typically occur every ten years. It has been mentioned in the introduction to this paper that there was an intense commemorative activity in most European capitals and Washington for the 50th anniversary of the Marshall Plan in 1997/98.

The more the American postwar contribution to Austria's economic (and political) reconstruction recedes into the distance, the less Austrian governments seem to remember it. This has not always been the case. The generation of founding fathers of the Second Austrian Republic showed intense gratitude to America for the blessings of the Marshall Plan. For the tenth anniversary of the Marshall Plan in Austria, the Raab Government published the 368-page book *Zehn Jahre ERP in Österreich, 1948–1958*. This report was an extensive documentary on the many projects ERP counterpart investments funded during the period of the Marshall Plan. The dedication of the book read: "To the unknown American taxpayer, to whose contribution the Austrian economy is indebted for the millions invested toward reconstruction." On March 18, 1959, Austrian Ambassador Platzer presented a copy of the book personally to President Eisenhower. The President was touched by this act of Austrian gratitude and so was the American public when it was informed about the book by a press release sent out through an American PR firm. 191 articles were published in American local, regional and national newspaper about this unusual act of gratitude by a recipient country of U.S. aid. The American public assumed that foreign aid went down dark holes and recipient nations were ungrateful (Stiefel in Bischof/Stiefel/Richter, 205–221).

16 Charles S. Maier has ruminated about excessive memory, see "A Surfeit of Memory? Reflections on History, Melancholy and Denial," *History & Memory* 5, no. 2 (Fall/Winter 1993): 136–152; on Cold War memory see David Lowe and Tony Joel, *Remembering the Cold War: Global contest and national stories* (Milton Park: Routledge, 2013).

In subsequent years, Austrian gratitude for Marshall aid diminished, even though in 1961 the American government transferred total assets of 11.2 billion Austrian Schillings of counterpart funds to the Austrian government. In 1962 the Austrian government established the *ERP-Fonds* in Vienna to continue investing these funds in the Austrian economy (to the tune of more than one billion öS a year). One can argue that through the ERP Fund, the Marshall Plan has been active in Austria to this day.[17] The 50th anniversary celebration in New Orleans mentioned at the beginning of this essay sparked a crucial initiative, namely the establishment of the Austrian Marshall Plan Foundation in 2000. This Foundation now makes sure that Austrian memory of the Marshall Plan is kept alive. For the 60th anniversary of the Marshall Plan in 2007, the ERP Fund agreed with the American Ambassador Susan McCaw to sponsor a scholarship program for 1,000 Austrian and American students over a period of ten years (2008–2018) to be handled through the Austrian Marshall Plan Foundation.[18] The Foundation also sponsored a conference in Vienna on the public diplomacy of the Marshall Plan. The papers were subsequently published in the volume *Images of the Marshall Plan*, which also had a DVD of Marshall Plan movies and documentaries enclosed in the back pocket (Bischof/Stiefel/Richter). The Austrian Marshall Plan Foundation is making plans for an adequate commemoration of the 70th anniversary of the Marshall Plan in 2017.

Finally, the Marshall Plan is frequently touted as a model for large-scale reconstruction programs, be it in the Third World/Global South,[19] or in Eastern Europe after the end of the Cold War. Barry Machado has analyzed and summarized the arguments that suggest that the Marshall Plan was unique to Western Europe in a time of crisis after the war (Machado, 113–123). Similar conditions are unlikely to prevail again, which makes it highly unlikely for a successful major aid program could occur under similar circumstances, which are, as Richard Bissel has put it: "skills, habits, motivations, customs, and procedures required for the operation of a modern economy" (cited in Machado, 118). Vast recuperating or failing economies usually do not bring such preconditions to the table.

---

17 The story of the *ERP-Fonds* is well summarized by Kurt Löffler and Hans Fussenegger, "The Activities of the ERP Fund from 1962 to 1998," in CAS 8, 15–55 (on the 1961 transfer of funds, see 24).

18 See <https://globale3.studioabroad.com/_customtags/ct_FileRetrieve.cfm?File_ID=14698> (18. Dec. 2015).

19 Austrian Chancellor Bruno Kreisky had been a lifelong champion of a Marshall Plan for the Third World to initiate economic growth and increase productivity, culminating in the Cancun Summit of 1981, see Ferdinand Lacina, "The Marshall Plan—A Contribution to the Austrian Economy in Transition," in CAS 8, 13.

Select Bibliography

Behrman, Greg. *The Most Noble Adventure: The Marshall Plan and the Time When America Helped Europe*. New York: Free Press, 2007.

Bischof, Günter, and Dieter Stiefel with Hannes Richter (digital editor), eds. *Images of the Marshall Plan in Europe: Films, Photographs, Exhibits, Posters* (TRANSATLANTICA 3). Innsbruck: StudienVerlag, 2009.

-------. "Der Marshall-Plan in Österreich/The Marshall Plan in Austria," in Österreich *Baut Auf/Rebuilding Austria*, ed. Helmut Lackner and Georg Rigele. Vienna: Technical Museum, 2005, 12–66; repr. in Günter Bischof, *Relationships/Beziehungsgeschichten: Austria and the United States in the Twentieth Century* (TRANSATLANTICA 4). Innsbruck: StudienVerlag, 2014, 103–138.

--------. "Marshall-Plan und Westintegration," in *Menschen – Regionen – Unternehmen: Festschrift für Franz Mathis zum 60. Geburtstag*, ed. Helmut Alexander, Elisabeth Dietrich-Daum, and Wolfgang Meixner. Innsbruck: *innsbruck* university press, 2006, 31–48.

Bland, Larry, Mark Stoler, Sharon Ridenour Stevens, and Daniel Holt, eds. *The Papers of George Catlett Marshall*, vol. 6: *"The Whole World Hangs in the Balance" January 8, 1947 – September 30, 1949*. Baltimore: Johns Hopkins University Press, 2013.

De Grazia, Victoria. *Irresistible Empire: America's Advance through Twentieth-Century Europe*. Cambridge, MA: The Belknap Press of Harvard University Press, 2005.

Gehler, Michael. *Vom Marshall Plan zur EU: Österreich und die europäische Integration von 1945 bis zur Gegenwart*. Innsbruck: StudienVerlag, 2006.

Machado, Barry F. *In Search of a Usable Past: The Marshall Plan and Postwar Reconstruction Today*. Lexington, VA: George C. Marshall Foundation, 2007.

Mills, Nicolaus. *Winning the Peace: The Marshall Plan & America's Coming of Age as a Superpower*. New York: John Wiley & Sons, Inc., 2008.

Seidel, Hans. *Österreichs Wirtschaft und Wirtschaftspolitik nach dem Zweiten Weltkrieg*. Vienna: Manz, 2005.

Telser, Simone Agnes Elisabeth. "Fremdenverkehr und Marshallplan in Österreich: Wiederaufbau bis 1952," PhD. diss., University of Innsbruck, 2008.

Tweraser, Kurt. *US Militärregierung Oberösterreich 1945–1950*, vol. 2: *Industriepolitik*. Linz: Oberösterreichisches Landesarchiv, 2009.

National Holiday 2005.
Press Conference, "50 Years Neutrality."
SPÖ Party Leader Alfred Gusenbauer, Historian Gerhard Jagschitz und Alexander Van der Bellen from the Green Party.
Vienna, Barbara Gindl, 10 26 2005
Credit: APA PictureDesk

Volume 9: Günter Bischof/Anton Pelinka/Ruth Wodak. *Neutrality in Austria*. New Brunswick, NJ: Transaction 2001

Austrian Neutrality in the 21st Century

Paul Luif

Introductory Remarks

Growing up during the Soviet occupation in the eastern region of Austria (in Burgenland), it was just natural to see neutrality, the key to the withdrawal of the totalitarian regime's troops, in a very positive way. Neutrality also helped to make contacts with relatives in Hungary easier. Still, the Iron Curtain remained, having artificially divided an area which did not know borders for hundreds of years.

There can be no doubt that, after its introduction in 1955, the idea of neutrality had gained a very positive connotation from Austria's population, especially in the east. In addition, for a researcher like me, neutrality and peace were closely connected—until I read a book actually dealing with "neutrality and peace."[1] The author argued that in former times, neutrality limited the area of war and increased the opportunity for peace. But in the industrial era, neutrality cannot be a real abstention from war, since warring states depended on the financial and industrial support of the neutrals. Writing in 1935, the author especially criticized the United States, which tried to isolate itself from the impending war in Europe. The author hoped that Franklin D. Roosevelt would introduce a policy change.[2] But after several Neutrality Acts passed by Congress (1935, 1936 and 1937),[3] FDR declared on 3 September 1939: "This nation will remain a neutral nation."[4] In hindsight, it would have been better for the smaller European states to form an alliance with the UK and the US in the 1930s and not to opt for

1 Nicolas Politis, *La neutralité et la paix* (Paris: Librairie Hachette, 1935); see also Paul Luif, "Neutralität und Frieden. Grundlegende Bemerkungen zu Geschichte und Gegenwart," in Österreichische Neutralität und Friedenspolitik I: Dialog – Beiträge zur Friedensforschung, no. 6 (1986): 17–76.

2 Politis, *Neutralité*, 130 and 153.

3 John N. Petrie, *American Neutrality in the 20th Century: The Impossible Dream* (Washington, D.C.: National Defense University, January 1995), 69.

4 Quote taken from Norman A. Graebner, "The Long American Struggle for Neutrality," in *Neutrality in History/La neutralité dans l'histoire*, ed. Jukka Nevakivi (Helsinki: SHS/FHS, 1993), 45–58, here 53.

neutrality; during World War II, most of them were occupied by Hitler's and/or Stalin's troops.[5]

Events in international relations during the 1980s and 1990s were problematic from a "neutral" point of view. In the early 1980s, protests against the stationing of NATO's SS20 missiles in Western Europe took place in neutral Austria; the earlier military build-up of Warsaw Pact countries had obtained significantly fewer critical comments here. At the same time, Austria's neutrality came under pressure from the US and reduced the leeway of its "active neutrality" policy. A case in point were the problems with the Americans concerning the transfer of high technology to the East via Austria.[6] The tragic events in (formerly) Yugoslavia in the 1990s showed that UN Peacekeeping was not always sufficient to end conflicts. Sometimes military intervention (and not neutral abstention), even without a mandate from the Security Council (cf. Kosovo), could be necessary to stop the mass killings of innocent people.

Austria's Neutrality After the Cold War

With this background, I wrote the rather critical article on Austria's permanent neutrality in 1999 and revised it in January 2000; it was then published in 2001.[7] The title spoke about neutrality's "demise," but in the last paragraph I warned that "*Totgesagte leben länger*" (the presumed dead live longer).

In the second half of the 1990s, Austria's international status was hotly debated. Already in 1990, after the end of the Cold War, the leader of the FPÖ, Jörg Haider, had questioned the relevance of the State Treaty from 1955 as well as its closely connected permanent neutrality. In 1997, probably also in view of the pending first enlargement of NATO, the ÖVP demanded Austrian NATO membership and with it the abandonment of Austria's neutral status. In contrast, most politicians from the SPÖ (and the Greens) strongly opposed any change of this status.

By this time, EU membership (as of 1 January 1995) had changed the content of Austria's neutrality. It was now narrowly defined and reduced

5 See Ger van Roon, *Small States in Years of Depression. The Oslo Alliance 1930–1940* (Assen/Maastricht: Van Gorcum, 1989).

6 The US administration threatened to stop providing high technology to Austria's already ailing nationalized industry—an argument which did not fail to influence the ruling Socialists and make them more forthcoming to the American demands. But it did take quite some time until Austria fully adhered to the so-called COCOM rules; see Paul Luif, "USA-Österreich: Der Konflikt um den Technologietransfer," in *Zukunft* (December 1985): 17–20.

7 Paul Luif, "Austria's Permanent Neutrality—Its Origins, Development, and Demise," in CAS 9, 129–159.

to three N's: non-participation in wars, no adherence to military alliances and no stationing of foreign troops on its soil. In view of this membership and to allow Austria to fully participate in the EU's Common Foreign and Security Policy (CFSP), an article was added to the Federal Constitution (Article 23f, now Article 23j). The Amsterdam Treaty from 1997 made the so-called "Petersberg tasks" part of the CFSP (then Article J.7, now Article 43 of Treaty on European Union—TEU); they included "tasks of combat forces in crisis management, including peacemaking" (i.e. wage war to make peace). Austria amended its Federal Constitution accordingly.

Specialists in public and international law began to talk about Austria as not being a "neutral" state anymore; "non-alignment" was now seen as the correct designation of Austria's international status.[8] During the—ultimately unsuccessful—negotiations on a new coalition government between the SPÖ and the ÖVP in November/December 1999, the leaders of the SPÖ were ready to accept the proposal by the ÖVP to include a mutual defense clause in the EU treaties and thus scrap Austria's neutrality completely.[9] As soon as the ÖVP formed a government with the FPÖ, the Social Democrats again insisted on full-fledged neutrality.

In my article in *Contemporary Austrian Studies*, I alluded to the possible misinterpretation of the EU's dynamics as well as to the neglect and writing off of Article 5 of the North Atlantic Treaty, its mutual defense clause.[10] Soon afterwards, the dynamics of the EU led to the adopting of the Treaty establishing a Constitution for Europe in 2004 and with it a mutual defense clause. This Treaty did not come into force, but the Lisbon Treaty (from 2007, in force 2009) includes an identical paragraph (Article 42.7 TEU). In 2003 Heinz Gärtner, examining Austria's neutrality still maintained: "The EU has specifically limited its security aims to peacekeeping, rising at most

8 See Theo Öhlinger, "BVG Neutralität," in *Bundesverfassungsrecht. Loseblattausgabe*, ed. Karl Korinek and Michael Holoubek (Vienna: Springer, 1999), 18: "Neutralität ist juristisch kein zutreffendes Etikett der Stellung Österreichs in der Staatengemeinschaft mehr." For Öhlinger, the notion of a "differentiated neutrality" instead of "integral neutrality" would be less exact than the concept of a mere "*Bündnislosigkeit*" (emphasis in the original). Non-alignment in this sense is not identical to the policies of the Movement of Non-Aligned States, which includes mostly Third World countries.

9 This willingness to abandon neutrality was reported in the newspapers at that time and has been confirmed in several articles by Heinz Gärtner, "who as member of the internal SPÖ-working group on security policy had inside information about the ongoing discussions on neutrality"; quoted from Helmut Kramer, "Österreichs Beitrag zur europäischen und globalen Sicherheit. Ein Plädoyer für mehr Selbstbewusstsein im Bekenntnis zu aktiver Neutralitäts- und Friedenspolitik," in *Wieviel Sicherheit braucht Friede? Zivile und militärische Näherungen zur österreichischen Sicherheitsstrategie*, ed. Thomas Roithner, Johann Frank, and Eva Huber (Vienna: Lit Verlag, 2013), 89–100, here 95 (all translations in this article by Paul Luif).

10 Luif, "Austria's Permanent Neutrality," 148–149.

to peace-enforcement with combat troops, if necessary. No mutual security guarantee is written into the European treaty, nor can one be obtained in the near future."[11]

In line with his argument about the end of territorial defense, the same author wrote on "the old-style NATO based on collective defense and balance of power"; for him "crisis management" was the "more important concept."[12] Gärtner came to the following conclusion in the 2001 article: "Austria does not need security guarantees along the lines of Article V [Article 5 of the North Atlantic Treaty] because no major attack on Austrian territory is likely. Therefore, membership in a collective defense system does not automatically increase Austria's security."[13]

The explanation of NATO's (as well as a possible EU) collective defense system would also have to include the analysis of the security of Austria's partners, an issue which the author did not discuss. The Ukraine crisis was only the latest event to show how important territorial defense and Article 5 are.

The "Re-Birth" of Neutrality

The new ÖVP/FPÖ government issued in 2001 a "*Sicherheits- und Verteidigungsdoktrin*" in which it declared Austria "*bündnisfrei*" (non-aligned, as Finland and Sweden).[14] It left the option of NATO membership open, but stated that there would have to be a referendum before Austria could join NATO.[15]

Chancellor Wolfgang Schüssel (ÖVP) declared on Austria's National Day, 26 October 2001, that neutrality, like *Mozartkugeln* or *Lipizzaner* are not adequate for the "complex reality as the 21st century gets under way."[16] These remarks prompted a flurry of criticism by the opposition, but also in the media. The influential mass circulation daily, *Kronen Zeitung*, read at that time daily by more than 40 percent of Austrians, started a crusade against Schüssel's attack on neutrality. It asserted that 80 percent of Austrians were for the maintenance of neutrality. The tabloid was only satisfied when

11 Heinz Gärtner, "European Security: The End of Territorial Defense," in *The Brown Journal of World Affairs* 9, no. 2 (2003): 1–13, here 2.

12 Heinz Gärtner, "Neutrality Must Change," in CAS 9, 115–128, here 118.

13 Ibid., 126.

14 Sicherheits- und Verteidigungsdoktrin. Analyse-Teil. Expertenentwurf, Bearbeitungsstand 23.01.2001.

15 Sicherheits- und Verteidigungsdoktrin. Allgemeine Erwägungen. Beschluss des Nationalrates vom 12.12.2001, <http://www.bka.gv.at/2004/4/4/doktrin_d.pdf> (23 Jan. 2016).

16 "Schüssel und Fischler: Absage an 'alte Schablone' Neutralität," *Die Presse*, 27 Oct. 2001.

Schüssel stated that NATO membership would only happen after a positive referendum—and that would not be on the agenda at the moment.[17]

In spring 2003, in the context of the Iraq crisis, as the United States invaded the country without UN Security Council mandate, the ÖVP/FPÖ government "rediscovered" neutrality. US war planes were not allowed to fly over Austrian territory; Secretary of Defense Donald Rumsfeld had already criticized Austria in February 2003 for blocking the transport of US troops from Germany to Italy.[18] Heinz Fischer (SPÖ) won the presidential elections of April 2004 because his defense of neutrality was more credible than the position of Benita Ferrero-Waldner (ÖVP) who had first supported NATO membership and later proposed solidarity in Europe but neutrality outside Europe.[19] So representatives of the ÖVP started again to support neutrality. In 2005, the splinter-party of Jörg Haider, the BZÖ, still was somewhat critical of neutrality, whereas the "new" FPÖ under Heinz-Christian Strache began to strongly defend neutrality.[20]

The new "grand coalition" government of SPÖ and ÖVP developed a new Austrian Security Strategy (Österreichische Sicherheitsstrategie). In July 2013 the report on this Strategy was passed by the Austrian Parliament (*Nationalrat*) with the votes by the SPÖ, ÖVP and also the FPÖ and the Team Stronach. The Strategy twice mentions "neutrality," both times in connection with Austria's EU membership. There is no NATO option; Austria will cooperate with NATO, but only in non-Article-5 operations.[21]

Specialists of public and international law have acknowledged that neutrality has now "obtained to some extent a legal upgrading."[22] From

17 See my discussion in Paul Luif, "'Die alten Schablonen ... ob das Mozartkugeln, Lipizzaner oder die Neutralität sind – greifen in der komplexen Wirklichkeit des beginnenden 21. Jahrhunderts nicht mehr.' Die Diskussion über die Neutralität," in *Die umstrittene Wende. Österreich 2000-2006*, ed. Robert Kriechbaumer and Franz Schausberger (Vienna/Cologne/Weimar: Böhlau, 2013), 551–584, here 567–569.

18 "Rumsfeld: Österreich blockiert Truppenverlegung. Außenministerin Ferrero ergreift Partei für Berlin und Paris. Russland: Chefinspektor Blix sieht keinen Fortschritt bei Irak-Abrüstung," *Der Standard*, 14 Feb. 2003, 1.

19 Erich Witzmann, "Die Wahlmotive: Neutralität als großes Plus Fischers," *Die Presse*, 26 April 2004.

20 For details see Luif, "Die alten Schablonen," 571–574.

21 See Österreichische Sicherheitsstrategie. Sicherheit in einer neuen Dekade – Sicherheit gestalten, Wien, 2013 <https://www.bka.gv.at/DocView.axd?CobId=52099> (23 Jan 2016), and Parlamentskorrespondenz Nr. 641, 3 July 2013.

22 Theo Öhlinger, "Neutralität und EU-Mitgliedschaft. Verfassungs- und völkerrechtliche Determinanten der österreichischen Sicherheitspolitik," in *Strategie und Sicherheit 2014. Europas Sicherheitsarchitektur im Wandel*, ed. Johann Frank and Walter Matyas, (Vienna/Cologne/Weimar: Böhlau, 2014), 775–784, here 784. Öhlinger bases this on the new wording in Article 23f of the Federal Constitution.

a political scientist's view the preservation of neutrality is the "most convenient" position for the political parties, although the functions of neutrality in international relations "tend to approach zero."[23]

Why is Neutrality so "Popular"?

The "*Kronen Zeitung* effect" could be a hint how the popularity of neutrality is maintained. Other indicators are textbooks for pupils which stress neutrality and websites for schools which provide mostly links to supporters of neutrality.[24] It is appropriate to take a closer look at the attitude of Austrians toward neutrality.

An analysis of a public opinion poll from 2010 showed that 80 percent of the persons asked supported the statement "Neutrality is important, because Austria can only through it participate in peacekeeping operations." Even a larger percentage (84 percent) favored the statement "Austria should conduct an active neutrality policy through offering international good offices [*gute Dienste*] and mediating in conflicts." Austrians favor international peacekeeping of its military, but only a minority of them would support "bigger military contributions than has been the case so far" (32 percent). Military assistance by the armed forces for another EU country would only be supported by 36 percent. Overall, the core image of the Austrian armed forces seems to be connected to "civil protection [*Katastrophenschutz*]."[25]

The attitudes of the respondents of public opinion polls sometimes depend on the wording of the questions. One poll from March 1998 showed that 51 percent of Austrian would support NATO membership; the question included the statement that NATO is a "mutual assistance pact" and thus would assist Austria in case of an armed attack.[26] This polling result was used by the then-Senator Joe Biden in a debate in the US Senate in April 1998 to prevent the adoption of a three year moratorium

23 Anton Pelinka, "Die österreichische Außen- und Sicherheitspolitik. Eine kritische Würdigung," in *Strategie und Sicherheit 2012. Der Gestaltungsspielraum der österreichischen Sicherheitspolitik*, ed. Johann Pucher and Johann Frank (Vienna/Cologne/Weimar: Böhlau, 2012), 631–639, here 636–637.

24 This bias was even evident during the ÖVP/FPÖ government, when the conservative ÖVP was in charge of the education ministry; see Luif, "Die alten Schablonen," 578–579.

25 All data are from a representative telephone survey of 1,400 persons during July and August 2010. They are reproduced in: Günther Ogris, "Österreichs Sicherheitspolitik im Spiegel der Bevölkerungsmeinung," in *Strategie und Sicherheit 2012*, ed. Pucher/Frank, 813–824, especially 820–822.

26 "Keine Scheu vor dem Nato-Beistand," *Die Presse*, 10 April 1998; the survey was conducted by the market-Institut in March 1998, n=1000.

for further NATO enlargement after the accession of the Czech Republic, Hungary and Poland.[27]

Considering long-term trends, Reinprecht and Latcheva show that evaluations of neutrality among Austrians are "crucially influenced by current political events." Neutrality became less attractive with EU membership, whereas the Kosovo crisis (1999) and the terrorist attacks on 9/11 (as well as the Iraq war in 2003) strengthened support for neutrality.[28] In analyzing public opinion polls more closely, the authors distinguish between the historical role of neutrality, which is seen very positively by the Austrians. The evaluations of neutrality in the contemporary political context are more discriminating. In addition, emotional discourse barely seems to converge with politico-strategic discourse on the part of the elites.[29] The results of the empirical/quantitative analysis confirm the assumed connection between historical neutrality and national identity. Historical neutrality "has proven to be a key component both of emotional commitment to Austria … and of a nationalistic attitude syndrome marked by an overestimation of the Austrian nation."[30]

Critically, Reinprecht and Latcheva maintain that the "state doctrine of perpetual neutrality made it easier 'to steal out of history' and fail to acknowledge historical responsibility." The historically formed idea of neutrality has a strong influence upon the development of contemporary attitudes towards neutrality; today's discussion "is shaped by mythological and historicizing ideas."[31] Public discourse is less concerned with neutrality as a "concept of national security than with safeguarding a myth."[32] The enormous reservations shared by the Austrian population regarding NATO membership have become evident in comparison with the countries of East Central Europe.[33]

27 "In fact, Austrian public opinion is already changing. Earlier this month when the Austrian public was informed of NATO's Article 5 guarantees, for the first time in a national poll a majority of Austrians said that Austria should abandon its neutrality and join NATO. So if the Austrian government decides to follow public opinion, would we then want to tell the Austrians, 'Sorry, no applications accepted until the year 2002?'" *Congressional Record*: April 30, 1998 (Senate), page S3841. For details see Paul Luif, "Mitteleuropa und Österreich in der Europäischen Union," in *Die Dimension Mitteleuropa in der Europäischen Union. Geschichte und Gegenwart*, ed. Michael Gehler, Paul Luif, and Elisabeth Vyslonzil, (Hildesheim/Zürich/New York: Georg Olms Verlag, 2015), 279–315, here 300–301.

28 Christoph Reinprecht/Rossalina Latcheva, "Neutrality and Austrian Identity: Discourse on NATO and Neutrality as Reflected in Public Opinion," in *NATO, Neutrality and National Identity: The Case of Austria and Hungary*, ed. András Kovács and Ruth Wodak (Vienna/Cologne/Weimar: Böhlau, 2003), 439–460, here 444.

29 Ibid., 442 and 447.

30 Ibid., 454.

31 Ibid., 456–457.

32 Ibid., 458

33 Ibid., 446.

Political Parties and Neutrality

In view of the analysis by Reinprecht and Latcheva, it is no surprise that the FPÖ, probably the most "nationalistic" party in the Austrian Parliament, has also become the most fervent supporter of neutrality. For its leader, Heinz-Christian Strache, the FPÖ is obviously the only party which "upholds for good reasons the neutrality concept." His defense of neutrality incorporates criticism of the EU and the United States; in addition, he warns of an "economic warfare" against Russia.[34]

For the Austrian Chancellor Werner Faymann (SPÖ), neutrality is no "out-of-date model" (*Auslaufmodell*).[35] It is an "essential part" of Austria's national character and thus constitutes a "national interest by itself." His colleague, Defense Minister Gerald Klug (SPÖ) adds that neutrality is a "distinguishing feature" or "unique selling point" for Austria in the European Union.[36] Foreign Minister Sebastian Kurz (ÖVP) uses the same expression and admonishes Austrians to not be ashamed of neutrality. Kurz pointed out that the Iran nuclear negotiations took place in Vienna and Ukraine asked for information about neutrality.[37]

The leader of the Green's parliamentary group, Eva Glawischnig, titles her contribution in the Schöpfer volume with the same phrase I used 14 years ago (without acknowledging it). She warns the EU that Austria's neutrality law will show its impact in case the EU should dare to act outside the rules of the UN Charter.[38] This is similar to the admonishing by the former SPÖ minister Caspar Einem, who on the one hand has argued that neutral Austria could participate in a future European army, since that would not be identical to joining a military alliance. On the other hand, should this army start a war without a UN Security Council mandate, Austria would have to use its veto (EU decisions having military implications must

34 Heinz-Christian Strache, "Immerwährende Neutralität – Zwischen Identitätsstiftung und Vermittlungsauftrag," in *Die österreichische Neutralität. Chimäre oder Wirklichkeit?*, ed. Gerald Schöpfer (Graz: Leykam, 2015), 61–66, here 65–66.

35 Werner Faymann, "Die Neutralität ist kein Auslaufmodell," in *Die österreichische Neutralität*, ed. Schöpfer, 33–34.

36 He uses the German word "*Alleinstellungsmerkmal*" which has both meanings, see Gerald Klug, "Der Stellenwert der österreichischen Neutralität im 21. Jahrhundert," in *Die österreichische Neutralität*, ed. Schöpfer, 41–43, here 41.

37 Kurz was born in 1986 and is thus one of the youngest foreign ministers in the world; see Sebastian Kurz, "Die Neutralität ist kein Hindernis: Wir übernehmen international Verantwortung und üben Solidarität," in *Die österreichische Neutralität*, ed. Schöpfer, 37–39, here 39.

38 Eva Glawischnig, "Totgesagte leben länger," in *Die österreichische Neutralität*, ed. Schöpfer, 67–70, here 69.

be taken unanimously).[39] Only the chairman of the NEOS' parliamentary group regards neutrality as "outdated."[40]

Even representatives of Austria's business community (be it SMEs or bigger companies) as well as trade union leaders support neutrality. Austrian business spokespersons were not pleased when the EU (with Austria's support) decided about a number of economic sanctions against Russia in the context of the Ukraine crisis. Economic sanctions "are no suitable means for easing of tensions."[41]

The EU is with its Article 42.7 a political (and many would say also a military) alliance. Strangely enough, Austrian politicians are always talking about "solidarity" and demand an even stronger security cooperation in the EU (for instance, to avoid the reinforcement of NATO, where Austria is not a member), but at the same time support the geopolitical interests of this alliance only as long as neutrality (whatever that means) will not be affected. These contradictions bring problems with trust, sincerity and credibility.[42]

Conclusion: Austria without Close Cooperation Partners

The classic dilemma of neutrality, to "sit on the fence" in situations of military aggression or grave violations of human rights, was to be solved by "active" neutrality during the Cold War. The newer version is "committed" neutrality (*engagierte Neutralität*).[43] Austria's neutrality requires a committed participation in international crisis management and in cooperative security. A neutral country can act, in certain conflicts, more credible as mediator and provider of good offices.[44] Heinz Gärtner even thinks that the EU

39 Caspar Einem, "Welche Probleme eine europäische Armee bringt," *Die Presse*, 1 April 2015.

40 Matthias Strolz, "Die Neutralität aus Sicht von NEOS," in *Die österreichische Neutralität*, ed. Schöpfer, 71–72.

41 Christoph Leitl, "Frieden stiften ohne Waffen! Was kann Neutralität heute?," in *Die österreichische Neutralität*, ed. Schöpfer, 75–87, here 86.

42 See also Gunther Hauser, *Neutralität und Bündnisfreiheit in Europa. Sicherheitspolitische Herausforderungen für neutrale und bündnisfreie Staaten in Europa zu Beginn des 21. Jahrhunderts*, WIFIS-aktuell, Vol. 52 (Opladen/Berlin/Toronto: Barbara Budrich, 2015), 57.

43 A similar notion was already used by Franz Karasek, an ÖVP politician and Secretary General of the Council of Europe from 1979 to 1984. See Franz Karasek, "Für eine engagierte Neutralitätspolitik," in *Neue Fakten zu Staatsvertrag und Neutralität*, ed. Andreas Khol, Alois Mock, and Ludwig Steiner (Vienna: Politische Akademie, 1980), 321; taken from Andrew Earl Harrod, "Felix Austria?: Cold War Security Policy between NATO, Neutrality, and the Warsaw Pact, 1945–1989," Thesis, Fletcher School of Law and Diplomacy, 2007, 763.

44 Heinz Gärtner, *Thesen zur engagierten Neutralität* (Vienna: Österreichisches Institut für Internationale Politik oiip), Policy Paper 4/2015, 4.

could "come closer" to the "principles of neutrality" if it would adhere to two conditions: "First, if it [the EU] waives the mutual defense clause (Art. 42.7) among the member states, [a clause] which could abrogate neutrality. The mutual defense clause should remain reserved to NATO. Second, if it ties its missions which require the use of force, to the authorization of the UN Security Council according to Chapter VII [of the Charter]."[45]

Only a few months after these conditions were spelled out, François Hollande, the French President, invoked Article 42.7 TEU because of the terrorist attacks in Paris of November 13, 2015.[46] The EU member states could simply not ignore France's requests.[47] The UN Security Council Resolution 2249 of November 20, 2015 stated in Point 5 that UN member states should "take all necessary measures ... to prevent and suppress terrorist acts committed specifically by ISIL." Chapter VII was not mentioned. This posed problems for Austrian neutrality.[48] Austria planned to assist France by sending some 15 soldiers to Mali (UN-Mission Minusma), to extend the stay of five advisors in the Central African Republic (Eumam), and provide air transport to EU and UN missions in Africa.[49] These activities will probably not damage neutrality from a legal point of view, but the EU clearly did not waive its mutual defense clause. Austria obviously did not invoke the "Irish clause" which would allow Austria not to participate in activities under Article 42.7.

This relatively tepid response to the request by the French President indicates the cautious behavior of Austria in international military matters. Austria's Defense Minister would not give in to strong US pressure to send more than a handful of troops to Afghanistan.[50] This in contrast to non-aligned Finland and Sweden which had sent more than 100 soldiers to

45 Ibid., 6.

46 The statement of the French President was quite dramatic: "*La France est en guerre. ... J'ai demandé au ministre de la Défense de saisir dès demain ses homologues européens au titre de l'article 42-7 du traité de l'Union qui prévoit que lorsqu'un Etat est agressé, tous les Etats membres doivent lui apporter solidarité face à cette agression car l'ennemi n'est pas un ennemi de la France, c'est un ennemi de l'Europe.*" François Hollande, Discours du président de la République devant le Parlement réuni en Congrès, Versailles, le 16 novembre 2015 [François Hollande, Speech to Parliament convened in Congress, Versailles, 16 November 2015] <http://www.elysee.fr/declarations/article/discours-du-president-de-la-republique-devant-le-parlement-reuni-en-congres-3/> (23 Jan. 2016).

47 Thierry Tardy, "Mutual defence—one month on," Issue Alert, European Union Institute for Security Studies, December 2015, 1 <http://www.iss.europa.eu/uploads/media/Alert_55_Article_42.7.pdf> (23 Jan. 2016).

48 Ralph Janik, "IS und Neutralität: UN-Resolution lässt Zweifel offen," *Die Presse,* 23 Nov. 2015.

49 "UN-Einsätze: Heer hilft mit Herkules," *Die Presse,* 23 Dec. 2015.

50 "Austria Rejects US Pressure to Send Afghan Troops," *New York Times/The Associated Press,* 17 Dec. 2009, or "Darabos wehrt sich massiv gegen US-Kritik," *Die Presse,* 6 Dec. 2010.

Afghanistan.[51] Sweden reinforced its bonds to NATO by sending eight fighter jets to the NATO-led air campaign in Libya, whereas Austria did not participate at all.[52] Sweden and Finland, but not Austria, take part in exercises of the NATO Response Force, fulfill functions at NATO's headquarters and participate in the Strategic Airlift Capability (SAC) initiative, with aircrafts operating out of the Pápa Air Base in Hungary.[53]

Austria declared its readiness to participate in the *Partnership Interoperability Initiative* of NATO, initiated at the NATO Summit in Wales, September 2014. But Austria was not invited to the "enhanced opportunities" of the Initiative, which has given other partners, like Finland and Sweden, the possibility for close consultations. It has made it possible for them to influence NATO's planning process, guarantee them participation in NATO exercises and tasks in NATO's headquarters.[54]

But even more detrimental for Austria is its lack of close cooperation partners in the EU, as empirical data shows. In an analysis of the 25 EU member states in 2006, states representatives of twenty-two countries in the Council working group said they had close cooperation partners, only officials from Ireland, Slovenia, and Austria did not have such partners.[55] As a result, Austria had problems with, for example, reducing EU transit traffic or troubles with the "sanctions" of the EU 14 in 2000.

Austria is not part of the Visegrad Group which comprises the Czech Republic, Hungary, Poland and Slovakia.[56] This Group represents "Central Europe" in the EU and NATO. Even if these countries do not always have identical positions in EU or NATO issues, the intensive exchange of

---

51 Tanja Vasama, "Afghanistan: Now it's Finland's war, too," *Helsingin Sanomat. International Edition*, 20 June 2009.

52 "Europe's Cold War neutrals now taking sides, timidly, as they redefine security policy," *Washington Post/The Associated Press*, 9 April 2011.

53 Gerhard Jandl, "Neutralität und österreichische Sicherheitspolitik," in *Die österreichische Neutralität*, ed. Schöpfer, 193–206, here 203, and information from NATO.

54 Jandl, "Neutralität und österreichische Sicherheitspolitik," 203.

55 See Daniel Naurin, *Network Capital and Cooperation Patterns in the Working Groups of the Council of the EU*, EUI Working Paper RSCAS 2007/1 (Badia Fiesolana: European University Institute, 2007), in particular Figure 4 on page 16. This fact is regularly confirmed in talks with Austrian officials involved in EU decision-making.

56 See my discussion on the reasons why Austria is a "loner" in Central Europe in: Paul Luif, "Mitteleuropa und Österreich in der Europäischen Union," in *Die Dimension Mitteleuropa in der Europäischen Union. Geschichte und Gegenwart*, ed. Michael Gehler, Paul Luif, and Elisabeth Vyslonzil (Hildesheim/Zürich/New York: Georg Olms Verlag, 2015), 279–315. The Austrian alternative to the Visegrad Group, the "Regional Partnership," including besides the Visegrad countries Austria and Slovenia, was terminated in 2011; see Paul Luif, "Austria and Central Europe," in *Regional and International Relations of Central Europe*, ed. Zlatko Šabič and Petr Drulák (Basingstoke/New York: Palgrave Macmillan, 2012), 83–103, here 90.

information among ministers and officials of the different ministries gives the Visegrad Group advantages Austria lacks. Small countries usually do not have enough resources to gather all relevant information. The alternative often mentioned for Austria, "ad-hoc coalitions," are not too useful in the EU context, because most decisions made are "package deals" where countries exchange benefits to each other over time and over different issue areas. Another alternative, cooperation among the neutral and non-aligned members in the EU,[57] is questioned by other authors;[58] the Nordic neutrals (Finland, Sweden) simply have their primary contacts in the Nordic Group.

This "isolation" of Austria in international relations, in particular inside the EU, is practically never mentioned when discussing Austrian foreign policy or its neutrality, although neutrality seems to be one of the important reasons for this state of affairs. In the book on Austrian neutrality recently edited by Gerald Schöpfer, the authors, be it politicians or researchers, practically ignore Austria's neighbors in Central Europe, though articles analyze the Soviet Union and Switzerland.[59] A book dealing with the "leeway of Austria's security policy" has a section on the "view from the outside." But in these chapters only the views from the EU, the US, Russia, Switzerland, Turkey and Israel are discussed.[60]

This neglect of Austria's "natural partners" in Central Europe is nothing new. I already remarked at the end of 2003 concerning Austrian newly "discovered" neutrality: "The Austrian government's defence of neutrality might win the voters at home, but experts such as Paul Luif, predict it will not win them many allies within the EU."[61]

Two retired diplomats who have been practitioners and close analysts of Austrian foreign policy for many years characterize neutrality in 2015 this way: "In view of the predominant public opinion one regards neutrality as a taboo which one does not want to touch, although it is hard to deny that it has become hollowed out and meaningless."[62]

57 For example, Kramer, "Österreichs Beitrag," 99.

58 See for example Pelinka, "Die österreichische Außen- und Sicherheitspolitik," 633, and Jandl, "Neutralität und österreichische Sicherheitspolitik," 203 (concerning the cooperation of the WEP-5 in relation to NATO).

59 See Schöpfer, ed., *Die österreichische Neutralität.*

60 Pucher/Frank, eds., *Strategie und Sicherheit 2012*, section 6: "Anhang: Österreichs Sicherheitspolitik – Ein Blick von außen," 761–809.

61 Sarah Johnson, "Has Neutrality become a dirty word within the EU?," in *Insight Central Europe*, 12 December 2003 <http://www.incentraleurope.com/ice/issue/48491>. The Internet site where this statement was published (based on an interview) does not exist anymore. It was a cooperation of several radio stations, including the Austrian ORF, in Central Europe. This cooperation was soon cancelled after 2003.

62 Franz Cede and Christian Prosl, *Anspruch und Wirklichkeit. Österreichs Außenpolitik seit 1945* (Innsbruck/Vienna/Bozen: StudienVerlag, 2015), 35.

Select Bibliography

Cede, Franz, and Christian Prosl. *Anspruch und Wirklichkeit. Österreichs Außenpolitik seit* 1945. Innsbruck/Vienna/Bozen: StudienVerlag, 2015.

Gärtner, Heinz. "European Security: The End of Territorial Defense," *The Brown Journal of World Affairs* 9, no. 2 (2003): 1–13.

-------. "Thesen zur engagierten Neutralität." Vienna: Österreichisches Institut für Internationale Politik oiip, Policy Paper 4/2015.

Hauser, Gunther. *Neutralität und Bündnisfreiheit in Europa. Sicherheitspolitische Herausforderungen für neutrale und bündnisfreie Staaten in Europa zu Beginn des 21. Jahrhunderts* (WIFIS-aktuell, Vol. 52). Opladen/Berlin/Toronto: Barbara Budrich, 2015.

Hilpold, Peter. "Österreichs Neutralität nach Lissabon," *Österreichische Juristenzeitung*, no. 13 (2010/65): 590–598.

Kramer, Helmut. "Österreichs Beitrag zur europäischen und globalen Sicherheit. Ein Plädoyer für mehr Selbstbewusstsein im Bekenntnis zu aktiver Neutralitäts- und Friedenspolitik," in *Wieviel Sicherheit braucht Friede? Zivile und militärische Näherungen zur österreichischen Sicherheitsstrategie*, ed. Thomas Roithner, Johann Frank, and Eva Huber. Vienna: Lit Verlag, 2013, 89–100.

Luif, Paul. "Austria and Central Europe," in *Regional and International Relations of Central Europe*, ed. Zlatko Šabič and Petr Drulák. Basingstoke/New York: Palgrave Macmillan, 2012, 83–103.

-------. "'Die alten Schablonen ... ob das Mozartkugeln, Lipizzaner oder die Neutralität sind – greifen in der komplexen Wirklichkeit des beginnenden 21. Jahrhunderts nicht mehr.' Die Diskussion über die Neutralität," in *Die umstrittene Wende. Österreich 2000–2006*, ed. Robert Kriechbaumer and Franz Schausberger. Vienna/Cologne/Weimar: Böhlau, 2013, 551–584.

-------. "Mitteleuropa und Österreich in der Europäischen Union," in *Die Dimension Mitteleuropa in der Europäischen Union. Geschichte und Gegenwart*, ed. Michael Gehler, Paul Luif, and Elisabeth Vyslonzil. Hildesheim/Zürich/New York: Georg Olms Verlag, 2015, 279–315.

Naurin, Daniel. *Network Capital and Cooperation Patterns in the Working Groups of the Council of the EU* (EUI Working Paper RSCAS 2007/1). Badia Fiesolana: European University Institute, 2007.

Ogris, Günther. "Österreichs Sicherheitspolitik im Spiegel der Bevölkerungsmeinung," in *Strategie und Sicherheit 2012. Der Gestaltungsspielraum der österreichischen Sicherheitspolitik*, ed. Johann Pucher and Johann Frank. Vienna/Cologne/Weimar: Böhlau, 2012, 813–824.

Öhlinger, Theo. "Neutralität und EU-Mitgliedschaft. Verfassungs- und völkerrechtliche Determinanten der österreichischen Sicherheitspolitik," in *Strategie und Sicherheit 2014. Europas Sicherheitsarchitektur im Wandel*, ed. Johann Frank and Walter Matyas. Vienna/Cologne/Weimar: Böhlau, 2014, 775–784.

Pelinka, Anton. "Die österreichische Außen- und Sicherheitspolitik. Eine kritische Würdigung," in *Strategie und Sicherheit 2012. Der Gestaltungsspielraum der österreichischen Sicherheitspolitik*, ed. Johann Pucher and Johann Frank. Vienna/Cologne/Weimar: Böhlau, 2012, 631–639.

Pucher, Johann, and Johann Frank, eds. *Strategie und Sicherheit 2012. Der Gestaltungsspielraum der österreichischen* Sicherheitspolitik. Vienna/Cologne/Weimar: Böhlau, 2012.

Reinprecht, Christoph, and Rossalina Latcheva. "Neutrality and Austrian Identity: Discourse on NATO and Neutrality as Reflected in Public Opinion," in *NATO, Neutrality and National Identity: the case of Austria and Hungary*, ed. András Kovács and Ruth Wodak. Vienna/Cologne/Weimar: Böhlau, 2003, 439–460.

Schöpfer, Gerald, ed. *Die österreichische Neutralität. Chimäre oder Wirklichkeit?* Graz: Leykam, 2015.

Tardy, Thierry. "Mutual defence – one month on," Issue Alert, European Union Institute for Security Studies, December 2015, <http://www.iss.europa.eu/uploads/media/Alert_55_Article_ 42.7.pdf> (23 Jan. 2016).

Austria's EU Council Presidency.
Informal Meeting of the EU Foreign Ministers in Klosterneuburg.
Austrian Foreign Minister Ursula Plassnik with Danish Foreign Minister Per Stig Moller.
Klosterneuburg, Roland Schlager, 05 27 2006
Credit: APA PictureDesk

Volume 10: Günter Bischof/Anton Pelinka/Michael Gehler. *Austria in the European Union*. New Brunswick, NJ: Transaction 2002

Austria in the European Union

Gerda Falkner[1]

Introduction

Austria's EU membership turned twenty in the year 2015. So much has happened during these years that it now seems hard to figure the country outside the EU.

That state was different during the debates preceding accession, in particular before Austria had even joined the European Economic Area. Before the EEA agreement transferred a significant amount of the EC's economic acquis to the EFTA states, developing an alternative future had still seemed imaginable, particularly since also the EU itself was by then smaller and less developed. By now, all of Austria's neighboring states, except Switzerland (which has its bilateral agreements but is in fact mostly a policy-importer without a voice in the EU's decision-making), have joined the Union and even the Balkan states are members or have membership perspectives. That makes imagining an alternative to the EU seem a bit like political science fiction.

However, these are times when the multiple crises of European integration may possibly—in a, from today's perspective, worst-case scenario—make it indispensable to (again) consider alternatives, or to imagine at least a standstill of what before was an "ever closer" integration process. Even a spill-back in some areas of the European integration process seems rather likely, by the time of this writing, notably concerning the free movement across borders in the Schengen zone.

---

1 Parts of this text build on earlier publications such as "The EU14's 'Sanctions' Against Austria: Sense *and* Nonsense," *ECSA Review (European Community Studies Association USA)* 14, no. 1 (2001): 14–20; "Zur 'Europäisierung' des österreichischen politischen Systems," in *Politik in Österreich. Das Handbuch*, ed. Peter Gerlich et al. (Vienna: Manzsche Verlags- und Universitätsbuchhandlung, 2006), 82–94; "Austria: Frictions and Mixed Feelings," in *The European Union and the Member States*, ed. Eleanor E. Zeff and Ellen B. Pirro (Boulder CO/London: Lynne Rienner, 2006), 237–252 (with Lisa Hunt); "The Europeanization of Austria and Ireland: Small is Difficult?," in *Member States and the European Union*, ed. Simon Bulmer and Christian Lequesne, (Oxford: Oxford University Press, 2005), 209–228 (with Brigid Laffan).

The EU has profoundly changed since 1995: consider the Treaty reforms, the Euro, the Eurozone crisis and its ensuing deepening via additional European Central Bank powers, and the banking union and economic governance competences for the EU (e.g. via the European Semester, which puts a corset on national spending processes). But the world has changed, too; crucial challenges, like fighting climate change and ensuring the stability of financial markets, are now global in nature. It is therefore no surprise that the importance of rule-making at levels beyond the nation state has indeed increased significantly over time (Falkner/Müller 2014). A globalized world requires international rules, which are increasingly supplied both at EU and global levels. Therefore, the nation state no longer suffices to safeguard the well-being of citizens. Contrary to what populist politicians in many EU member states—including Austria—now insinuate, without the EU, the individual member states would by no means stand alone as powerful shapers of their own fate. They would still depend on international cooperation, but they would have much less voice and influence on global policies than they can have now, when they form a much larger chorus as the EU. This is particularly true for the small alpine Republic of Austria, with its less than eight million inhabitants.

But what exactly has changed in Austria due to EU membership? The remainder of this article will report what experts in the field concluded.

Austria in the EU: Effects on the Political System

Based on the referendum of 12 June 1994, where more than three million Austrians opted for membership (66 percent of the votes cast), Austria turned from "nation state" to "member state" (Alberta Sbragia), trading autonomy for voice and co-decision rights in the EU.

Membership in the European Union entailed significant adaptations to the traditional Austrian political system (Falkner 2006). Even the democratic principles of the Austrian constitution were affected:

Law-making competences were henceforth to be shared between the Austrian Parliament and the EU's Council of Ministers, the latter of which now almost always acts jointly with the European Parliament.

Austria's principal of the division of political powers changed, since national executives now dominated the legislative process at the EU level.

EU membership also influenced the rule of law principle, since the Austrian Constitutional Court's monopoly to interpret Austrian law was restricted to purely national affairs. In the EU, the European Court of Justice enjoys primacy in the interpretation of EU law.

Moreover, the federalist principle of Austrian constitutionality was deeply affected, since many competences of the regions were shifted to the EU.

Finally, one of the most notable features of the Austrian political system, the so-called system of social partnership, was significantly affected by EU membership, with many competences shifted outside of its central and influential position.

To counter-act these expected effects of EU accession, the Austrian constitution was amended. The directly elected first chamber of the Parliament (the *Nationalrat*) was attributed powers to exercise (in international comparison, rather strict) control over government actions at the European level. Article 23e of the Austrian constitution now specifically states that the relevant government minister is required to keep the Parliament informed about all EU-related matters. Most importantly, the Austrian Parliament may adopt a binding opinion that restricts government representatives in EU-level negotiations. Only for compelling reasons of foreign and integration policy ("*aus zwingenden außen- und integrationspolitischen Gründen*," Art. 23e para. 2) may a member of government depart from such a binding statement, and only after hearing the Parliament a second time.

Though far-reaching in theory, this provision has not in practice meant a major change to the expected shift in power from the Parliament to the government: the instrument is scarcely used, since parties in government usually have no interest in it, and Austrian parliamentarians have traditionally been bound by strict party discipline and lack individual resources for their work. It also needs mentioning that the particular features of EU-level negotiations, with all their dynamism and complexity, do not easily lend themselves to control by politicians who are not at the table. By the time of the adoption of the above-mentioned provisions in 1994, the government did not avail of the two-thirds majority needed to adopt constitutional acts. Therefore, votes from the opposition parties were needed to adapt the Austrian constitution to EU membership, and they demanded the control rights. However, "constitutional majority" for the parties in government was re-established in the next elections.

Similarly, the nine constituent units of the Austrian federal system (the *Bundesländer* or *Länder*) knew that their already relatively limited powers would be encroached upon significantly, both by shifts in the level of decision-making from the sub-national to the supranational level, and by the absence of any co-decision power for the *Bundesländer* as sub-national entities at the EU level. Again, steps were taken to ameliorate this situation in a similar way to that which was done to protect the powers of the federal Parliament. Article 23d of the Austrian constitution and a special state-*Bundesländer* agreement regulated the participation of the lower level units in relevant EU-related decision-making. They require due information of the *Länder* and give them powers to issue binding opinions. Even so, the unanimity required for these mandates binding the governmental negotiators in the EU Council is a high hurdle for the *Länder*, whose interests often differ widely. Therefore, *Länder* mandates on the government have been very rare, too. Moreover, the national position sometimes gets decided before representatives from the *Länder* can agree on a common position since, in practice, the *Länder* have even more difficulty in keeping up to date with EU negotiations than the Parliament does.

While it is important that the government has to inform Parliament and *Länder* about all relevant EU matters, this need for information has led to an overflow of reading material for the national-level politicians. In the first year of Austrian EU-membership, the Parliament was informed of 17,317 EU legislative matters. Unfortunately, the law only provided for the transmission of relevant documents, not for their analytical summary, and hence the Parliamentarians—at least initially—felt quite overwhelmed. Over time, however, the Austrian Parliament has developed into one of the most active national institutions regarding the "subsidiarity check" of new legislation proposed by the EU Commission. This is not primarily a means to control their own government, but rather it presents an opportunity to get involved in EU politics—if only with a "negative" thrust bringing down (and not promoting) initiatives with the argument that the lower levels' competences should not be impinged (see also Dossi 2015).

In any case, the counter-steering of political effects on the Austrian system via constitutional reform has in essence remained a rather dead letter. However, this has not triggered much controversy. Related complaints from within the governing parties remained very few, since party discipline levels are high in Austria in the case of the social democrats' SPÖ and the Christian-democrats' ÖVP (and those two parties have been in government together most of the time: 1945–1966, 1987–2000, 2007–present/2016). On the level of the political discourse, those two parties' post-war dominance has only been broken with the upsurge of the Freedom Party (FPÖ) and its populist, nationalist and, in recent times, unequivocally anti-EU integration attitudes. They are at present the third largest party (20.5 percent; SPÖ: 26.8 percent, ÖVP: 24 percent), but quickly gaining according to opinion polls, and "committed to our homeland of Austria as part of the German-speaking linguistic and cultural community, to the groups of people native to our country and to a Europe of free peoples and fatherlands" (FPÖ party program, "Austria First"). A critical but constructive leaning towards European integration characterizes the Green party, which has fought hard to use existing means to exercise control over government activities in Brussels. The newest stable party in the Austrian Parliament, the NEOS (2013: 5 percent), take a clearly pro-European stance.

That counter-steering measures preceding EU adhesion showed little effect is no different when we turn to the "social partnership," Austria's deeply rooted, though informal, system of corporatist cooperation of the centralized peak associations of labor and management with the government in developing public policies. Both the structural (interest group set up) and the procedural (involvement in policy-making) dimensions of corporatism were extremely well developed in Austria. There are a number of hierarchically organized interest groups set up by Austrian law where membership is obligatory. The classic social partner institutions in Austria are thus the Chamber of Business (*Wirtschaftskammer Österreich*), the Chamber of Labor (*Bundesarbeitskammer*), the Conference of Presidents of the Chambers of Agriculture (PRÄKO), and the encompassing Austrian trade union confederation (ÖGB). These participants in the "social partnership" used to work together on a constant basis, in both an informal and formal capacity, since World War II. It was not uncommon in Austria for the government and the social partners to negotiate draft legislation before it was approved (or rather, rubber-stamped) by Parliament. Clearly, the shift of competences to the EU cut many issues out of that cooperation.

However, the major Austrian interest group federations received some favors before EU membership, such as rooming in the Austrian Representation in Brussels. But they were not, in the end, allowed to be present in Council negotiations. And yet, again, the counter-steering of expected effects was hardly effective, although it needs mentioning that other, internal developments (like the center-right government after the year 2000) have meanwhile made the model of "social partnership" less relevant as well (see also Karlhofer/Tálos 2005). The "social partners" had very actively campaigned for joining the EU, in the 1994 referendum, and they still have a clear pro-European posture. That they hardly complain about their loss of influence seems understandable in the context of their close proximity to the two parties of the grand coalition government, which gives at least peak personnel special relations and insights into the government's EU-related actions and opinions.

Austria in the EU: Conflict and Compromise

This section will outline the worst conflict between Austria and the EU (below a). It will also discuss Austria's more general approach as an EU member, which has frequently been criticized as being rather passive and as not following up on former Chancellor Bruno Kreisky's active foreign policy approach, which had made Austria a well-known part of the international community back in the 1970s (below b).

a) A rather peculiar moment in Austria's history of EU membership was Austrian government formation in the year 2000 and the EU's reaction to this. A few days before the new Austrian center-right government between ÖVP and FPÖ (whose infamous chairman Jörg Haider was not, however, in the government) was formally agreed on 4 February 2000, the Portuguese EU Council Presidency issued a statement "on behalf of fourteen Member States" out of the then-fifteen. It announced a list of what were de facto, though not de jure, "sanctions," i.e. that "The governments of the fourteen Member States will not promote or accept any official bilateral contacts at political level with an Austrian government integrating the FPÖ, there will be no support for Austrian candidates seeking positions in international organizations, Austrian Ambassadors in EU capitals will only be received at a technical level."

At that time, the Treaty on European Union (TEU) included only provisions on the suspension of membership rights in case of "the existence of a serious and persistent breach" of basic principles. It is important to note that this procedure was at no point initiated against Austria, since it was almost uncontested among the EU 14 that Austria was not "in serious and persistent breach" of the Treaties' basic principles. The other EU governments were, however, concerned that this might be the case at some point in the future, under a government including the FPÖ. From the perspective of a close political community, where the members of national governments make up the main decision-making body and can block many crucial initiatives, at times even unilaterally, this seems a legitimate concern and reacting to the formation of the new Austrian government made sense.

However, the wisdom of the specific form of reaction seemed questionable: Considering the EU provisions in force, it would have been a clear breach of the Treaty provisions if "EU sanctions" had been imposed on Austria. Many even thought that the Fourteen's multiple "bilateral" action was premature, because the Union's basic rules do not only contain the clear procedures for potential sanctions outlined above, but also provisions on the respect of the national identities of the Member States (then Art. E TEU) and prohibiting any discrimination for reasons of nationality (e.g. Art. 12 TEC). From this perspective, the Fourteen's "bilateral" measures seemed questionable, at least in the spirit of the Treaties. Furthermore, their design was criticized for its initially open-ended character and the lack of an exit option, other than a breakdown of the Austrian center-right government. The Presidency, an institution of the Union, was used to proclaim the multi-national (but not "EU") decision. Content-wise, the second measure (non-support of Austrians in international organizations) has been discussed most controversially. Point two of the "sanctions" could harm persons who had never in their life voted for the FPÖ or who had even protested against the center-right government—despite the fact that one of the EU's major policies is non-discrimination on grounds of nationality!

Five months after the imposition of the "sanctions," the Fourteen developed an ad-hoc exit strategy based on a report by three "wise men." These criticized the FPÖ, (for methods of campaigning and for intimidation of political critics via litigation in court, to give a few examples), but confirmed the general opinion that the new government had not acted against European values. On that basis, the "sanctions" were lifted without any follow-up procedure or qualification. It should be mentioned, however, that the Austrian government had threatened to hold a referendum on blocking EU reforms if the sanctions continued. In any case, the Austrian government came out of this episode domestically rather stronger and more unified than was initially the case. The same is true for the ÖVP and the breakdown of the center-right government in autumn 2002. After serious internal upheavals within the Freedom Party (the FPÖ members of government were sidelined by more right-wing and "Haiderist" members in an extraordinary party convention), the ÖVP became the strongest Austrian party and was therefore, in the second ÖVP-FPÖ government formed in late February 2003, in a more powerful position than before. This also meant that the ÖVP could pursue its European integration stance more easily than before. By the time of the new government formation (which happened to fall into the crucial phase of the ten accession treaty preparations in Brussels), the ÖVP indeed had its pro-enlargement policy accepted by its to-be coalition partner.

The decision to include the FPÖ in a coalition government was highly controversial within Austria from the beginning. However, the decision by the other fourteen EU member states to de facto sanction Austria for this move failed to bring about a change in the composition of the new government, and may have, ironically, contributed to an erosion of support for the EU within Austria, even among those who did not sympathize with the FPÖ.

Altogether, the EU's attempt to intervene in the formation of the Austrian government in 2000 became probably the most prominent and controversial case of Austria having an impact on the EU, although indirectly and hardly on purpose: at the Nice Summit for EU Treaty reform in December 2000, the EU15 decided that the Union can henceforth already intervene if there is a danger of serious breach of Treaty principles (by addressing appropriate recommendations or setting up a Committee of Wise Persons to report on the case). That the member state in question must be heard before such a measure can be taken had been promoted by the Austrian delegation.

Until now, however, these provisions have not been applied, in practice. A lack of problems with sticking to the basic principles of the Treaties is not the cause, but rather the fact that there are now several rather nationalist governments within the EU and in many places a trend towards populism. As a consequence, the needed unanimity except one vote for sanctions seems out of reach—too many governments now oppose, in principle, any "intervention from outside" into what they define as national affairs. This has meant that states like Hungary, under the Orbán government, and Poland, governed by the law-and-justice party, could recently attack pluralist control in their countries quite openly and promote explicitly an "illiberal democracy" without having to seriously fear a consequence for their rights under the EU Treaties.

b) Austria is generally considered a member state with comparatively little impact on the EU level. That is not necessarily an effect of its small size and consequently few votes, which could be counter-steered by diplomatic effort and genius, but seems to relate to a lack of interest by many Austrian politicians. As Sarah Mayer (2015) highlights in her studies of the Austrian political discourse on the EU, the joint effort of the major political parties predating the Austrian membership referendum was rather short-lived. Back then, the parties in government, jointly with the social partner organizations and dominant media like the *Kronen Zeitung*, had formed a very dominant coalition promoting a yes-vote in the referendum, not only by taking a very active part in the political discourse, but even by using means of advertisement and side-lining more critical actors. Once Austria had become a member state, and particularly after the "sanctions" against the center-right government, the mainstream parties allowed the political debate to shift towards topics such as the loss of sovereignty and national identity, as promoted by the EU sceptics. The latter are now no longer only in the FPÖ but, crucially also in, for example, the highly relevant major daily newspaper in Austria, the *Kronen Zeitung*—and this seems to have had a strong impact on the vote-seeking politicians.

A decisive moment was the "letter to the *Kronen Zeitung*" in 2008 by two leading figures in the social democratic SPÖ, then-Chancellor Alfred Gusenbauer and then-designated head of party Werner Faymann (now Chancellor). Although a few weeks earlier the SPÖ had still rejected a referendum on the ratification of the Lisbon Treaty, the party was now informed by their leaders via this letter published in the *Kronen Zeitung* that henceforth any changes to the EU's Treaties that might affect Austrian interests should be put to a public vote—as the FPÖ had traditionally requested. The ÖVP used this occasion to break the governmental coalition and call elections, although this seemed more an issue of tactics than of true EU commitment. Even though the SPÖ softened its stance again later, the coalition governments of SPÖ and ÖVP have since been characterized by using EU-related topics for intra-coalition quarrels, rather than by pursuing a joint vision of European integration (Mayer 2015: 294).

To act in concert would seem all the more important, since the Austrian electorate has meanwhile turned into one of the most EU-skeptical within the Union: by the time of the most recent EP elections, Austrian EU membership was judged a good thing by only 42 percent (a bad thing: 29 percent, neither: 27 percent; ÖGfE/AUTNES-Nachwahlanalyse 2014).

Even with regard to the recent, major challenge of hundreds of thousands of refugees, mainly from the Syrian war, coming to the EU (often under life-threatening conditions, since they have no safe, legal way of entering), Austria's record as an EU member state is not too impressive. When Austria still was at the outer borders of the free-travel Schengen zone, it vociferously requested burden-sharing within the EU. Later, when Austria was surrounded by many Schengen partners, it made no significant efforts to help Italy and Greece cope with their highly over-proportional influx of refugees—at least not before 2015, when many refugees started to move towards the wealthier EU member states, such as Austria, and most EU member states finally voted for at least some degree of distribution of refugees within the EU (albeit a quite limited one, compared to the overall numbers, and one that is to date not being implemented).

It is true that the government in Vienna joined German chancellor Angela Merkel's approach of opening borders when a human tragedy was about to happen in Hungary and along the Balkans in autumn 2015. However, it bears mentioning that the expectation was that people would only pass through Austria to Germany and the Nordic countries. When almost 100,000 refugees asked for asylum here, the discourse quickly turned towards how to most effectively keep people out of the country, and finally the social democratic Chancellor Faymann gave in to his conservative coalition partner: a partial fence along the southern border was built (in Austrian politics for a while called a "construction with side parts" to prevent using the notion of fencing out asylum seekers) and border controls were re-established with Austria's Schengen partner Slovenia. In vain, the Austrian EU Commissioner Hahn had warned member states that unilateral action would trigger a domino effect.

Concluding Outlook

To change the EU-skeptical discourse, as dominated by the *Kronen Zeitung* and the political right wing, the ensuing rather critical outlook of the electorate, and the rather passive approach of the leading politicians vis-à-vis EU affairs seems the crucial (and giant) challenge regarding Austria in the EU. The matter is urgent, since the EU is now confronted with a major crisis. Therefore, a nation-first orientation of the parties in the political center is not only disadvantageous from the strategic point of view, (since the chances of being a member state are not being realized in full whilst autonomy has already been given up), but could unduly support those forces both inside and outside of this country that want to stop or even end European integration—exactly at times when common solutions to major humanitarian and political challenges would seem crucial from a problem-solving perspective.

Select Bibliography

Dossi, Harald. "20 Jahre EU-Mitgliedschaft: Erwartungen und Erfahrungen," in *20 Jahre EU-Mitgliedschaft Österreichs*, ed. Andreas Maurer, Heinrich Neisser, and Johannes Pollak. Vienna: Facultas Verlag, 2015, 250–261.

Falkner, Gerda, and Patrick Müller, eds. *EU Policies in a Global Perspective: Shaping or Taking International Regimes?* London/New York: Routledge, 2014.

Karlhofer, Ferdinand, and Emmerich Tálos, eds. *Sozialpartnerschaft – eine europäische Perspektive?* Münster: Lit-Verlag, 2005.

Maurer, Andreas, Heinrich Neisser, and Johannes Pollak, eds. *20 Jahre EU-Mitgliedschaft Österreichs*. Vienna: Facultas Verlag, 2015.

Mayer, Sara. "Wer kämpft noch für Europa?" in *20 Jahre EU-Mitgliedschaft Österreichs*, ed. Andreas Maurer, Heinrich Neisser, and Johannes Pollak. Vienna: Facultas Verlag, 2015, 307–323.

"ÖGfE/AUTNES-Nachwahlanalyse zur Europawahl," in *Österreichische Gesellschaft für Europapolitik (ÖGfE)*, 23 July 2014 <http://oegfe.at/wordpress/blog/2014/07/23/oegfeautnes-nachwahlanalyse-zur-europawahl/> (1 Feb 2016), and much other useful reading on the *ÖGfE* website <http://oegfe.at/wordpress/oegfe-policy-briefs/>.

Austrian chancellor Kurt Schuschnigg pays tribute to Engelbert Dollfuß.
Opening ceremony for the Dollfuß residential homes in Gänserndorf.
Gänserndorf, Wilhelm Willinger, 05 24 1936
Credit: Austrian National Library

Volume 11: Günter Bischof/Anton Pelinka/Alexander Lassner, eds. *The Dollfuss/Schuschnigg Era in Austria.* New Brunswick, NJ: Transaction, 2004

Dictatorship, Fascism and the Demise of Austrian Democracy

Tim Kirk

Almost a century on from its creation at the end of the First World War, there has been something of a surge of interest in the history of the First Austrian Republic, which has often seemed to stand in the shadow of the more glamorous culture of *fin-de-siècle* Vienna, or the more dramatic political history of the Weimar Republic. In particular, the controversial history of the destruction of democracy in the early 1930s and the establishment of the Dollfuss-Schuschnigg dictatorship has been overshadowed by the Anschluss and the history of Nazi Austria, not least since the Waldheim affair of the 1980s focused attention on the country's wartime past. Yet in many ways the history of the preceding, "home-grown" dictatorship has remained a much more difficult and controversial subject for Austrians. Few know very much about the dictatorship or how it came about, and discussion of the period has been hampered by the political controversy it still invariably generates.

In this context, the renewal of interest in the political culture—and political legacy—of the "Dollfuss-Schuschnigg era in Austria" since the publication of the volume on that subject in this series thirteen years ago is very much to be welcomed, and not least for the refreshing open-mindedness with which a new generation of historians has sought to question and overturn received wisdoms and old methodologies. Perspectives have shifted considerably, and a tendency to construct contemporary history in terms of affairs of state and institutions, parties, and programs has given way to new approaches, above all an emphasis on everyday experiences and preoccupations that transcend both national boundaries and the chronological milestones of high politics. The work of Tara Zahra and others on indifference to nationalism in the late imperial period and the successor states has enormous implications for how we understood popular political mentalities in the age of fascism and dictatorship;[1] and the work of

1 Tara Zahra, *Kidnapped Souls: National Indifference and the Battle for Children in the Bohemian Lands, 1900–1948* (Ithaca: Cornell University Press, 2008); see also the collection of articles edited by Tara Zahra and Pieter Judson, *Austrian History Yearbook* 43 (2012).

Robert Gerwarth and others on the transnational roots and networks of the paramilitary political violence is a reminder that from the outset Austria stood in the cross-currents of the formation and development of fascism and authoritarianism in central Europe, that its own fascisms were shaped as much by European developments as by domestic circumstances.[2]

A further important shift has been the development of a much more critical engagement with the historiography of the period. It has frequently been observed, and with good reason, that study of the history of Austria's First Republic has been dominated by the political agendas of the Second, and above all by the perceived need to preserve the domestic political peace that eluded the pre-war generation. Not unlike the Weimar Republic, the Austrian First Republic has frequently been set up as an experiment in democracy that was doomed to fail on account of the uncompromisingly entrenched positions of its leading political actors, and has stood as a warning of what happens when political consensus breaks down. In this comfortable narrative of flawed democracy and inevitable destinies, responsibility for the destruction of parliamentary democracy is shared, and the dictatorship is presented not as fascist itself, but as a defense against the fascism of the Nazis. For most historians of the period, this has long since ceased to be a convincing account of events.[3]

As new, more critical approaches to the history of the First Republic have revealed its positive impact on the lives of many Austrians, such "useful" narratives, and the motives behind them, have been increasingly questioned by a younger generations of researchers, often in doctoral dissertations, project reports, and conference papers. Among the most important recent contributions to the field are two very substantial collections of essays. The first of these, entitled simply *Österreich 1933–1938*, is the product of a conference held in 2011, and jointly organized by the Institute of Contemporary History and the Faculty of Law at Vienna University.[4] It offers an interdisciplinary range of approaches both to the history of the period and its post-war impact, from the origins of the dictatorship and the nature of its constitution, to issues of interpretation, restitution, and rehabilitation since the war. As a collaboration between legal scholars and

2 Robert Gerwarth, "The Central European Counterrevolution: Paramilitary Violence in Germany, Austria and Hungary after the Great War," *Past and Present* 200 (2008): 175–209; Robert Gerwarth and John Horne, eds., *War in Peace: Paramilitary Violence in Europe after the Great War* (Oxford: Oxford University Press, 2013).

3 See Jill Lewis, "Conservatives and Fascists in Austria, 1918–1934," in *Fascists and Conservatives*, ed. Martin Blinkhorn (London: Unwin Hyman, 1990), 98–117, here 114.

4 Ilse Reiter-Zatloukal, Christiane Rothländer and Pia Schölnberger, eds., *Österreich 1933–1938. Interdisziplinäre Annäherungen an das Dollfuß-/Schuschnigg Regime* (Vienna: Böhlau, 2012).

historians, it is particularly strong on the fundamentally unconstitutional ways in which the dictatorship was established and operated, using illegal property confiscations as an instrument of repression and political control.[5] The dictatorship was established not by constitutional means, but by violence, and critics of the regime and its policies were dealt with peremptorily. When Dollfuss was interrupted at a rally with the cry "Herr Bundeskanzler, you are violating the constitution," the speaker was unceremoniously removed by a violent mob, bleeding from his nose and ears.[6] Others ended up in the "detention camp" at Wöllersdorf, as opposition was suppressed and political dissent was criminalized.[7] A particular strength of this collection is its attention to the divisive post-war legacy of the dictatorship, including the grudging rehabilitation of such political victims, whose convictions were eventually annulled by the Rehabilitation Law of 2011.[8]

The second collection, also based on a conference in Vienna, draws on an equally impressive range of contributors, and with surprisingly little overlap. It complements the first volume in so far as it aims to provide a historiographical snapshot of the field, drawing on work in progress in order to take stock of new approaches and interpretations.[9] The editors argue that while the political controversy surrounding the subject is still very discernible—and academic arguments about the nature of the regime frequently spill over into the press—the acrimony has nevertheless receded in recent years, and it should now be possible to discuss the regime on a purely scholarly basis. They too see Austria's experience between the wars as inseparable from broader political developments across the continent. The country was at the epicenter of the conflict between fascism and democracy; and although its dictatorships, both before and after 1938, were to a large extent shaped by external circumstances, events in Austria itself helped in turn to shape and influence political developments taking place abroad. Taken together, the contributions to these two volumes constitute a challenging reappraisal of the "corporate state," and one that constitutes

5 See Ilse Reiter-Zatloukal, "Repressivpolitik und Vermögenskonfiskation 1933–1938," in ibid., 61–76; and Christiane Rothländer, "Die Durchführungspraxis des politisch motivierten Vermögensentzugs in Wien 1933–1938," in ibid., 77–93.

6 Thomas Olechowski and Kamila Staudigl-Cheicowicz, "Die Staatsrechtslehre an der Universität Wien 1933–1938," in ibid., 227–241, here 232.

7 Pia Schölnberger, "'Ein Leben ohne Freiheit ist kein Leben.' Das Anhlatelager Wöllersdorf 1933–1938," in ibid., 94–107.

8 Ilse Reiter-Zatloukal, "'Unrecht im Sinne des Rechtsstaats' – Das Aufhebungs- und Rehabilitierungsgesetz 2011," in ibid., 327–346.

9 Florian Wenninger and Lucille Dreidemy, eds., *Das Dollfuß/Schuschnigg-Regime 1933–1938. Vermessung eines Forschungsfeldes* (Vienna: Böhlau, 2013).

part of a continuing process of questioning the founding mythologies of the Second Republic, from both within and beyond the academy.[10]

By their nature, however, conference collections draw on a diversity of views and approaches, and despite the gradual withdrawal from political positions, there is still a measure of disagreement, or at best a difference of emphasis, on quite how the dictatorship is to be defined, and on how we should compare it with other, similar regimes elsewhere in Europe, a dilemma epitomized in the formulation of R. John Rath many decades ago: "The First Austrian Republic—Totalitarian, Fascist, Authoritarian, or What?"[11] As Gerhard Botz has rather pointedly observed in his own most recent contribution to the debate, it is telling that contributors to the same volume have not managed "to agree on a name for their subject: authoritarian, *(berufs)ständisch* (corporatist) or Austrofascist (with or without quotation marks) are used."[12] Researchers themselves, of course, are only too aware of the tendency to dwell on definitions, and if there is a measure of agreement among the contributors here, it is that more solid empirical research is needed on all aspects of the history of the regime. And there is no shortage of unused or underused archival material; Georg Hans Schmitt, for example, has found the party archive of the ÖVP and former Christian Social Party, housed in the Karl von Vogelsang Institute, to be an underused resource and one which, in addition to its collections of records and political publications and its press archive and library, is particularly rich in visual material, with over three thousand posters and some twenty thousand photographs. Perhaps the most important new resource, however, is the collection *Vaterländische Front und Bundeskanzleramt*. This comprises 400 boxes of documents formerly held in a special archive in Moscow, and returned to the Austrian state archives in 2009. The contents cover not only the establishment and development of the Fatherland Front, but various aspects of the regime's activities, including its relationship with the Church.[13]

10 See also Stephan Neuhäuser, ed., *"Wir werden ganze Arbeit leisten..." – Der austrofaschistische Staatsstreich 1934* (Norderstedt: Books on Demand GmbH, 2004).

11 R. John Rath, "The First Austrian Republic—Totalitarian, Fascist, Authoritarian, or What?," in *Beiträge zur Zeitgeschichte. Festschrift Ludwig Jedlicka zum 60. Geburtstag*, ed. Rudolf Neck and Adam Wandruszka (St. Pölten: Verlag Niederösterreichisches Pressehaus, 1976), 163–81.

12 Gerhard Botz, "The Coming of the Dollfuss-Schuschnigg Regime and the Stages of its Development," in *Rethinking Fascism and Dictatorship in Europe*, ed. António Costa Pinto and Aristotle Kallis (Basingstoke: Palgrave, 2014), 121–153, here 121.

13 Georg-Hans Schmitt, "'Im Namen Gottes, des Allmächtigen': christlich – deutsch – berufsständisch. Ausgewählte Aspekte über den Stand und die Perspektiven der Forschung über das christlich-soziale Lager in den Jahren 1929 bis 1938," in *Das Dollfuß/Schuschnigg Regime*, ed. Wenninger and Dreidemy, 141–158, here, 146–7.

Extensive use is made of the Moscow material by Emmerich Tálos in his long awaited comprehensive study of the Austrofascist political system, a book that builds on several decades of research and expertise in the field and will doubtlessly be the single most valuable work of reference on the subject for the foreseeable future.[14] Tálos systematically analyzes the workings of the regime, relating its propaganda claims and political structures to the realities of life under the dictatorship. He begins with a lengthy discussion of the origins of the regime in the political and economic crisis in Austria during the early 1930s and concludes with a relatively short discussion of its demise in 1938. At the center of the study is an account of the dictatorship that reveals its hollow "corporate" institutions as mere window dressing, imposed and controlled from above by an authoritarian executive, which was in turn supported by the real pillars of the regime: the Fatherland Front (*Vaterländische Front*, VF), the paramilitary organizations, and above all the Catholic Church. The term "corporate state" reflected the self-image the regime wanted to project, he argues, not the reality of the Austrofascist political system. There is no doubt for Tálos that the regime was fascist: Mussolini's Italy was a model from beginning to end, and the *Duce* himself a political mentor to Dollfuss.[15] The Austrian regime did not come to power with the help of a popular mass movement, but attempted to create one instead in the wake of a coup d'état. Unfortunately, any ambition that the movement might have had to make of the VF a flamboyant avant-garde in imitation of other more successful fascist movements was frustrated by the indifference of the people, but also by the regime's continuing insistence on a financial orthodoxy, which helped prolong the economic depression in Austria until well into the 1930s. Kept short of funds by a parsimonious government, the Fatherland Front had to restrict itself largely to cheaper activities, such as snooping on its fellow citizens.

New work brings new insights, and some of the most fascinating ones are from the very same Fatherland Front snoops. In the absence of elections or free public opinion the regime—like other dictatorships—had to gauge the impact of its policies by relying on reports on popular morale in the provinces from its own rank and file, and Tálos uses these reports to assess

14 Emmerich Tálos, *Das Austrofaschistische Herrschaftssystem. Österreich 1933–1938* (Vienna: LIT Verlag, 2013). A sixth edition of the collection of essays on Austrofascism edited by Tálos and Wolfgang Neugebauer in 1984, long the standard work on the subject, appeared a year earlier: Emmerich Tálos and Wolfgang Neugebauer, eds., *Austrofaschsimsus. Politik-Ökonomie-Kultur 1933–1938* (Vienna: LIT Verlag, 2012).

15 See the recently republished correspondence between the two: Wolfgang Maderthaner, ed., *"Der Führer bin ich selbst": Engelbert Dollfuss – Benito Mussolini, Briefwechsel; mit weiterführenden Beiträgen zum Austrofaschismus von Emmerich Tálos und Wolfgang Maderthaner* (Vienna: Löcker, 2004). The exchange was originally published as an appendix to Julius Braunthal, *The Tragedy of Austria* (London: Gollancz, 1948).

the reception of the regime. What he finds is revealing: high expectations of change initially, and in the Fatherland Front itself enthusiasm both among functionaries and ordinary members. Within a couple of years, however, it seems to have become clear that the early promise of the regime would remain unfulfilled, and the buoyant mood had dissipated somewhat, even among the regime's own supporters. By the summer of 1935, reports from VF branches in the provinces were openly pessimistic about the political reliability of the population: estimations of "patriotic" political support for the regime in Salzburg and Styria hovered between twenty and forty percent; in the Tyrol VF membership "existed only on paper"; and the political outlook for the regime in suburban Vienna was bleakest of all. One of the main reasons for this widespread popular disillusionment was the continuing economic stagnation. Among the working class in particular, the long-term unemployment that affected virtually every family was combined with deteriorating wages and conditions for those in work, as well as welfare cuts, employer chicanery, and political repression. Disaffection was widespread not only among Social Democrats in the suburbs of Vienna, but among the regime's own supporters in the provinces as well, as a report from a "loyal" VF branch in Laa an der Thaya makes clear: "Workers can find no justice in this state. We must become Communists if the bosses are going to walk all over us just as they like. What has happened so far is a sham."[16] If the objective of corporatism was to transcend the class conflict in modern industrial society over which Catholic ideologues fretted so much, its introduction in Austria was an abject failure.

Central to the regime's plans for integrating workers into the 'corporate state' was the so-called unity union (*Einheitsgewerkschaft*), and trades unionists per se were not treated with quite the outright open hostility reserved for the regime's straightforwardly political enemies in the Social Democratic Party, as Paul Pasteur shows in his recent study of trade unions under the dictatorship. Originally published in French in 2002, Pasteur's work is based on a wide range of archival sources in both Vienna and Amsterdam, (where Otto Leichter's papers are deposited), along with a number of personal memoirs from the period, and it constitutes an important contribution both to the history of the regime and the history of the labor movement.[17] The containment of organized labor was, after all, one

16 Tálos, *Das austrofaschistische Herrschaftssystem,* 452.

17 Paul Pasteur, *Unter dem Hakenkreuz. Gewerkschafter und Gewerkschafterinnen in Österreich 1934–1938*. Translated from the French by Sonja Niederacher (Innsbruck: StudienVerlag, 2008), originally published as *Être syndiqué(e) à l'ombre de la croix potencée. Corporatisme, syndicalisme, résistance en Autriche, 1934–1938* (Rouen: Publications de l'Université de Rouen, 2002).

of the principal goals of the Austrofascist project; what happened to trade unionists and how they responded should be central to our understanding of what the dictatorship was about, and to what extent it succeeded in its aims. The events of 1934 were the most serious reverse the Austrian labor movement had suffered since its years of illegality in the late nineteenth century, and the initial response was one of widespread disorientation and an optimistic hope that the regime would not survive. While the overwhelming majority of trade unionists were resolutely oppositional, few were prepared to engage in illegal activity, and some functionaries optimistically believed that they might be able to collaborate with the regime—despite the swift call from the exiled Social Democratic leadership in Brno for a boycott of the regime's government union and all its works. Their hopes were dashed, however, despite (qualified) overtures from their Christian Social colleagues; on this issue at least, the *Heimwehren* clearly had the upper hand within the regime's power cartel and scuppered the chances of a rapprochement between regime and workforce. The labor movement's achievements during the First Republic now proved very fragile to say the least, and incapable of surviving the suppression of democratic institutions, while Christian Social promises of new "corporate" institutions to represent the position of the workforce remained unfulfilled. Instead, employer-friendly regulations were introduced, wages were driven down, and conditions in the workplace deteriorated, above all for women workers and apprentices, who were left increasingly at the mercy of unscrupulous and above all unregulated employers.[18] The regime's "unity union" was at best ineffectual, at worst an indifferent bureaucracy; and when it came to strikes and other conflicts in industrial relations, it was never clear whether the regime's response would be mediation or repression.[19] Pasteur draws some telling conclusions about the experience of trade unionists under the "Christian authoritarian corporate state." (He eschews the term "Austrofascism.") The Social Democrats were eventually forced to abandon some of their long held positions, and—following the example of the Communists—engage with the official union, thereby laying the foundations for a different kind of corporatist approach to industrial relations after the war. But in any case, he reminds us, ideological affiliations did not map straightforwardly onto Austria's class structure: national identity, gender, and attitudes to religion were also important elements in the formation of political loyalties.

18 Pasteur's findings echo those of Everhard Holtmann, *Zwischen Unterdrückung und Befriedung. Sozialistische Arbeiterbewegung und autoritäres Regime in Österreich 1933–1938* (Vienna: Verlag für Geschichte und Politik, 1978).

19 See Christian Koller, "Streiken im austrofaschistischen 'Ständestaat' 1934–1938," *Vierteljahresschift für Sozial-und Wirtschaftsgeschichte* 96, no. 3 (2009): 320–335.

To add complexity to the mix, the Nazis were present all the while in the background, consolidating and extending their influence. In fact, the ambivalence and fluidity of positions on the Austrian right during the 1930s has increasingly become the focus of new research. Julie Thorpe's innovative study of Pan-Germanism in the Austrofascist state finds that political allegiances during this period were far less clear-cut than "conventional wisdom" would have us believe. In particular, she dispenses with the widely accepted tripartite model of Austrian politics proposed by Adam Wandruszka in the 1950s. The *Lager* theory, she argues, was a convenient post-war construction, accepted by the left because it helpfully blurred distinctions between Social Democrats and Communists. It also provided a kind of legitimacy for the League of Independents (VdU), the party in which most former Nazis were concentrated. Above all, however, it created a false sense of political distance between the "Catholic conservative" Christian Social Party and the German Nationalists, concealing the extensive common ideological ground between the two 'camps' and overlooking their close collaboration in the anti-Socialist "bourgeois bloc" coalition governments of the 1920s. For Thorpe, this (deliberate) blurring of the political boundaries has fuelled the myth that while the German Nationalist camp supported the Nazis, the conservatives under Dollfuss and Schuschnigg "acted as a bulwark against fascist movements in Austria."[20] Beginning with an examination of the origins of popular politics in the nineteenth century, she sets out to show that our understanding of the history of Pan-Germanism in Austria is mistaken. The activities of Georg von Schoenerer notwithstanding, the 'Pan-German movement' did not constitute a discrete, if marginalized third political force, alongside the more formidable organizations of the Christian Social Party or the labor movement. It was at once far too pervasive and far too fragmented to be meaningful a political 'camp' in its own right, and should be seen instead as the unifying ideology underlying Austrian politics. It meant different things to different people, from political or economic union to shared cultural values, but it spanned the entire political spectrum up to 1938.

Thorpe's studies of the regional press under Dollfuss and Schuschnigg show that while editors and journalists could not express open support for the Nazis, they were able to articulate German nationalist sympathies that were shared by supporters of the dictatorship, and to a large extent the regime itself. She argues that Austria was already a fascist state before 1938, and one that shared an "entangled" history with both Fascist Italy and

20 Julie Thorpe, *Pan-Germanism and the Austro-Fascist State, 1933–1938* (Manchester: Manchester University Press, 2011), 8.

Nazi Germany. This transnational approach to fascism, she suggests, makes the nation state redundant in any case as a point of reference in the broader process of 'fascistization' that swept across Europe in the 1930s, reconfiguring political alliances according to necessity, and leaving a variable imprint on national societies that depended on local circumstances. Austria's particular geographical position meant that it was caught in the cross current of German and Italian fascism, a circumstance that was reflected in the separate but overlapping development of its indigenous fascist movements. The image of an "authoritarian" Austria, which the Catholic Church prevented from becoming fully fascist, is misleading, Thorpe argues. It has its roots in the regime's own propaganda self-image, and its acceptance is based on inadequate comparisons with church-state relations in the ostensibly more secular fascist states of Italy and Germany, or for that matter with other right-wing dictatorships of the period. She has expanded on her approach to the definition of fascism in an article for the *Journal of Contemporary History* in 2010, in which she provides both an overview of the literature on the subject and a summary of her own research findings.[21]

Fundamental to Thorpe's argument is that there was substantial common ideological ground between the 'black' camp (Catholic conservatives and Austrofascists) and the 'brown' camp (German Nationalists and Nazis), which most accounts of Austrian contemporary history have preferred to keep separate. Janek Wasserman's study of the radical right in Vienna during the First Republic endorses this interpretation.[22] In the first instance it is a welcome reminder that not all was red in 'Red Vienna.' Although it was a bastion of the Social Democratic Party, whose Austromarxist theorists forged intellectual alliances with scholars in a number of disciplines on the basis of shared Enlightenment values, it was also home to a powerful group of right-wing intellectuals. The city was just as much a center of conservative politics. It had been run before the war by the Christian Social Party, which continued to dominate national governments from the very beginning of the Republic; it was also the seat of an archbishop and the center of the country's Catholic hierarchy; and it was home to the Republic's social and political elites, senior officers and civil servants, *Besitz- und Bürgertum*, very few of whom had much instinctive sympathy with the Social Democrats and their experiments.

To take our cue from Karl Kraus and his excoriation of the city's "lightweight" right-wing intelligentsia, would be to make the same mistake

21 Julie Thorpe, "Austrofascism: Revisiting the 'Authoritarian State' 40 Years on," *Journal of Contemporary History* 45, no. 2 (2010): 315–343.

22 Janek Wasserman, *Black Vienna. The Radical Right in the Red City, 1918–1938* (Ithaca: Cornell University Press, 2014).

as their more progressive contemporaries. For if cultural history has been kinder to Kraus than to the *Reichspost*, it nevertheless remains the case that the right-wing press, and not just the daily papers, but also more intellectual periodicals such as *Die schönere Zukunft* and *Das neue Reich,* had a much wider readership, and wielded more influence among the propertied and educated middle classes than *Die Fackel.* It would be an understandable mistake, however. Vienna's right-wing intellectuals were themselves rather pessimistic in the wake of the defeat of the empire, the collapse of the economy and a democratic revolution, which left them feeling dispossessed and disorientated. Nevertheless, conservative ideology enjoyed a remarkable resurgence during the 1920s, and Wasserman traces its development, alternating his focus between the attempts of the Austro-Marxists to establish a new progressive hegemony among the capital's intellectuals, and an increasingly confident, if fissiparous group of right-wing scholars, journalists and pamphleteers: a "Black Vienna" that went from strength to strength. The study concludes with the rise of Austrofascism and the triumph of Black Vienna, which flourished as never before under Dollfuss and Schuschnigg, but became impatient with the perceived weakness of the "corporate state" and increasingly receptive towards Nazi ideology. This radicalization was epitomized by the response of right-wing intellectuals to the 1936 murder of Moritz Schlick, professor of philosophy at Vienna University, by a former student who had been receiving psychiatric treatment. Johann Sauter, a political scientist and disciple of Othmar Spann, but also one of Schlick's colleagues at the university, published an anonymous article about the incident in the pages of *Die schönere Zukunft*. In it he maintained that the student, not Schlick, was the real victim in the affair, and that the murder was the outcome an ideological struggle between the world of materialism, Bolshevism, freemasonry and Jewishness on the one hand, and that of true *völkisch* values on the other. Most of the Black Viennese camp, Wasserman argues, was already embarked on the road towards fascism and Anschluss by the early 1930s.

Wasserman concludes his study with some reflections on the relationship of Black Viennese intellectuals with the Austrian victim narrative of the post-war period. Despite their increasing acceptance of a more *völkisch* fascism, many of the "Black Vienna" intellectuals were arrested and imprisoned after the Anschluss, among them Spann himself, who had some difficulty convincing the Nazis he actually agreed with them. After the defeat of Nazism, these intellectuals were able to recast their inter-war work as apolitical, and themselves as victims of Nazi persecution. Moreover, their position was now strengthened by the absence of left-wing intellectuals, who were encouraged neither to return to Vienna after the war, nor to resume their work. In the absence of a critical counter-narrative, rehabilitated former fascists were able to construct a contemporary history that attributed the destruction of democracy in the First Republic to the failures of democracy itself, blaming the Social Democrats for not rallying to the 'patriotic' cause, and joining their persecutors in a common front against Hitler.

At the very birth of Austria's post-war victim mythology, however, is the figure of Dollfuss himself, the originator of the dictatorship, and yet ostensible first victim of Nazi oppression, struck down by assassins for his resistance to fascism. The 'usable past' created by Dollfuss' martyrdom is one which operates very effectively on a number of levels, defining fascism as something external and threatening, but above all something other than Dollfuss himself or his dictatorship. To question the Dollfuss myth and its contribution to the founding mythology of the Second Republic is still, it seems, to invite howls of outrage and indignation from the conservative politicians and historians who have so much invested in it. This is precisely what Lucile Dreidemy has done in her recent "biography of the posthumous," which sets out to deconstruct the Dollfuss myth systematically and comprehensively, and to examine the ways in which the dictator's legacy has been instrumentalized for political ends.[23] She begins with his death in 1934, which was immediately exploited by the regime for propaganda purposes in text and image both ritual and memorial. The hand of the Catholic Church was evident from the outset, and the quasi-canonization of Dollfuss furnished the new regime with an instantly recognizable, if rather morbid, iconography replete with suggestive allusions to the death of Christ, and encouragement for a cult of the hitherto largely unknown St. Engelbert. The representation of Dollfuss as "soldier" and "fighter," and above all as a hero in the struggle against Nazism, enabled his supporters to depict him as a victim rather than a perpetrator of fascism, thereby cleverly identifying Nazism as fascism, and the dictator as an anti-fascist resister. As Dreidemy points out, Dollfuss' own approach to Austria's relationship with Nazi Germany was much more ambivalent. Nevertheless, the Dollfuss myth enabled Austrian conservatives to promote the idea in the United States that Austria was the "first victim of Nazism" long before it was incorporated in the Moscow Declaration of the Allies in 1943. The strategic importance of the victim thesis was perceived as so important for the political stability and international rehabilitation of Austria, Dreidemy argues, that the erstwhile enemies of the "civil war" now collaborated in

23 Lucille Dreidemy, *Der Dollfuß-Mythos. Eine Biographie des Posthumen* (Vienna: Böhlau, 2014).

suppressing discussion of the period, with the Social Democrats compelled to accept a thesis of "shared responsibility" for the destruction of democracy. It is not clear why the SPÖ continued to turn a blind eye to the compromise despite its powerful political position during the Kreisky years—Kreisky had been a victim of the regime himself—and in spite of provocative attempts by ÖVP to breathe new life into it, recasting the "Führer with a friendly face" of Austrofascist propaganda as the "democratic farmer" of the semi-scholarly apologetics of the post-war period. This consensual agreement made the Dollfuss dictatorship a taboo subject and seriously hindered scholarly discussion of the period until the Waldheim scandal distracted attention from it, leaving Dollfuss a "discreet but stable presence" in Austrian political life. Renewed attention, Dreidemy argues, came with the advent of the ÖVP-FPÖ coalition in February 2000, but culminated earlier, in 1998 with the opening of a Dollfuss museum in the house where he was born at Texing in Lower Austria, creating a modern shrine, as Dreidemy pointedly observes, behind the pretext of popular education.

The publication of Dreidemy's book, which was based on her doctoral research in Vienna, was as much a political as an academic occasion. The polemical tone of the final section in particular, on the enduring determination of his apologists to preserve and reinvigorate the Dollfuss myth, prompted an equally polemical response in the conservative press. Writing in *Die Presse*, Andreas Khol, a senior figure in the ÖVP and former president of the *Nationlrat*, accused her of writing "polemic disguised as scholarship," and leaped to the defense of the "respected political scientist" Karl Gottfried Kindermann (whose controversial account of "Hitler's defeat in Austria" Dreidemy had eviscerated) and Gudula Walterskirchen, a journalist on *Die Presse* and author of a sympathetic anniversary biography of Dollfuss in 2004;[24] and Kindermann himself was prompted to respond in the newspaper's online commentary section to Dreidemy's "grotesque" characterization of many of the dictator's biographers as hagiographers and apologists.[25]

In light of these responses, the rather optimistic suggestion that the political explosiveness of the subject has diminished somewhat seems a little premature, but the increasing divergence of scholarly consensus from popular history and political biography is increasingly discernible.[26] Much of the haggling that remains is around the term "Austrofascist," used by

24 Andreas Khol, "Dollfuß heute: keine Spur von Kult und Mythos. Zu einer neuen, verstörenden Biografie des Autokraten aus Frankreich," *Die Presse*, 28 Nov. 2014.

25 See the commentary section of "Dollfuß-Kult: ein Toter as ewiger 'Führer,'" in *Die Presse*, 18 November 2014 <http://diepresse.com/home/kultur/literatur/4598499/DollfussKult_Ein-Toter-als-ewiger-Fuhrer?_vl_backlink=/home/kultur/index.do> (23 Feb. 2016).

26 Wenninger and Dreidemy, *Das Dollfuß/Schuschnigg-Regime*, 7.

some to define the regime as wholly fascist and comparable with Italy and Germany, and by others to refer only to elements of it. In practice there is a measure of agreement on a number of issues. Most historians and political scientists would agree that the regime was internally heterogeneous—whether one sees the cartel of power players as the "limited pluralism" of an authoritarian state or the "polycracy" familiar from Nazi Germany. There is also agreement that the regime developed over time, an approach which is compatible with the notion of a broader process of "fascistization" that swept across Europe during the 1930s, leaving a political imprint that varied according to local circumstances, but whose overall tendency was towards a fuller, more pervasive acceptance of fascism. In that context Austria was—arguably—subject to the vicissitudes of the more powerful political currents around it. In any political snapshot of the authoritarian regimes of the 1930s, including Italy and Germany, there is a fluid combination of fascist and conservative forces, which can be interpreted variously, depending on the balance in a particular state or the focus of the historian. Where Janek Wassermann, for example, has found an ideological convergence between Austria and Germany that prepared the road for Anschluss, Gerhard Botz has interpreted the same period, which was characterized by the "uncontrolled growth of corporations" as a bureaucratization of the regime and an effective "de-fascistization."[27]

The focus of much of the new work is on identifying a new kind of common ground across Europe. Julie Thorpe finds the term "para-fascism" useful in this context, as a designation which to suggests a difference of degree rather than one of substance between regimes such as Italy and Germany and those elsewhere, which—according to Aristotle Kallis, who has used the term most extensively—adopted the trappings of fascism without sharing the "revolutionary ideological vision" of the "core" fascist regimes.[28] Historians of fascisms beyond Italy and Germany have found the term particularly useful and applied it to regimes where fascism was present but which did not become fully fascist. For Miguel Ángel del Arco Blanco, for example, who has compared the "corporate state" with the early Franco regime and concluded that "para-fascism" was the norm and "full fascism" the exception in inter-war Europe.[29] The concept of para-

27 Botz, "The Coming of the Dollfuss-Schuschnigg Regime," 144.

28 Thorpe, "Austrofascism," 326; Aristotle Kallis, "'Fascism,' 'Para-Fascism' and 'Fascistization': On the similarities of Three Conceptual Categories," *European History Quarterly* 33, no. 2 (2003): 219–249, here, 220.

29 Miguel Ángel del Arco Blanco, "La marea autoritaria: nacimiento, desarrollo y consolidación de regímenes parafascistas en Austria y España," *Historia Actual Online* 12 (Winter 2007) 119–131.

fascism provides the basis for a discussion of the development of fascism across Europe that avoids polarization but, like many such definitions, it is as much about ideology as about the lived realities of the period. If there is a common thread to the new research in the field, it is an increasing impatience with prescriptive terminologies and typologies, and a renewed focus on the realities of political change: how and why the dictatorship was established, how it structured itself and operated politically; what it set out to achieve, and how far it succeeded; how it was experienced, and how people responded to it. What researchers have found is a fluidity of ideology and political loyalties, a landscape of the political right in interwar Austria characterized as much by shared values and political affinities as by disagreements; in short a politics which, ultimately, softened Austria up for the Anschluss, rather than served as a bulwark against it.

Select Bibliography

Dreidemy, Lucile. *Der Dollfuß-Mythos: Eine Biographie des Posthumen.* Vienna: Böhlau, 2014.

Neuhäuser, Stephan, ed. *"Wir werden ganze Arbeit leisten…": Der austrofaschistische Staatsstreich 1934.* Norderstedt: Books on Demand GmbH, 2004.

Pasteur, Paul. *Unter dem Hakenkreuz: Gewerkschafter und Gewerkschafterinnen in Österreich 1934–1938.* Transl. from the French by Sonja Niederacher. Innsbruck: StudienVerlag, 2008.

Reiter-Zatloukal, Ilse, Christiane Rothländer, and Pia Schölnberger eds. Österreich 1933–*1938: Interdisziplinäre Annäherungen an das Dollfuß-/Schuschnigg Regime.* Vienna: Böhlau, 2012.

Tálos, Emmerich. *Das Austrofaschistische Herrschaftssystem: Österreich 1933–1938.* Vienna: LIT Verlag, 2013.

----- and Wolfgang Neugebauer, eds. *Austrofaschsimsus: Politik-Ökonomie-Kultur 1933–1938.* 6th ed. Vienna: LIT Verlag, 2012.

Thorpe, Julie. *Pan-Germanism and the Austro-Fascist State, 1933–1938.* Manchester: Manchester University Press, 2011.

Wasserman, Janek. *Black Vienna: The Radical Right in the Red City, 1918–1938.* Ithaca: Cornell University Press, 2014.

Wenninger, Florian, and Lucille Dreidemy, eds. *Das Dollfuß/Schuschnigg-Regime 1933–1938: Vermessung eines Forschungsfeldes.* Vienna: Böhlau, 2013.

Prominent tourists.
Hillary Clinton and her daughter Chelsea visit Schönbrunn Palace.
Vienna, Harald Schneider, 07 12 1997
Credit: APA PictureDesk

Volume 12: Günter Bischof/Anton Pelinka, eds. *The Americanization/ Westernization of Austria*. New Brunswick, NJ: Transaction 2003

Austria and the United States Today: From Top Model America to America's Next Top Model?

Reinhold Wagnleitner[1]

A great deal of intelligence can be invested in ignorance when the need for illusion is deep.
Saul Bellow, *To Jerusalem and Back* (1976)

Amerika soll man kapieren, nicht kopieren.
Victor Gruen

Picture yourself, no, not in a boat on a river, but in the Marble Hall of Salzburg's Mirabell Palace on 14 September 2015 (just a short distance from the famous 'Do-Re-Me' *Sound of Music* scene in Mirabell Garden). We are not attending a wedding—although this is one of the most treasured wedding destinations worldwide—but a celebration of the 15th anniversary of the partnership between the Southern Chinese island Hainan and the State of Salzburg.

Heinz Schaden, the mayor of the city of Salzburg, and dignitaries from the government of Land Salzburg are waiting for the Chinese delegation led by the Deputy Governor of Hainan, Chaofeng Mao. But the proverbially punctual Chinese guests are delayed. They got stuck on the autobahn because Germany, reacting to the massive influx of refugees, had just introduced strict border controls at the frontier between Bavaria and Salzburg.

Two female singers and a male woodwind instrumentalist (member of the Chinese Communist Party, the program proudly announces), representatives of the LI group of Hainan, and the Abersee musicians (a male duo of guitar and accordion) perform Chinese and Austrian traditional music. The wait is shortened by a pushed up buffet and a most surprising musical cooperation. What popular songs unify Chinese and Austrian musicians? "Jingle Bells" and "Edelweiss"!

1 Dedicated to Anna and Ella.

Dear me, is that an example of Americanization? Or Westernization? Or Globalization, *Chinafication and Easternization*? Or, heaven forbid, the utmost form of wicked cultural imperialism, the Austrianization of the world? While it may be none of the above, the typical Austrian answer would be yes and no ("*jein*").[2] But then, what is typically Austrian anyhow (or European? or American, for that matter?) after more than a hundred years of the shock of America in Europe—and more than five hundred years of the shock of Europe in America, which had turned the new found land into an artifact of European expansion.[3]

Whatever it is, performing the song "Edelweiss" (from the *Sound of Music*, this for the Austrian readers) acted as the single most common denominator, uniting China and Austria (through America). After all, only two weeks later Xu Xi, the deputy general secretary of Beijing, in his opening remarks at another Chinese-Austrian colloquium in Salzburg referred to the really important background of the *Sound of Music* as a story of anti-Nazi resistance.[4]

While the global success of US-American culture clearly constitutes one of the most important chapters of contemporary history, it is surprising how comparatively small the exploits of US sports in Austria have been for a long time. After all, Austria's national baseball team is being coached by Japanese head coach Hiroyuki Sakanashi, and the real revolution did not occur through the introduction of US-American sports in Austria, but rather the replacement of Austrian marching music with Anglo-American rock and hip-hop as musical accompaniment of Austrian sports since the 1970s.

Before joining the European Union, Austria's contemporary political, economic, social and cultural relations had been strongly emblazoned by spotlights and projectors situated in New York, Hollywood and Washington. In 1995 two new additional spotlights were installed—Brussels and Frankfurt. Now Austrians could blame (real or imagined) negative developments not any more exclusively on Washington, Wall Street and Tinseltown, but the European Union and the European Central Bank.[5]

---

2 An Austrian wise cracker turned Barack Obama's slogan "Yes, we can" most fittingly into the Austrian "Yes, we can't!"

3 David W. Ellwood, *The Shock of America: Europe and the Challenge of the Century* (Oxford: Oxford University Press, 2012); Reinhold Wagnleitner, *Coca-Colonization and the Cold War: The Cultural Mission of the United States in Austria after the Second World War* (Chapel Hill/London: University of North Carolina Press, 1994).

4 "China Europe 2025: Eine gemeinsame Momentaufnahme der nächsten Dekade," (Second China Europe Conference organized by the Stiftungsinstitut für China-Europa-Beziehungen at Salzburg) 30 September 2015.

5 Not only Austria's international position changed, but also its image. See Günter Bischof, "Of Dwarfs and Giants: From Cold War Mediator to Bad Boy of Europe," in CAS 22, 13–54.

During the last twenty years, the image of the United States in Austria (and Europe) experienced a helter-skelter ride with the extremes of a fever curve on both ends of the scale: from the mostly positive figures during the era of Bill Clinton to the dumbfounded incredulity around the developments of the first election of president George W. Bush. After the terror attacks on 11 September 2001, the sympathies for the United States soared higher than ever before. *Le Monde* published an uncharacteristic editorial on 13 September 2001, titled "Nous sommes tous Américains." But then, the reaction of the Bush administration, the war in Afghanistan, the preparation and execution of the war against Iraq, drone warfare, the use of torture, illegal flights with assumed terrorists via various European countries, the prisons in Guantánamo, Bagram and Abu Ghraib, as well as the negligent and disastrous mismanagement after Hurricane Katrina, resulted in the greatest and sharpest decline of pro-American sentiment in known history.

In two publications of the largest international opinion polls ever conducted, the Pew Center for the People and the Press characterized world opinion towards the United States most befittingly: from "U.S. Image Slips" (December 2002) to "U.S. Image Plummets" (March 2003).[6] The Bush-Cheney administration remained unperturbed by this global upheaval. It nonchalantly invented an Old and a New Europe as well as a "coalition of the willing." The majority of Austrians, like many other Europeans, certainly was not willing to follow. During the remaining years of the Bush-Cheney administration, the international reputation of the United States continuously slid downhill. Even the Oval Office had to prick up its ears a few months before Barack Obama was elected. On 2 April 2008, the BBC published an international public opinion poll on views of a country's influence in the world. The good news: the USA was up to 35 percent positive answers (compared to only 31 a year before). The bad news was not only that the United States was still seen as a negative influence by 47 percent, but that the home of the brave had even slipped below Russia, which carried 37 positive percent. This was a first in polling history. One does wonder whether the White House was at least satisfied to come out ahead of North Korea (23), Iran (20), Israel (19), and Pakistan (18), especially when the leaders of the Coalition of the Unwilling had come

6 "What the World Thinks in 2002: How Global Publics View: Their Lives, Their Countries, The World, America," in *Pew Research Center*, 4 December 2002 <http://www.people-press.org/2002/12/04/what-the-world-thinks-in-2002/> (11 Jan. 2016); "America's Image Further Erodes, Europeans Want Weaker Ties, But Post-War Iraq Will Be Better Off, Most Say," in ibid., 18 March 2003 <http://www.people-press.org/2003/03/18/americas-image-further-erodes-europeans-want-weaker-ties/> (11 Jan. 2016).

out on top with 56 positive (18 negative), for Germany, and 50 positive (22 negative), for France. The fact that Japan also achieved 56 positive percent, equaling Germany's position on the top of all countries mainly viewed as positive globally, more than strongly indicated that something most peculiar had happened. Shortly into the new millennium, the one-time leading positive image of the United States had been transferred to the former top "bad guys" of the Second World War.[7]

In Austria this opposition to US-led aggression in the Middle East led to a decline of students wanting to study in the United States as well as a noticeable dwindling of students in American Studies (or history students studying US-American themes). Only this deep disillusionment, which was partly as irrational as the usual enthusiasm for anything American, can explain the initial stupendous support for presidential candidate Barack Obama—which went way beyond the support he received in the USA itself. My US-American students at Salzburg College, who had travelled in Europe disguised as Canadians (with the help of a Canadian flag on their backpacks) during much of the first decade of the 2000s, were rather surprised to be kissed and hugged by complete strangers (including Viennese taxi drivers!) immediately after the election of Barack Obama. The hype during Obama's first election campaign was so strong that Germans could be seen carrying posters proclaiming "Obama for Kanzler" during his speech in Berlin on 24 July 2008. About 200,000 showed up for the Democratic candidate, "who has brought rock-star charisma to electoral politics."[8] Eighty percent of Germans would have voted for Obama in that year.

While Obama's politics during his first administration partially reduced his saint-like status domestically and internationally, some of his rock-star charisma continued much longer outside the United States than at home. This became more than clear during his second election campaign in 2012. In a *BBC World* service poll of more than 21,000 people in twenty-one countries, President Barack Obama showed a dramatic lead over his challenger Mitt Romney: in France Obama led Romney 73 to 3 percent, in Australia 68 to 6, in Canada 65 to 8, in the United Kingdom 65 to 6, in Brazil 65 to 5, in Germany 64 to 8, in South Korea 58 to 8, in Mexico 46 to 6, in India 45 to 12, in Poland 36 to 18, and in China 38 to 18. The only country among the twenty-

7 "World Views U.S. More Positively," in *BBC*, 2 April 2008 <http://news.bbc.co.uk/2/hi/americas/7324337.stm> (9 Dec. 2015).

8 "US Elections: Obama wows Berlin crowd with historic speech," in *The Guardian*, 24 July 2008 <http://www.theguardian.com/global/2008/jul/24/barackobama.uselections2008> (9 Dec. 2015).

one polled that had Mitt Romney leading was Pakistan with 15 to 12.[9] In Austria, 80 percent would have voted for Obama, only 5 percent for Romney.[10] In early November 2012, a poll of 560,000 people in thirty-six countries revealed that Austrians, together with Belgians and Finns, were leading the pro Obama-faction with 93 percent pro-Obama (7 Romney). Only in Portugal, would more people have voted for Obama (94 versus 6 for Romney). All in all, 81 percent of those polled wanted Obama in office for four more years, whereas Romney received 19 percent.[11]

Soon these global fans of President Obama experienced an unanticipated blow. In June 2013, citizens of planet earth caught on to an organization, attempting (and partly succeeding) to eavesdrop and store all digital human communication supposedly in the interest of freedom, liberty, democracy, the free market economy and other indispensable "Western values": the US's National Security Agency (NSA) with a little help from its friends, the British Government Communications Headquarter (GCHQ), the German *Bundesnachrichtendienst* (BND) and other European secret services.

This Austrian was rather baffled by this ubiquitous display of global surprise and outrage as these uncovered machinations were anything but new or astonishing, and not only because of Austria's long history of secretly assisting Western intelligence gathering throughout the Cold War, despite its official status of neutrality. A simple reading of James Bamford's *The Puzzle Palace: Inside the National Security Agency America's Most Secret Intelligence Organization* published in 1982, thirty years before Edgar Snowden's revelations, would have sufficed. The USA's attempts at global data collection and analysis of course predated the foundation of the NSA in 1952.[12] The signal intelligence cooperation of the Five Eyes (Australia, Canada, New Zealand, the

9 "BBC poll: Rest of world favours Obama," in *BBC*, 23 October 2012 <http://www.bbc.com/news/world-us-canada-20008687> (9 Dec. 2015).

10 "Profil-Umfrage: Österreicher würden Obama wählen," 9 August 2012 <http://www.ots.at/presseaussendung/OTS_20120908_OTS0002/profil-umfrage-oesterreicher-wuerden-obama-waehlen> (9 Dec. 2015).

11 "Obama is popular across the globe. Poll finds non-Americans want President to win election," in *MailOnline*, 5 November 2012 <http://www.dailymail.co.uk/news/article-2227822/Obama-popular-globe-Poll-finds-non-Americans-want-President-win-election.html> (9 Dec. 2015).

12 David Talbot, *The Devil's Chessboard: Allen Dulles, the CIA, and the Rise of America's Secret Government* (New York: Harper, 2015); see also an interview with the author in *Salon*, 15 October 2015 <http://www.salon.com/2015/10/15/every_president_has_been_manipulated_national_security_officials_david_talbot_investigates_americas_deep_state/> (11 Dec. 2015).

United Kingdom and the United States of America), probably the most all-encompassing and comprehensive espionage confederacies in history, goes back to the Atlantic Charter (1941) and the UKUSA Agreement of 5 March 1946.

On the occasion of the building of new data storage centers in Bluffdale, Utah, and San Antonio, Texas, James Bamford summarized already in March 2012: "The NSA has become the largest, most covert, and potentially most intrusive intelligence agency ever."[13] Be that as it may, while the NSA had turned the Internet into the perfect global remote control, interestingly enough, only part of the US-American public was alarmed. Most US citizens were predominantly concerned about the invasion of their own privacy and the breach of civil liberties within the United States, if at all.

Once again, the extraordinary insularity of US-American voters became particularly conspicuous, because the NSA practices produced a global bombshell unperceived in the United States. The universal implications of this monitoring abomination, which resulted in the absolute loss of faith in the United States on a worldwide scale, tended to elude the US-American public. All of a sudden, Barack Obama's election slogan "Yes, we can" morphed into "Yes, we scan." The skeleton was out of the national closet and the fractures of its bones are globally visible. According to the late German Christian Democrat politician Philipp Mißfelder, this colossal dishonesty resulted in a dramatic deterioration of US-German relations. The German trust in the USA sunk even lower than at the beginning of the Iraq War.[14]

This breach of trust was not just a German (or Austrian) phenomenon. "Global Opposition to US Surveillance and Drones" the Pew Research Center for the People and the Press titled a global opinion poll of summer 2014: Greece 97 percent unacceptable (2 acceptable), Brazil 94 (4), Lebanon 92 (6), Egypt 91 (6), Jordan 91 (8), Tunisia 91 (8), South Korea 89 (10), Venezuela 88 (7), France 88 (12), Germany 87 (12), Russia 87 (10), Spain 87 (12), Chile 86 (9), Palestinian Territory 86 (7), Senegal 86 (10), China 85 (9), Japan 85 (10), Argentina 84 (9), Ukraine 83 (8),

---

13 James Bamford, "The NSA Is Building the Country's Biggest Spy Center (Watch What You Say)," in *Wired*, 15 March 2012 <http://www.wired.com/2012/03/ff_nsadatacenter/> (9 Dec. 2015).

14 "NSA-Affäre: Künftiger Amerikabeauftragter kritisiert US-Politik scharf," in *Der Spiegel online*, 16 January 2014 <http://www.spiegel.de/politik/deutschland/missfelder-kritisiert-us-politik-wegen-nsa-affaere-a-943873.html> (9 Dec. 2015); "NSA-Skandal: Deutscher Sonderermittler beschuldigt die USA," in *Die Zeit online*, 30 October 2015 <http://www.zeit.de/politik/ausland/2015-10/nsa-bnd-selektoren-bericht-sonderermittler-graulich> (11 Dec. 2015).

Vietnam 83 (9), Israel 82 (13), Peru 81 (10), Turkey 81 (9), Nicaragua 80 (14), Italy 76 (19), Mexico 76 (16), Columbia 74 (19), Tanzania 71 (25), Bangladesh 70 (23), United Kingdom 70 (25), Indonesia 67 (22), El Salvador 65 (29), and Thailand 65 (26).[15]

Even the staunchly conservative *Tiroler Tageszeitung* (founded in Innsbruck by the US Army in 1945) headlined in July 2013: "Erschüttertes Vertrauen (Unsettled Trust)."[16] That this global loss of trust in the United States—with drone warfare as a second major matter of dissonance[17]—is hardly ever discussed within the USA is illuminating, though hardly surprising.

However unsettled the trust in the self-proclaimed "benevolent hegemon" may have become, there are other players to consider. All of the world knows that companies like Google, Facebook, Apple, YouTube, and Microsoft (and this list is anything but complete) have been pushing over George Orwell's Big Brother as an anachronous amateur. On top of Hollywood, New York, and Washington, the planetary community has been forced to watch out for future

15 "Global Opposition to U.S. Surveillance and Drones, but Limited Harm to America's Image," in *Pew Research Center*, 14 July 2014 <http://www.pewglobal.org/2014/07/14/global-opposition-to-u-s-surveillance-and-drones-but-limited-harm-to-americas-image/> (9 Dec. 2015).

16 "'Erschüttertes Vertrauen': USA bestätigen Österreich NSA-Spitzelei," in *Tiroler Tageszeitung online* <http://www.tt.com/politik/innenpolitik/6862945-91/ersch%C3%BCttertes-vertrauen-usa-best%C3%A4tigen-%C3%B6sterreich-nsa-spitzelei.csp?tab=article> (2 Feb. 2016).

17 See "Global Opinion of Obama Slips, International Policies Faulted," in *Pew Research Center*, 13 June 2012 <http://www.pewglobal.org/2012/06/13/global-opinion-of-obama-slips-international-policies-faulted/> (15 Dec. 2015); "Widespread Opposition to Drones: Global Opposition to US Surveillance and Drones but Limited Harm to America's Image," in ibid., 14 July 2014 <http://www.pewglobal.org/2014/07/14/global-opposition-to-u-s-surveillance-and-drones-but-limited-harm-to-americas-image/pg-2014-07-14-balance-of-power-0-01/> (15 Dec. 2015): Venezuela 92 against (4), Jordan 90 (5), Greece 89 (6), Nicaragua 88 (9), Egypt 87 (4), Argentina 87 (5), Brazil 87 (7), Columbia 86 (9), Senegal 86 (11), Spain 86 (12), Palestine territory 84 (7), Turkey 83 (7), Japan 82 (12), Peru 81 (10), Malaysia 80 (6), Mexico 80 (14), Thailand 79 (12), Russia 78 (7), Vietnam 78 (12), Tunisia 77 (17), South Korea 75 (23), Indonesia 74 (10), Italy 74 (18), El Salvador 73 (12), France 72 (72), Lebanon 71 (23), Bangladesh 70 (22), Chile 68 (15), Philippines 67 (24), Tanzania 67 (27), Germany 67 (30), Pakistan 66 (3), Ukraine 66 (11), United Kingdom 59 (33), Poland 54 (32), China 52 (35), Ghana 47 (29), South Africa 46 (27), United States of America 41 (52), Nigeria 39 (42), Kenya 38 (53), India 36 (28), Israel 27 (65). See also "White House calls drone strikes against Americans on U.S. soil 'legal,' 'ethical' and 'wise' - even without evidence of a pending attack," in *Daily Mail online*, 5 February 2013 <http://www.dailymail.co.uk/news/article-2273643/White-House-calls-drone-strikes-Americans-U-S-soil-legal-ethical-wise--evidence-pending-attack.html> (15 Dec. 2015); "A War Waged from German Soil: US Ramstein Base Key in Drone Attacks," in *Der Spiegel online*, 22 April 2015 <http://www.spiegel.de/fotostrecke/photo-gallery-ramstein-s-role-in-the-us-drone-war-fotostrecke-125799-2.html> (15 Dec. 2015).

trends(and for being watched) to yet another space: Silicon Valley, "American Companies Are Getting Way Too Cozy With the National Security Agency." This is not my interpretation of a scandalous development but the title of an analysis by the *Pacific Standard* of 23 October 2014, with the fitting subtitle: "Newly released documents describe 'contractual relationships' between the NSA and U.S. companies, as well as undercover operatives."[18]

This constitutes a crucial and dangerous international predicament of the first order for the United States. It took Max Schrems, a Salzburg-born Austrian law student, to legally challenge Facebook with his initiative, "Europe versus Facebook," in Austrian, Irish and European courts. Occasionally the struggle David vs. Goliath works. On 6 October 2015, the European Court of Justice declared the European Union Commission's Safe Harbor decision as null and void, and this will have substantial consequences for the future. This ruling of the highest European court does not only declare the data transfer between the United States and Europe as illegal, because (European) data is not safe—neither in the United States territory, nor with US-American companies globally—but also, for the first time, this legal decision by the European Court of Justice represents a declaration of independence by the members of the European Union from the continuous practice of US companies to effectively and comprehensively ignore all European data security and privacy legislation.[19]

On 15 May 2015, the German weekly *Die Zeit* furnished a story about US-American machinations with the caption "Impotent Fury." It detailed the reaction of German members of government towards revelations about the collection of 1.3 trillion metadata (per month!) by the German secret service BND for the NSA. The data collected is based on at lest 45,000 selectors, including many German and other European companies.[20] We neither have to wonder about chancellor Angelika Merkel's reaction after being confronted with the tapping of her phone by the NSA, nor the derision dumped on French and Austrian

18 "American Companies Are Getting Way Too Cozy With the National Security Agency," in *Pacific Standard*, 23 October 2014 <http://www.psmag.com/politics-and-law/american-companies-getting-way-cozy-national-security-agency-92713> (11 Dec. 2015).

19 "Data Transfer Pact Between U.S. and Europe Is Ruled Invalid," in *International New York Times*, 6 October 2015 <http://www.nytimes.com/2015/10/07/technology/european-union-us-data-collection.html?_r=0> (11 Dec. 2015).

20 "NSA-Affäre – Ohnmächtige Wut: Über die amerikanischen Umtriebe hat die Regierung nicht so sehr das Volk belogen, sondern vor allem sich selbst," in *Die Zeit Online*, 15 May 2015 <http://www.zeit.de/2015/20/bnd-nsa-geheimdienst-affaere> (12 Jan. 2016).

politicians for, supposedly, not having been spied on.[21] Although the German government officially ended its cooperation with the NSA in May 2015, recent reports strongly indicate that the BND has reopened its collaboration in the spy center Bad Aibling, less than a hundred kilometers away from Salzburg.[22]

But there's more than digital security; as so much else, Austria's security situation (and foreign policy options) underwent quite a few permutations since the "end of the Cold War." In a superficial reading, the whole region oscillated between the liberating forces of US-American neoliberal market evangelists, plus military missionaries and the threats of aggressive, illiberal, militarist, nationalist Russian reactionaries, if not Soviet nostalgics. But the warning of NATO Secretary-General Anders Fogh Rasmussen that any incursion of Russia into the Crimean Peninsula and eastern Ukraine would be a "historic mistake" (on 8 April 2014) had a real historic antecedent which of course remained unheard and disregarded in the West nearly twenty years earlier.

Already in February 1997, George F. Kennan, the chief architect of Cold War containment made a clean sweep in *The New York Times*. According to the *eminence grise* of US foreign policy, the plans of the Clinton administration for "expanding NATO would be the most fateful error of American policy in the entire post-Cold War era." Kennan clearly envisioned the dire consequences of a triumphalist foreign policy by pushing NATO eastward, while the former antagonist (the Warsaw Pact) had evaporated: "Such a decision may be expected to inflame the nationalistic, anti-Western and militaristic tendencies in Russian opinion; to have an adverse effect on the development of Russian democracy; to restore the atmosphere of the cold war to East-West relations, and to impel Russian foreign policy in directions decidedly not to our liking."[23] And George F. Kennan was not alone. In an open letter to President Clinton, "fifty illustrious signatories opposed NATO enlargement" as "a policy error

21 "Governments and NGOs: Germany Spied on Friends and Vatican," in *Der Spiegel Online*, 7 November 2015 <http://www.spiegel.de/international/germany/german-bnd-intelligence-spied-on-friends-and-vatican-a-1061588.html> (10 Dec. 2015); "Secrets Must Remain Secret: Interview with German Intelligence Coordinator on NSA and Media Leaks," in *Spiegel Online International*, 14 August 2015 <http://www.spiegel.de/international/germany/nsa-interview-with-german-intelligence-coordinator-altmaier-a-1048072.html> (11 Dec. 2015); "NSA-Affäre: BND schaltete 25.000 NSA-Selektoren scharf," in *Der Spiegel online*, 15 May 2015 <http://www.spiegel.de/politik/deutschland/spiegel-bnd-affaere-weitet-sich-aus-a-1033881.html> (12 Dec. 2015).

22 "Abhörskandal: BND und NSA kooperieren wieder in Bad Aibling," in *Süddeutsche Zeitung*, 8 January 2016 <http://www.sueddeutsche.de/politik/abhoerskandal-bnd-und-nsa-kooperieren-wieder-in-bad-aibling-1.2810828> (11 Jan. 2016).

23 George F. Kennan, "A Fateful Error," *The New York Times* Op-Ed, 5 Feb. 1997.

of historic proportions" in June 1997. They predicted that open-ended NATO expansion, "will inevitably degrade NATO's ability to carry out its primary mission and will involve U.S. security guarantees to countries with serious border and national minority problems, and unevenly developed systems of democratic government."[24] The signatories did not only include US Senators Bill Bradley, Gary Hart, Mark Hatfield, and Sam Nunn, but also former Secretary of Defense Robert S. McNamara, President Ronald Reagan's Director for Eastern European and Soviet Affairs, Richard Pipes, and Paul H. Nitze, one of the chief architects of US-policy towards the Soviet Union since the 1950s.

It was a foresightful analysis of a foreseeable development. The Russian leadership, supported by a majority of the Russian people, reacted exactly as predicted. The increasing alienation as well as the eastern Ukrainian and Crimean crises can only be understood in the light of a series of Russian defeats. Initial Russian cooperation in the war in Afghanistan was promptly undermined by US-American intervention in Iraq, NATO enlargement, specifically the NATO Membership Action Plan for Georgia and Ukraine, the establishment of permanent US Army bases in Tajikistan, Kyrgyzstan, Kazakhstan, Turkmenistan, Uzbekistan, as well as other moves creating ever more instability, from the unilateral US withdrawal from the Anti-Ballistic Missile Treaty to the adoption of the military doctrine of full-spectrum dominance as well as a global, US-led Unified Combatant Command.[25] While all of this does not alter the fact that the Russian annexation of Crimea constitutes a substantial breach of international law, it may help to explain the constant growth of Russian fears, which led to a mentality of forming a corral.

But Russia is not the only power living in constant angst. In the spring 2012 issue of *Foreign Policy*, David Rothkopf located an enemy within the United States: "The United States is a bit like a 375-pound, middle-aged man with a heart condition walking down a city street at night eating a Big Mac. He's sweating profusely because he's afraid he might get mugged. But the thing that's going to kill him is the burger."[26]

Austria's security position is also changed by the continuous increase of refugees from Africa, the Near East and the Middle East. At the moment

---

24 "Open Letter to President Bill Clinton," 26 June 1997, in *Boston University* <http://www.bu.edu/globalbeat/nato/postpone062697.html> (9 Dec. 2015).

25 "The World with Commanders' Areas of Responsibility," in *United States Central Command,* 17 December 2008 <http://www.centcom.mil/images/stories/unified-command_world-map.jpg> (16 Jan. 2016).

26 David Rothkopf, "The Enemy Within," in *Foreign Policy*, May/June 2012 <http://www.foreignpolicy.com/articles/2012/04/23/the_enemy_within_0> (17 Jan. 2016).

of writing, Austria, Germany and Sweden are taking the brunt in central and northern Europe and everything is in flux. Final assessments will have to wait, no doubt. It is certain; not only Austria's social and political systems are under pressure. The whole European Union is in danger.

According to the UN, more than 60 million refugees are running for safety. The *World Migration Report* of 2015 counts 244 million people on the move altogether.[27] In the case of the Near and the Middle East, they are not only fleeing from the deterioration of longstanding inner-Islamic divisions, assorted local dictatorships, climate change, and dramatic population growth; they are also attracted by the allure of European (German) wealth. Countries comprising the West, as well as Russia, share a substantial portion of responsibility for this greatest migration since the Second World War. To mention but a few: from European imperialism and colonialism, which one hundred years ago (16 May 1916) culminated in the Anglo-French (and Tsarist Russian) Sykes-Picault Agreement, via the CIA coup against the Iranian government of Mohammad Mossadegh in 1953, as well as the support of the Mujahideen in Afghanistan before and after the Russian invasion.

Two of the latest interventions created the most recent conditions for opening the locks. The first was spearheaded by the George W. Bush administration (and the coalition of the willing) in the hapless war against Iraq in 2003 (and Afghanistan since 2001), which caused the whole region to sink into chaos. The lies about the reasons for war were as devastating morally as was the subsequent amalgam of historical amateurishness and ignorance, imperial hubris, aggressive boorishness, near complete desultoriness and sheer incompetence to negotiate political agreements acceptable to all religious and ethnic groups. This did not only create the fertile soil for the growth of the terror militia *Daesh* (Islamic State) in the first place, while the discrimination of young Muslims in Europe helped to recruit fighters. These wars also produced millions of Iraqi and Afghani refugees, who flooded Pakistan, Iran, Syria, Jordan, Lebanon, and Turkey. All of this, topped by unforeseeable (though not unpredictable) droughts and desertification, created the conditions for social deprivation, desperation, hopelessness, riots, rebellions, upheavals and revolutions, which were misunderstood as an "Arab Spring" in the West.[28]

27 International Organization for Migration, *World Migration Report 2015* (Geneva, 2015) <http://publications.iom.int/books/world-migration-report-2015-migrants-and-cities-new-partnerships-manage-mobility> (26 Jan. 2016).

28 Craig Welch, "Climate Change Helped Spark Syrian War Study Says," in *National Geographic*, 2 March 2015 <http://news.nationalgeographic.com/news/2015/03/150302-syria-war-climate-change-drought/> (10 Jan. 2016).

The second was the destruction of Muammar al-Gaddafi's rule in Libya, which was led by France and the United Kingdom (and supported by US and other NATO forces) from March to October 2011. The UN Security Council resolution 1975, which demanded a ceasefire and no-fly zone (tacitly accepted by Russia) was exploited to achieve regime change. Since then Libya has become a failed state and an open valve for refugees from sub-Saharan Africa to start their dangerous journey across the Mediterranean.

In general, the economic (political, social and cultural) dependency of Austria (and "the rest of the world") on the United States can be subsumed under the headings of the Washington Consensus, the Harvard Business Model, the unlimited dominance of US rating companies over national economies, the global arrogation of US patent law and other jurisdiction as overruling national law, tax evasion, tax havens and other privileges of transnational companies (nicknamed "Luxleaks"). In particular, this dependency became self-evident when within a couple of days in 2007–08, the US subprime mortgage crises morphed into a world financial crisis—as well as into a taboo. While no one dares to call it what it really is—a world economic crisis—at least some spectators have begun to wonder whether the whole Washington Consensus model does not deserve the epithet "subprime" as well.

At the moment, the secret negotiations between the United States and the European Union for a Transatlantic Trade and Investment Partnership (TTIP) are an appropriate case in point. These secret talks are highly controversial, the strongest opposition being raised in Germany and Austria. In Salzburg, even the present Catholic Archbishop is among its most vociferous critics. Proponents constantly argue that economic advantages for transnational companies will not come at the expense of "European values and identities." Critics, on the other hand, are wondering what kind of diplomatic spirit is prevailing when US Ambassador to the European Union, Anthony L. Gardner, makes clear "that TTIP is, if you'll pardon the expression, geopolitically pertinent." Why? It will "provide an economic equivalent to NATO" settling "the rules of world trade before others do it for us."[29]

Before all else, opponents dread the introduction of secret arbitrary courts, a massive lowering of European food and environmental safety

29 "What is TTIP and why we should be angry about it?" in *The Guardian online*, 3 August 2015 <http://www.theguardian.com/business/2015/aug/03/ttip-what-why-angrytransatlantic-trade-investment-partnership-guide> (11 Dec. 2015); "Kritik an geplantem Handelsabkommen TTIP," *ORF online*, 18 November 2015 <http://salzburg.orf.at/news/stories/2742889/> (11 Dec. 2015).

standards, a deterioration of health and education systems, social and labor rights, as well as a further constriction of European Union laws and national sovereignty—in short, a triumph of economy over politics. It is a truism that every seventh job in the European Union (thirty million) is dependent on exports (625,000 jobs in Austria). But the argument that the reduction of current trade barriers should be more desirable for consumers, workers, small businesses and not just international and multinational companies is open to substantial skepticism.

In particular, the market for global agribusiness and (genetically modified) seeds has been approaching oligopolistic prospects. At present this is exemplified by attempts of Monsanto (or Du Pont) to take over the Swiss giant Syngenta, while the other major players Dow Chemicals, Bayer and BASF, are watching behind the scenes. Monsanto has been threatening (not only) European biodiversity in food production through its genetically modified and patented seeds, e.g. corn Mon810, soybeans, sugar beet, cotton, canola, and a variety of other vegetables and flowers in more than 150 countries all over. It is to be hoped, that Roundup, the most used weed killer globally since the 1970s, is no link to a period when Monsanto (and Dow Chemicals) were the major producers of Agent Orange in the Vietnam War from 1965–69.[30]

It would be a first in world history that deregulation should actually raise food safety, boost environmental standards and data security, enhance international fair labor laws, abolish child labor plus discrimination in the workplace, and support the development of poorer countries: in short, the protection of (the) species—which is, at the moment, even more threatened by a new menagerie of gene-edited animals.[31]

Whatever the outcome, at least two things are quite clear. First: the Trans-Pacific Partnership (TPP), drafted between twelve countries on 5 October 2015, excludes China, constituting one of the multiple attempts to hold down that rising giant. Similarly, TTIP, if signed, would not only exclude Africa, Latin America and Asia, but also, secondly, continue the longstanding (and seemingly natural) global agenda setting of US and European economic, labor and social standards. A catch-22, if ever there was one.

China recently replaced Europe as the most important market for US-American movies. Whether the impact of this seminal development will

30 "Agent Orange: Background of Monsanto's Involvement," in *Monsanto* <http://www.monsanto.com/newsviews/pages/agent-orange-background-monsanto-involvement.aspx> (2 Feb. 2016).

31 "Gene-Edited Animals On Farms And Tables," *The New York Times International Weekly*, 7 Dec. 2015: 1, 3.

be as fundamental an influence on film themes, plots, characters etc., like Chinese investments in US-American industries, will have to be seen. What is also open is the question whether Wang Jianling's "Hollywood on the Yellow Sea" will achieve global film success after the takeover of the movie chain AMC and the studio Legendary.[32] The US-American movie, television, and video game business recently has been undergoing such drastic changes that the national label "American" may have become misleading. Still, although many movies are neither shot in California (or even in the United States), nor financed with US-American money anymore, they are still seen as "American" films worldwide and Hollywood still works as *the* identifier of the globally paramount US-American entertainment industry.

While only 130 of the 367 films shown in Austrian cinemas in 2011 originated in the United States, their market share was 76.5 percent, followed by German films with 10.4, and Austrian with 1.7 percent. This kind of proportion has been, more or less, prevalent during the last decades. In 2014, 125 US films (approximately 40 percent of films shown) attracted 70 percent moviegoers. Most important: of the top 50 movies, 43 were US-productions![33]

The situation in the "social" media dominion is also striking: in the end of 2015, the *Social Media Radar Austria* has 3.4 million Facebook users on its screen, 140,000 on Twitter, 340,000 on Instagram and 704,000 on LinkedIn.[34] The social, economic and cultural changes introduced by these "social" media, as well as the chances for cutting-edge US influences, are still

32 Willie Shih and Henry McGee, "Hollywood on the Yellow Sea," in *The Atlantic*, December 2015 <http://www.theatlantic.com/magazine/archive/2015/12/hollywood-on-the-yellow-sea/413185/> (11 Jan. 2015); "Matt Damon nun in chinesischem Sold," *Der Standard*, 13 Jan. 2016: 20.

33 "Kino und Filme 2011," in *marktmeinungmensch* <http://www.marktmeinungmensch.at/studien/kino-und-filme/>; "Österreicher gehen zweimal im Jahr ins Kino," in *Kurier*, 9 May 2013 <http://kurier.at/wirtschaft/unternehmen/oesterreicher-gehen-zwei-mal-im-jahr-ins-kino/11.819.172> (11 Jan. 2016); Filmwirtschaftsbericht Österreich 2014 <http://filmwirtschaftsbericht.filminstitut.at/14/kino/kinobesuche-und-filmverleih/> (11 Jan. 2016); "Krampus und der Rest der coolen Gang," in *orf.at*, 2 December 2015 <http://orf.at/stories/2312425/2312455/> (11 Jan. 2016); Fernsehereignis des Jahres 2008: "FM4 Exitpoll 2008: Teil zwei," in *FM4*, 30 December 2008 <fm4v2.orf.at/connected/225832/main> (11 Jan. 2016).

34 *Social Media Radar Austria* <http://socialmediaradar.at/> (11 Jan. 2016); "Anzahl der Nutzer von Facebook in Österreich in ausgewählten Monaten von April 2013 bis Dezember 2015 (in Millionen)," in *statista – Das Statistik-Portal*, January 2016 <http://de.statista.com/statistik/daten/studie/296115/umfrage/facebook-nutzer-in-oesterreich/> (11 Jan. 2016); "124% der 16jährigen ÖsterreicherInnen sind auf Facebook," in *Webmarketing Blog* <http://www.webmarketingblog.at/2012/08/09/124-der-16jahrigen-osterreicherinnen-sind-auf-facebook/> (11 Jan. 2016); "Top Web Apps in Austria," in *readwrite*, 12 October 2006 <http://readwrite.com/2006/10/13/austria_top_web_apps> (11 Jan. 2016).

under research. The same applies to the growing video streaming services Netflix, Amazon Prime Instant Video, Maxdome, Snap by Sky, Sky Online, Watchever, Flimmit A1 Videothek, and UPC On demand.[35]

At least in the business of popular culture, not all seems to be lost yet: In 2003, the domestic box office brought in $9.2 billion for US-based studios, while foreign markets generated $10.9 billion. In 2007, domestic was $9.6 billion, while international rose to more than $17 billion. As *The New York Times*, reporting the dramatic increase of US-American programs on major European networks from 214,000 to 266,000 hours between 2000 and 2006, proclaimed on 30 November 2008: "World Falls for American Media, Even as It Sours on America."[36] In the long run, this situation may be of utmost importance for US interests, because entertainment is the commercial equivalent of propaganda (Guo Xiaolu). None other than Frank Zappa recognized politics to function as entertainment division of big business.

The European world, particularly in Austria, also continued to fall for "typically American food." Europe has been the largest market for McDonald's for quite a while, with forty percent of its global sales. McCafé McDonald's not only competed with traditional cafes but, especially, with Starbucks. Interestingly enough, all of this happened while McDonald's experienced a substantial crisis with dropping sales in the United States, Asia, Africa, and the Near East. But business in Austria was especially dazzling. Between 2010 and 2014, it soared from 481 to 562 million Euro sales and from 146 to 158 million customers. According to *Euromonitor*, McDonald's not only has a strikingly positive reputation in Austria, but also one of the highest densities of restaurants per capita in all of Europe.[37] While the latest food trend has been the substantial growth of the market

35 "Netflix, Amazon and Co.: Streaming Angebote in Österreich im Überblick," in *derStandard.at*, 22 November 2014 <http://derstandard.at/2000008512517/Vom-Medien-Albanien-zum-Netflix-Land-Video-on-Demand-Oesterreich> (11 Jan. 2016).

36 Tim Arango, "World Falls for American Media, Even as It Sours on America," in *The New York Times,* 30 November 2008 <http://www.nytimes.com/2008/12/01/business/media/01soft.html> (11 Jan. 2015); See also "Chinese Embrace America's Culture but Not Its Policies," in *International New York Times*, 28 September 2015 <http://www.nytimes.com/2015/09/29/world/asia/china-united-states-culture-policy.html?hp&action=click&pgtype=Homepage&module=photo-spot-region&region=top-news&WT.nav=top-news&_r=0> (11 Jan. 2016).

37 "McDonald's: Heimatmarkt kriselt, blendende Österreich-Geschäfte," in *format.at*, 2 April 2015 <http://www.format.at/wirtschaft/mcdonald-heimatmarkt-oesterreich-geschaefte-5584764> (2 Feb. 2015); "McDonald's setzt in Österreich auf Veggie und Bestellterminals," in *Die Presse*, 13 August 2015 <http://diepresse.com/home/wirtschaft/international/4798982/McDonalds-setzt-in-Osterreich-auf-Veggie-und-Bestellterminals> (2 Feb 2015); "Marktanteile weiter ausgebaut,"in *orf.at*, 6 October 2011 <http://orf.at/stories/2082913/2082955/> (2 Feb. 2015).

for home meal replacement, which grows twice as fast as restaurants, the jury is still out in the final battle between Döner, Würstel and Burger.[38]

During the last decades, jazz, the blues, rhythm & blues, rock 'n' roll, and many other genres of US-American pop music have become an integral and quasi natural part of the Austrian soundscape. Since the 1920s, the standard of European ballroom dancing has been moving way beyond the Viennese Waltz. It now includes the Tango, Foxtrot, Slowfox, Quickstepp, Cha-Cha-Cha, Samba, Rumba, Paso Doble and Jive, and the formation of Austropop represents a declaration of independence from the German *Schlager*, not a secession from US-American models.

The American Century has at least as much to do with the global attraction of the "Sound of Freedom" as with U.S. economic, financial, and military power. While the latter have lost their glory for nearly everybody outside the elite circles profiting from the "Empire of the Fun," the leading position of jazz and U.S. popular music as unchallenged global creators of taste likewise has been challenged.[39] To name but a few of the most important elements contributing to the slow erosion of US-dominated popular culture: the British invasion of the United States, spearheaded by the Beatles, but by no means restricted to pop and rock music; when Miles Davis hired British guitarist John McLaughlin and bassist Dave Holland, as well as the Austrian keyboarder Joe Zawinul, for his *Bitches Brew* sessions in August 1969, the world of jazz would never be the same; the musical revolution created within the "Third World" and wonderfully represented by its first lead singer Bob Marley, whose "Them Belly Full, But We Hungry" was the appropriate battle cry (and the Jamaican influence on the development of hip-hop only continued the long-range influence of the Caribbean on U.S., and thereby world, music); the influence of the Munich Sound (e.g. Giorgio Moroder) on the development of disco (diagnosed, among others, as the death of rhythm & blues by Nelson George); and the massive influence of Kraftwerk (and, later, Techno) had on hip-hop and a myriad of global dance styles, which could now be produced on home computers. This caused a technological revolution in the field of music creation and production in general, not only in Austria. Digitization and the Internet overturned the paradigmatic control of distribution structures

38 "Burger gegen Würstel gegen Döner," in *derStandard.at*, 24 February 2011 <http://derstandard.at/1297818911870/Gefundenes-Fressen-Burger-gegen-Wuerstel-gegen-Doener> (2 Feb. 2015); Beate Hausbichler, "Am Esstisch rückt die Welt zusammen," *Der Standard*, 4 Nov. 2015: 7.

39 Alex Seago, "'Where Hamburgers Sizzle on an Open Grill Night and Day.' Global Pop Music and Americanization in the Year 2000," *American Studies* 41, no. 2–3 (2000): 119–136; Alex Seago, "The 'Kraftwerk-Effekt': Transatlantic Circulation, Global Networks and Contemporary Pop Music," *Atlantic Studies* 1, no.1 (2004): 85–106.

by global entertainment corporations. The cumulative effect of all the above has left no stone unturned—and the giant entertainment corporations reelin' (but not rockin').[40]

Scant room for bafflement exists when we consider the staggering global success of US-American popular culture. Still, a few stunners do remain in the domain of global transmission of musical (and political) communication. One certainly is the lasting influence of Malcolm X and US-American Islam on Austrian, German and Swiss Muslim youth via hip-hop since the 1990s. The experience of cultural and religious marginalization of young Upper Austrian Muslims' amalgamated experiences of individual discrimination created a collective identity of hip-hop culture, Islam, Malcolm X, the civil rights movement, and the struggle against social and cultural repression. Hip-hop became the bullhorn of ethnic and religious minorities in central Europe, just as it had been in the Bronx. Its messages became the soundtrack for many members of the Austrian Muslim Youth.[41]

The dissemination of US-American Islam and Malcolm X to young Innviertler Muslims via hip-hop typifies a rather stupefying example of "Americanization" indeed. But there it is. The soaring marginalization of an ever-larger cohort of young people worldwide has been accompanied by a parallel increase of global instant communication technology, causing a stupendous amplification and circulation speed. Nearly a century before, jazz became the classical music of globalization exactly because of a similar development, the improvement of the means of mass communication (radio, records and movies).

Now hip-hop is the mouthpiece of global dissent. Although the genre frequently deteriorated to demonstrations of wealth and status in the United States, it metamorphosed into the vernacular of dissatisfaction from Rio to Paris, from Berlin to Beirut, and from Ulan Bator to Ried im Innviertel. To paraphrase Ned Sublette, it was the world that made (the music of) New Orleans. It is only fitting, that it is New Orleans, which remakes the soundscapes of the world.

---

40 Reinhold Wagnleitner, "Jazz – the Classical Music of Globalization, Or: When the Cold War Morphed into the Cool War," in *Is It 'Cause It's Cool?' Affective Encounters with American Culture*, ed. Astrid M. Fellner, Susanne Hamscha, Klaus Heissenberger, and Jennifer J Moos (Vienna/Berlin/Münster: LIT Verlag, 2014), 51–73; Reinhold Wagnleitner, "'The Empire of the Fun': Pop Culture and Geopolitical Aesthetics," in *On the Idea of America: Perspectives from the Engelsberg Seminar 2009*, ed. Kurt Almquvist and Alexander Linklater (Stockholm: Axel and Margaret Axson Foundation, 2010), 79–83.

41 Farid Hafez, "'Von Harlem ins Hoamatland': Hip Hop, Malcolm X und muslimischer Aktivismus in der Alpenrepublik," *Arbeiten aus Anglistik und Amerikanistik* 38, no. 2 (2013): 213–234.

The global success of US-American pop culture constitutes an essential chapter of contemporary life. It can be argued that the only culture unifying all youngsters in the European Union is US-American pop culture. At present more than 70 percent of younger Austrians are able to carry on a conversation in English (more than in most other EU countries).[42] Yet thinking about future probabilities, we should always be aware of Angela Chen's caveat that "when it comes to making predictions, most experts are not more accurate than a dart-throwing chimp."[43] The late William Pfaff—he will be sorely missed—laconically summed up the reasons for the global decline of enthusiasm for the "model America": "The international credit collapse that began in America in 2008 cooled enthusiasm for a deregulated capitalist economic and trading system centered upon the United States."[44] The strange case of the disappearance of the American middle class may lead to a situation even more surprising.[45] We could face an even stranger situation, where the attraction of the "model America" might be reduced to the significance of the mother of all model shows, "America's Next Top Model." But even that ended on 4 December 2015.

42 Jakub Marina's map of the percentage of people speaking English in the EU by country <https://jakubmarian.com/map-of-the-percentage-of-people-speaking-english-in-the-eu-by-country/> (26 Jan. 2015).

43 Angela Chen, "Seeing into the future. Does Philip Tetlock Hold the Key to Accurate Predictions?" in *The Chronicle of Higher Education*, 5 October 2015 <http://chronicle.com/article/Philip-Tetlock-s-Tomorrows/233507> (15 Dec. 2015).

44 William Pfaff, *The Irony of Manifest Destiny. The Tragedy of America's Foreign Policy* (New York: Walker & Company, 2010), 11.

45 Paul Mason, "The strange case of America's disappearing middle class," in *The Guardian online*, 14 December 2015 <http://www.theguardian.com/commentisfree/2015/dec/14/the-strange-case-of-americas-disappearing-middle-class> (15 Dec. 2015).

Corpus Christi Holiday.
Religious procession in Bergheim.
Bergheim, Franz Neumayr, 06 04 2015
Credit: APA PictureDesk

Volume 13: Günter Bischof/Anton Pelinka/Hermann Denz, eds. *Religion in Austria*. New Brunswick, NJ: Transaction 2004

Religion in Austria Revisited

Paul M. Zulehner

Sociology of religion in Austria is in good condition. A survey that stretches back over forty years is available. The long-term project was started in 1970 and is entitled "Religion in the Life of Austrians." The survey has been conducted every ten years.[1] The five waves together show a dramatic development from a predominantly Catholic to a pluralistic country. In addition, there are three gender studies from 1992, 2002 and 2012. Their main topic was not religion, but types of gender roles and their development over twenty years.[2] Among the personal data, there is a lot related to religion and Church. Furthermore, the results of the European Value System Study are helpful. Austria took part in this longitudinal project in 1991, then in 1999 and 2008.[3] Hermann Denz, who unfortunately died much too early in 2008, belonged to the Austrian research board in all three waves. The sociological Research Community and I miss him very much.

In 2010, it was a time-sensitive decision to analyze Muslims in Austria within a special sample. This analysis made it possible to have a look at the growing cultural tensions between a part of Austria's population and Muslims immigrants, who came in the last decades to Austria from, for instance, Anatolia in Turkey. Demonstrations of anti-Islamic groups in all European countries are signs of these tensions. In the newest study, we wanted to know better the different migrant-generations of Muslims: Are there changes in their belief system and lifestyle from the first to the following generations?

The aim of this contribution is to clarify whether the situation of religion in Austria, presented in Volume 13 of *Contemporary Austrian Studies*, is the same as in 2005. Alternatively, are there new developments, embedded in a more and more inestimable evolution of the globalized world?

1 Paul M. Zulehner, *Verbuntung. Kirchen im weltanschaulichen Pluralismus: Religion im Leben der Menschen 1970–2010* (Ostfildern: Schwabenverlag, 2011).

2 Petra Steinmair-Pösel and Paul M. Zulehner, *Gleichstellung in der Sackgasse? Frauen, Männer und die erschöpfte Familie von heute* (Vienna: Styria Premium, 2014).

3 The data of all studies and the questionnaires are available at <http://www.zulehner.org/site/forschung>.

"Colorization" ("*Verbuntung*") Continues

The ideological scene in Austria is in transition. The era in which Christianity in its Catholic variation was the only permitted religion is definitively over. The end of the Constantine era has come. In the past, Christianity was the religion of the state. Whoever wanted to be a citizen in that "christentümlichen" culture had to be a Christian. To belong to the Church und to be a Christian was "fate." That situation was sharpened in the time after the Reformation in 1517, when the Emperor decided to which Christian confession to which the subjects had to belong.

In a long historical process with enormous fights and tensions, religious freedom was won. To belong to a religion is no longer a cultural fate, but a personal choice. The ability to choose increases religious mobility. Citizens decide whether to stay in the Church into which they are christened as children by their parents. They can also leave their Church without any social restraints and disadvantages. Therefore, it is to be expected that every year Church members leave their community without causing a stir. Mostly this is not sparked by failures of the Church. It is part of the historical transition from "fate to choice" (Peter L. Berger).[4] Some members leave their Church because of severe irritations like the abuse of children by priests and monks, the discrimination of women in some Christian Churches, and the pre-modern language of some preachers. In addition, leaving the Church can mean saving money. Nevertheless, the much more important reason is the lack of gratifications: those who do not know "for what" they remain a Church member leave the Church.

4 Peter L. Berger and Anton C. Zijderveld, *In Praise of Doubt: How to Have Convictions Without Becoming a Fanatic* (New York: Harper One, 2010); Peter L. Berger, *The Many Altars of Modernity: Toward a Paradigm for Religion in a Pluralist Age* (Boston: De Gruyter Mouton, 2014).

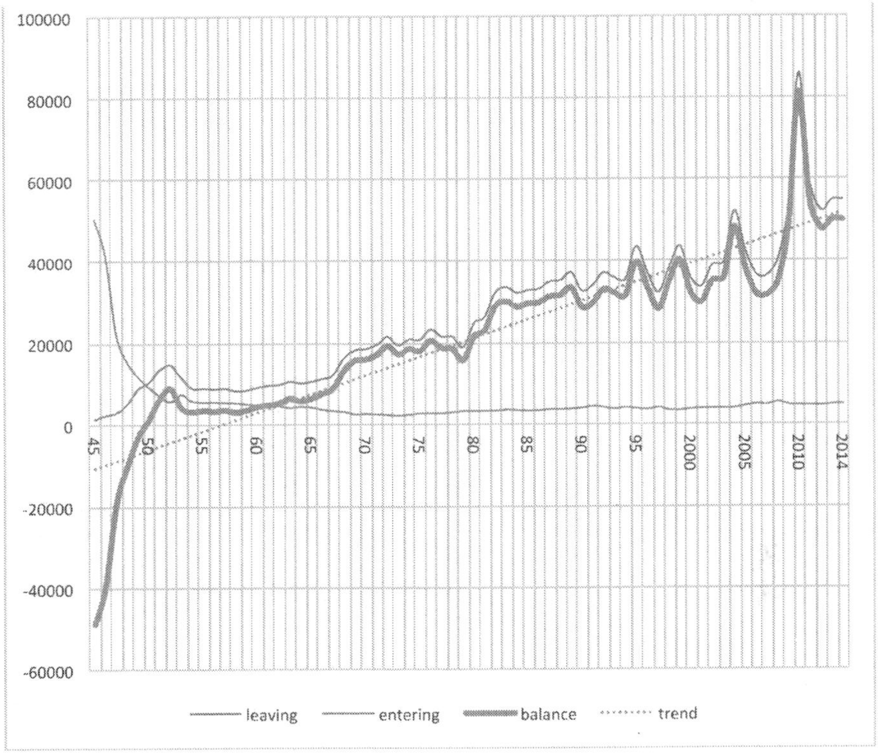

Graph 1: A constant number of members leave the Church every year

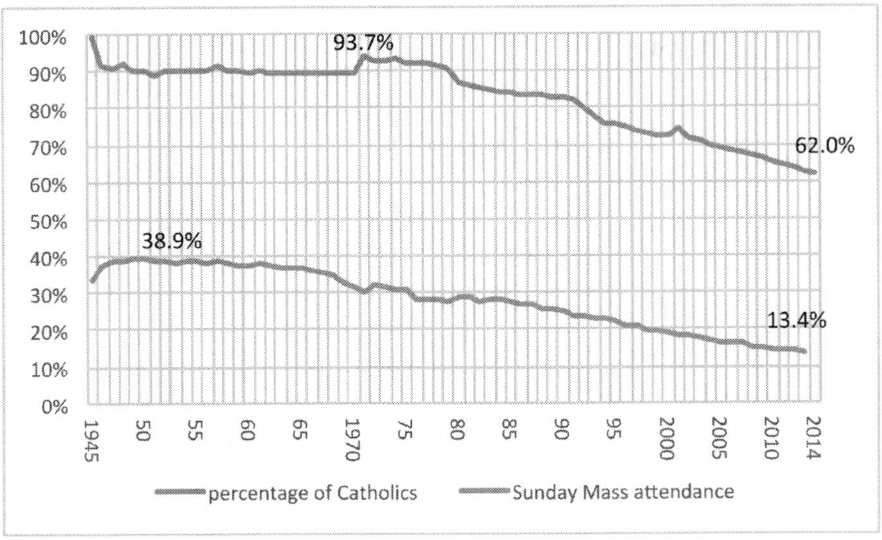

Graph 2: The percentage of Church members and Sunday Mass attendance decrease continuously

For many years, above all in the 1970s, the leading experts of sociology of religion interpreted this development as secularization. Their principle was the more modern the more secularized, the less religious society is. Our survey data over forty years shows that not even in Europe does modernization secularize the culture. The result of modernization is not a secularized culture, but a culture with a colorful variety of religions, worldviews and lifestyles.

Four Types

Here are empirical data documenting this process of colorization or pluralization of the modern Austrian culture in the last four decades. Based on several socio-religious items we formed four types.

To elucidate the four types, we correlate them with central socio-religious items.

Table 1: Correlations

	I am a religious person.	I pray	If I do not succeed to know God and to love him, my life will be meaningless.	I do not care if there is a God.	Attends mass every Sunday.	You can be a good Christian without attending Sunday mass.
secular	19%	2%	2%	37%	1%	88%
skeptical	70%	30%	12%	9%	14%	86%
religious	89%	65%	69%	7%	38%	93%
churchly	94%	86%	85%	2%	88%	6%
all	68%	42%	38%	12%	29%	77%

Data Base: Surveys 1970–2010

Table 2: Consent of the four types to Christian positions

	There is a God, who revealed himself in Jesus.	The resurrection of Christ gives meaning to my life.	The future lies in the reign of God, which Jesus proclaimed.
secular	13%	5%	6%
skeptical	59%	41%	44%
religious	82%	75%	77%
churchly	82%	78%	81%
all	55%	42%	45%

Data Base: Survey 2010

Table 3: Shift in the last forty years

	secular	skeptical	religious	churchly
1970	9%	32%	36%	23%
1980	21%	32%	34%	13%
1990	23%	39%	27%	11%
2000	26%	39%	27%	8%
2010	26%	45%	24%	5%

Data Base: Surveys 1970–2010

The table shows that the *churchly persons* have high percentages not only in relation to the religious items, but also on Church commitment. They attend Sunday mass and think that without going to Mass on Sunday you cannot be a good Christian. These persons are the devoted Church members. The socio-religious level is extremely high.

The *religious type* finds that Church commitment is not necessary. Those people do not go to Church on Sundays. They are convinced that you can be a good Christian without going to Sunday mass.

The so-called *secular type* tends to be atheistic. They do not care if there is a god. Conducting a meaningful life for them has no relation to a god. They do not pray or go to Sunday service. They do not accept the Church's doctrine about Jesus Christ.

The *skeptical type* differs from the secular. Most of the skeptical feel they are religious. A third of them pray often. Half of them accept the Church's teaching about Jesus Christ.

The following table shows a creeping shift over the last forty years from the religious and the churchly type not only to the skeptical, but also in part to the secular type. Nevertheless, no single type disappears. A modern citizen's beliefs are now deinstitutionalized and de-churched; instead, these beliefs are personalized. For many, this personalization does not lead to atheism or secularity: this is the case only for a quarter of individual belief-stories. Only 37 percent of respondents do not care if there is a God.

Deinstitutionalization produces destabilization, and therefore skepticism. If one of the types should be defined as modern, then we have to choose the skeptical type. To be modern is to be skeptical. Alternatively, in a positive sense: to be a seeker. Danièle Hervieu-Léger coined the term *pèlerins*, pilgrims, for them.[5] In this sense, spirituality is "in"—it is a megatrend of our times. But this spirituality is a highly privatized spirituality without Church; sometimes, it forms short-term communities with rituals and gurus.

Mobility characterizes modern religiosity/spirituality. In religious terms, we can say that it is a time for conversions. People change their religious orientation more often during their lifetime than in times before. Some leave the Church; later on, some enter again. Others approach Buddhism or Islam, or they look around for spiritual rituals, like healing services or esoteric wisdom.

Muslims in Austria

For many centuries in Europe, in order to avoid religious and political violence, religion was a private matter. It seems that nowadays religion is returning to the public stage. A re-politicization of religion is happening.

One reason is that the Islamic community in many countries of Europe—in Austria too—is increasing rapidly. Therefore, in the last survey in 2010 about "Religion in the Life of the Austrians," we implemented a special sample for first, second, or third generation Muslims living in Austria. We wanted to know about Muslims, whose roots are in the pre-modern culture of Anatolia, or those who immigrated from the Balkans or Africa, and how they live and believe. Another important question was if lifestyle and belief systems of Muslims changed from the first to the following generations. Of

5 Danièle Hervieu-Léger, *La religion en mouvement, le pèlerin et le converti* (Paris: Editions Flammarion, 1999).

high interest was a look at the gender roles of male and female Muslims in the different generations. In addition, we analyzed the relation between the native Austrians and the migrant Muslims.

Here follow some highlights of our research, which help us to understand some aspects of the recent politics in relation to religion in Austria and Europe in the last years.

Types of Islamic Practice in Austria

The commitment of Muslims in their religious community differs very much. To form a typology, we took a series of items:

about belief: the five pillars of Islam: declaration of faith, obligatory prayer, fasting in the month of Ramadan, compulsory giving, pilgrimage to Mecca;

about practice: services in the Holy Nights, go to the Mosque on Fridays, and;

about the possession of holy things: the holy book of Quran, holy stone, prayer mat, lucky charm.

Based on these items, we identified three types of Muslims: the practicing (48 percent), the open (27 percent), and the secular (25 percent).

Graph 3: Three types of Muslims

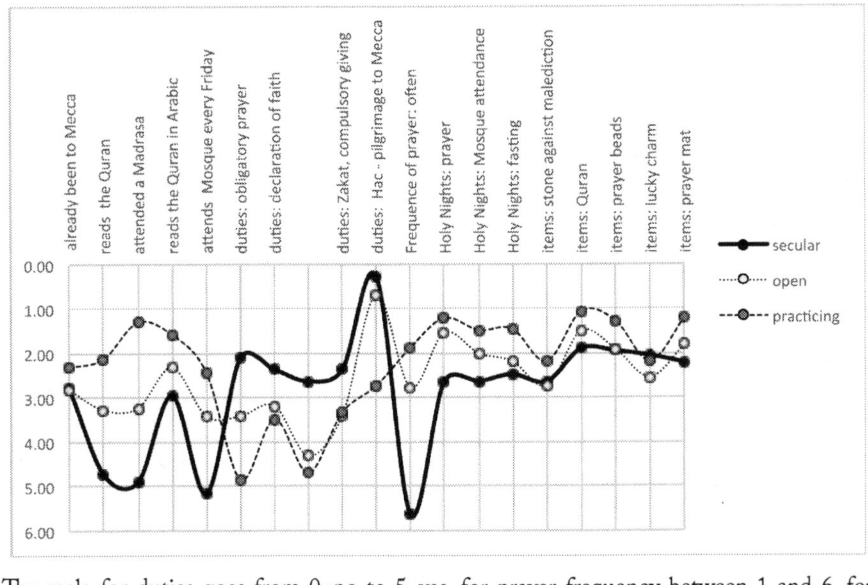

The scale for duties goes from 0=no to 5=yes, for prayer frequency between 1 and 6, for possessions between 1 and 3, for others between 1 and 5. 2010

The distribution of these three types in the various social strata is different: more men than women are practicing, school education generally reduces the percentage, and from the first to the second generation the percent practicing is cut in half. Therefore, the older the Muslims are, the more they belong to the practicing type.

Graph 4: The practicing type according to social items

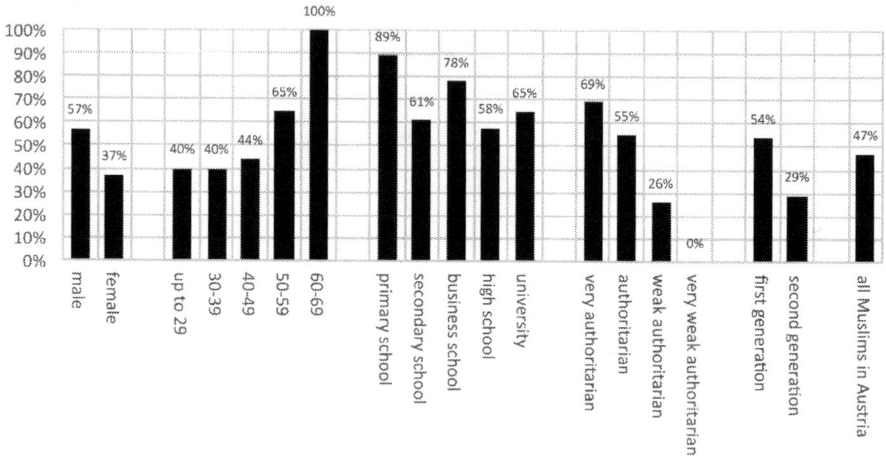

Source: Religion in the Life of Austrians 2010

Authoritarianism has a major impact. Authoritarianism is a personality characteristic: an authoritarian person is submissive. They feel that those who are above them in the hierarchy are right. They do not build their own stable identity, but they borrow it from strong leaders or structured groups. There are many authoritarian persons in pre-modern cultures, as in Anatolia, where many of the Muslims in Austria come from.

The religiosity, which they bring with them as migrants from their homeland to Austria, is characterized by an authoritarian manner. The correlation between the Islamic belief system and authoritarianism is very strong. This is the case with the first generation: when Muslims live for a longer time in Austria's modern culture, authoritarianism decreases quickly. The percentage of those who are religious and authoritarian together falls from 61 percent in the first generation to 39 percent in the second one.

Table 4: Religiosity and authoritarianism of Muslims in the first and the second generation

		religious + authoritarian	religious + non-authoritarian
men	1. generation	78%	6%
	2. generation	58%	11%
	all men	74%	7%
women	1. generation	40%	25%
	2. generation	26%	54%
	all women	35%	34%

Source: Religion in the Life of the Austrians – Muslims, 2010

The modern culture of Austria is changing the inner structure of Islamic religiosity gradually. The Muslims who live in Austria are creating in their own life a modern version of Islam. It is a change within the Islamic religious culture from bottom up, long before the religious leaders of the Islamic community modernize the official teaching. Are the grassroots Muslims in Austria forming a "European Islam," which is compatible with the modern values of Europe such as freedom or gender roles?

That seems to be the case and we can bring good empirical arguments for it. We own data about the gender roles of Muslims in Austria, and this data again describes the different generations. Muslims of the first generation have a very traditional concept of the role of man and woman (43 percent). Contrarily, the Muslim women of the second generation tend more and more overall to a modern gender role, more than their male counterparts do. Muslim women are the forerunners in this development. That is understandable, because women are the winners of modernization of the lifestyle.

Graph 5: Gender roles according to sex and generation of migration

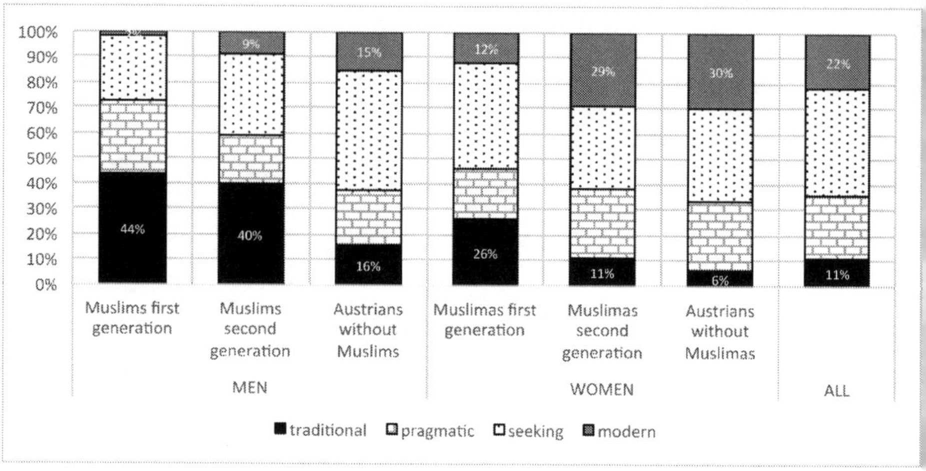

Source: Austrian Gender Survey 2012

"Cultural Christians"

In European countries, an anti-Islamic mood has emerged in the last years. Demonstrations against an Islamization of Europe were organized. The hub of that movement was Eastern Germany. The organization is named PEGIDA (Patriotic Europeans Against the Islamization of the Occident). Historically, for them Europe is a Christian continent. This should not be changed by migration of Muslims from different Islamic regions of the world.

In the 2010 study "Religion in the Life of Austrians," we focused on this topic. How do Austrians perceive the growing Islamic population in Europe—and in Austria? For Austrians, how compatible is modern European culture with Quran-based Islamic values?

With a series of items, we could identify three types of relationships between Christianity and Islam. The first type opts for a peaceful and productive dialogue between both religions, their leaders, and their members in the local communities (31 percent). Then there are the so-called "Cultural Christians" ("*Kulturchristen*"). They are convinced that, "a self-aware Christianity is important for Europe." On average 56 percent of Austrians think so. Within the "Cultural Christians," there a two subtypes. The one is peaceful (40 percent), the other militant (29 percent).

Table 5: Three types in respect of the relationship between Islam and Christianity in Europe

	militant Cultural Christians	for religious dialogue	peaceful Cultural Christians	all
Islam is per se a peaceful religion but extremists abuse it for their own aims.	72%	78%	82%	78%
The moral values of Islam are traditional and old-fashioned. They are not suitable in the Europe of the 21st century.	86%	62%	69%	74%
Islam is, as Christianity and Judaism, a world religion. As such it stands for peaceful cohabitation.	53%	57%	61%	57%
A self-aware Christianity is important for Europe.	81%	0%	82%	56%
At the same time, one can be a Muslim and a good democrat.	29%	41%	81%	50%
Islam is a violent religion, which favours the emergence of radicalised groups and terrorism.	66%	38%	33%	46%
Christian Churches should take a harsher stand against Islam.	79%	7%	0%	32%

Source: Religion in the Life of the Austrians – Muslims, 2010

In 2010 in Austria we found 31 percent who stand for a peaceful religious dialogue, 29 percent were militant and 40 percent were peaceful "Cultural Christians." The distribution varies corresponding to the political preference. Those who are prone to the Freedom Party (FPÖ) tend to be militant "Cultural Christians." Those who sympathize with The Greens (*Die Grünen*) opt for peaceful religious dialogue. This explains the politics in relation to migration and integration of these two parties. The Freedom Party takes an extremely xenophobic stance, while The Green Party stands for welcome and integration. However, this is only the mainstream among the voters of these two parties. The following table shows that the sympathizers of all political parties are split, even polarized. Half of the sympathizers with the People's Party (ÖVP), which has historically a proximity to the Catholic Church, stands for a peaceful relation to Islam while supporting the dominance of Christianity in Europe.

Table 6: Relationship between Islam and Christianity according to the political preference

	for religious dialogue	peaceful Cultural Christians	militant Cultural Christians
Social Democratic Party (SPÖ)	30%	36%	34%
People's Party (ÖVP)	21%	**47%**	32%
Freedom Party (FPÖ)	32%	25%	**43%**
The Greens (Die Grünen)	**49%**	35%	17%
Coalition Future Austria (BZÖ)	22%	31%	**47%**
all Austrians	29%	40%	31%

Source: Religion in the Life of Austrians 2010

Summarizing, we see that the transformation of the ideological landscape of Austria continues noiselessly. Churches, religions and atheistic organizations have to learn dialogue. Tolerance will be more and more a needed virtue in the society. Otherwise, ideological tensions and fights could arise. In addition: the privatization of religion is over. Religion is back on the political stage.

Daffodil Fest in Bad Aussee.
Conchita Wurst with Daffodil Princess Julia Pfanzeltner (OÖ), Daffodil Queen Theresa Pliem (ST), and Daffodil Princess Marlies Pilz (OÖ).
Bad Aussee, Barbara Gindl, 06 01 2014
Credit: APA PictureDesk

Volume 15: Günter Bischof/Anton Pelinka/Dagmar Herzog, eds. *Sexuality in Austria*. New Brunswick, NJ: Transaction 2006

Sexuality in Austria: An Update

Dagmar Herzog

An extraordinary amount has happened in the field of the history of sexuality in Austria-Hungary and Austria since the special issue of *Contemporary Austrian Studies* 15 (2007) was being prepared in the fall of 2005. At the time, I had noted that Austria could be an especially logical focus for exploring the history of sexuality—and this not least because it was home to both Sigmund Freud and Adolf Hitler—but had also observed that the history of sexuality in Austria was only just at that moment beginning to emerge from the shadow of the history of sexuality in Germany, a history into or under which it had for too long been amalgamated or subsumed. And one of the points of that special issue, with its eight contributors spanning the length of the twentieth century, was to highlight the distinctiveness of Austrian developments. The anthropologist and historian Matti Bunzl, a contributor to that issue—with a marvelous piece on what it took to "queer" Austria adequately to smooth its entry into the European Union in 1995—remarked in 2007 in his introduction to a three-essay Forum on the history of sexuality within the *Austrian History Yearbook* (a kind of companion to the CAS volume): "The history of Austrian sexualities remains full of substantial gaps."[1] We can say with certainty that in this past decade, study of the history of sexuality in Austria has not just come into its own, but is flourishing.

In the special issue, Pieter Judson's investigation into the (lamentably homophobia-reinforcing) consequences of an unexpectedly metastasizing crisis surrounding a cache of child pornography found in 2004 on one (!) Polish seminarian's computer at St. Pölten and Julia Woesthoff's brilliant

1 Matti Bunzl, "Desiderata for a History of Austrian Sexualities," in *Austrian History Yearbook* 38 (2007): 48–57, here 50. The essays in the Forum are by Scott Spector (also a contributor to the CAS special issue), Nancy Wingfield, and Keely Stauter-Halstead. Another important publication in 2011 was the more literary-criticism-oriented anthology *Contested Passions: Sexuality, Eroticism, and Gender in Modern Austrian Literature and Culture*, eds. Clemens Ruthner and Raleigh Whitinger (New York: Peter Lang, 2011), very helpfully reviewed by Britta McEwen in *Journal of Austrian Studies* 46, no. 2 (2013). The most recent literary and art historical approach is Esther K. Bauer, *Bodily Desire, Desired Bodies: Gender and Desire in Early Twentieth-Century German and Austrian Novels and Paintings* (Evanston: Northwestern UP, 2014).

diagnosis of the histrionic (and often misogynist) media reportage on binational marriages in the run-up to and aftermath of the passing of the new Foreigner Police Law of 2006 (with its sharpened scrutiny and penalization of so-called "fictitious marriages" entered into for the sole sake of acquiring citizenship) had already taken the study of Austrian sexual politics into the twenty-first century. But since then, and inevitably, several further politically volatile issues have brought the topic of sexuality in Austria recurrently also into the international news.

Foremost among these were the scandals surrounding hundreds of past incidents of sexual abuse of children by Catholic priests and members of religious orders (and the cover-ups and collusion by church authorities that had kept those incidents from view for decades) that erupted across numerous western European nations starting in January 2010. In Austria, more than 800 individuals came forward to report incidents of institutional abuse (by now the number has climbed to 1,700) as, also in 2010, a record number of 87,000 persons formally quit their church membership in indignation.[2] Even before the bishops in Germany had formulated a response, the church leadership in Austria had mobilized a Victim Protection Advocacy Office, responsible for coordinating financial restitution payments as well as therapy for survivors. Psychologists at the University of Vienna, working with the Advocacy Office, have since produced a careful study of traumatic sequelae based on survivor testimonies and evaluations.[3] A non-aligned Austrian organization—the "Platform for Those Affected by Church Violence"—criticized the Advocacy Office's work, and ran its own hotline, which also garnered several hundred calls; this project too led to a substantive formal report detailing the kinds of abuse suffered and proposing some perspectives on the structural sources of the problem.[4] Although one effect of the avalanche of scandals is that the society as a whole has become more sensitized to various dimensions of

2 Sylvia Westall, "Over 800 Complaints to Austrian Catholic Church Sexual Abuse Commission," in *Reuters*, 13 April 2011, <http://blogs.reuters.com/faithworld/2011/04/13/over-800-complaints-to-austrian-catholic-church-sexual-abuse-commission/> (18 Nov. 2015); "Fünf Jahre 'Klasnic-Kommission,'" in *ORF.at*, <http://religion.orf.at/stories/2703515/> (18 Nov. 2015).

3 Brigitte Lueger-Schuster, "Psychotraumatologische Fragestellungen zu Gewalt und Missbrauch in der Katholischen Kirche," final report of a research project at the Institute of Applied Psychology: Health, Development, Enhancement and Intervention, University of Vienna, November 2012, <http://ppcms.univie.ac.at/fileadmin/usermounts/luegerb8/Abschlussbericht_20121207.pdf> (18 Nov. 2015).

4 "Abused, Ignored, Slandered: Victims of Church-related Violence/ Bericht der Unabhängigen Hotline für Betroffene kirchlicher Gewalt," in *betroffen.at – Plattform Betroffener kirchlicher Gewalt*, 18 November 2010 <http://www.betroffen.at/wp-content/uploads/2010/11/PKpressetext-englisch.pdf> (18 Nov. 2015); see also the organization's website: <http://www.betroffen.at/>.

the issue of child abuse in all sites—including within families—there was no question that as a closed and authoritarian institution, and one that insists on propounding restrictive sexual mores, the Church's reputation and self-understanding has been deeply damaged.

Meanwhile, and as though happening on a different planet—although for some of the same geographic and economic reasons that are currently, as of the fall and winter of 2015, causing Austria to be a crucial reception and transit area for the multiple hundreds of thousands of refugees fleeing the crises in Syria and other war zones—Austria, bordering as it does on Slovenia, Hungary, Slovakia, and the Czech Republic, has over the last ten years, specifically as membership in the European Union has expanded eastward, also been a major destination for sex workers from the former Soviet bloc.[5] Additionally, in the past decade, significant numbers of African, especially Nigerian, sex workers have joined what had previously been a population of sex workers with a disproportionate percentage of Latin American origin. Much of the journalistic coverage as well as academic scholarship has addressed the phenomenon of prostitution in the context of increasingly serious, though many times also misplaced, European Union-wide concerns about trafficking.[6] (Of the more than 5,000 female sex workers officially registered in Austria, 85–90 percent have a migratory background.)[7] Important work has also been done on the phenomenon of roadside prostitution near the national border areas.[8]

Another area of scholarly productivity involves the history of homosexuality. A remarkable study is the dissertation by Anita Kurimay, "Sex in the 'Pearl of the Danube'" (2012), demonstrating that early twentieth-century Budapest was not only a far queerer but in general a far wilder and freer example of sexual modernity than any specialist on Paris or London or Berlin might have guessed.[9] In addition to the publication of an updated

5 Rutvica Andrijasevic, "Ost-, ostmittel- und südosteuropäische Prostituierte in West-, Mittel-, Nord- und Südeuropa seit den 1980er Jahren," in *Enzyklopädie Migration in Europa: Vom 17. Jahrhundert bis zur Gegenwart*, ed. Klaus J. Bade et al. (Munich: Wilhelm Fink Verlag, 2007).

6 David Signer, "'Diese Frauen sind nicht naiv'" (interview with Laura María Agustín), in *Neue Zürcher Zeitung*, 26 July 2009 <http://www.nzz.ch/diese-frauen-sind-nicht-naiv-1.3196618> (19 Nov. 2015).

7 Petra Wagner and Judith Winter, "Sexualdienstleistung in Österreich," in *Soziales Kapital* 11 (2014).

8 Bernhard Pichler, "Sexarbeit in Österreich," PhD. diss, University of Vienna, 2010; Jürgen Nautz and Birgit Sauer, eds., *Frauenhandel: Diskurse und Praktiken* (Göttingen: Vandenhoeck und Ruprecht, 2008).

9 Anita A. Kurimay, "Sex in the 'Pearl of the Danube': The History of Queer Life, Love, and its Regulation in Budapest, 1873–1941," PhD. diss, Rutgers University, 2012, for which Kurimay won the University of Minnesota's Center for Austrian Studies Dissertation Prize.

and revised edition of his classic *Kultur der Begierde* (2002, rev. 2009), the preeminent Austrian historian of sexuality Franz X. Eder—also a contributor to the CAS special issue of 2007—published an outstanding synthesis of the development of homosexual rights in Austria between 1870 and 1970. Not least in view of the—rather unusual in the international context—fact that not just male homosexuality but also lesbianism was criminalized in Austria, and in view of the longstanding dearth of specialized research, the sections of Eder's *Homosexualitäten* (2011) on the Nazi and the postwar eras are especially instructive.[10] Eder here also makes the point that the Austrian government has yet to follow the German Bundestag's example and apologize for and undo the convictions of men and women prosecuted for homosexuality in the Nazi era.[11] There is much more that remains to be explored historically. A detailed regional study of Nazi persecution of homosexuals in Oberösterreich was provided by Albert Knoll and Thomas Brüstle; an exhibit catalogue on homosexual lives in the Steiermark was produced by Maria Froihofer et al.[12] Martin Gössl, a prolific young scholar, has also published *Von der Unzucht zum Menschenrecht* (2011), a valuable volume of primary documents.[13] In addition, Gössl has written an interesting essay on the exceedingly long and winding path to gay and lesbian equality in postwar Austria, while Ulrike Repnik—drawing also on first-person interviews—has told the story of the gay and lesbian activist movements.[14]

But also the gains that have been made in the last twenty years are not completely secure. The 2014 flap over Austrian pop star and drag queen Conchita Wurst being chosen as icon for Bank Austria's advertising campaign, for instance, suggested that transsexuality and homosexuality

10 Franz X. Eder, *Kultur der Begierde* (Munich: C. H. Beck, 2009), 2nd rev. ed.; Franz X. Eder, *Homosexualitäten: Diskurse und Lebenswelten 1870–1970* (Vienna: Bibliothek der Provinz, 2011).

11 See the call for exoneration in "HOSI Wien fordert Entschädigung für homosexuelle NS-Opfer – Offener Brief an Bundesparteiobmänner von ÖVP und FPÖ," in *Homosexuelle Initiative (HOSI) Wien*, 4 May 2003, <http://www.hosiwien.at/hosi-wien-fordert-entschadigung-fur-homosexuelle-ns-opfer/> (18 Nov. 2015).

12 Albert Knoll and Thomas Brüstle, "Verfolgung von Homosexuellen am Beispiel Oberösterreich in der NS-Zeit," in *Frauen- und Geschlechtergeschichte des Nationalsozialismus: Fragestellungen, Perspektiven, neue Forschungen*, ed. Johanna Gehmacher and Gabriella Hauch (Vienna: Studienverlag, 2007); Maria Froihofer et al., eds., *L[i]eben und Begehren zwischen Geschlecht und Identität* (Vienna: Löcker, 2010).

13 Martin J. Gössl, *Von der Unzucht zum Menschenrecht: Eine Quellensammlung zu lesbisch-schwulen Themen in den Debatten des österreichischen Nationalrats von 1945 bis 2002* (Graz: Edition Regenbogen, 2011).

14 Martin J. Gössl, "Die Kontinuität einer Abnormität: Erklärungen zur Trägheit einer schwul-lesbischen Gleichberechtigung in Österreich," in *When We Were Gender: Geschlechter erinnern und vergessen, Analysen von Geschlecht und Gedächtnis in den Gender Studies, Queer-Theorien und feministischen Politiken*, ed. Guggenheimer et al. (Bielefeld: transcript, 2013); Ulrike Repnik, *Die Geschichte der Lesben- und Schwulenbewegung in Österreich* (Vienna: Milena, 2006).

were still awkward topics for many.[15] And the eruption of debate in 2015 over the government's new plans for sex education in the schools—which critics vehemently complained not only shunted parents to the side but were more generally aimed at substituting the traditional family model with (in their view unwarranted, even alarming) appreciation for "sexual diversity," and which also, critics fretted, would indoctrinate children in social constructionist understandings of "gender" (to critics' minds a slippery slope leading to "in the final analysis a dissolution of the bipolar organization of the sexes and therewith to dissolution of marriage and family as a connection between man and woman with (their own) children")—was an indication that it was premature to assume a basic cultural consensus in Austria on the value of sexual self-determination.[16]

A further cluster of work concerns the development of "sexual knowledges." Tracie Matysik's *Reforming the Moral Subject* (2008) adds unique elements to our understanding by embedding early twentieth-century legal, psychoanalytic, feminist and antifeminist arguments about sexual ethics in a discussion of broader concerns about social responsibility and freedom in an era of war and new anxieties about materialism and secularization.[17] Social reform and sex and marriage counseling clinics in interwar Vienna are the subject of an excellent book by Britta McEwen.[18] Yet more new aspects will be brought to light when Kirsten Leng's groundbreaking book on female sexologists in the German-speaking lands is published next year. Among Leng's subjects are the fascinating Austrian figures of Rosa Mayreder, Grete Meisel-Hess, and Sofie Lazarsfeld.[19] And for devotees of the history (and prehistory) specifically of psychoanalysis, it is worth mentioning that the first four volumes of a new *Gesamtausgabe* of the writings of Sigmund Freud have just been published by the Psychosozial Verlag in 2015. These volumes cover the years 1877–1894; among the intriguing inclusions are 200 reviews Freud wrote during that time.[20]

15 For example, see "Österreich: Bürger wehren sich gegen politisch und medial verordneten Gender-Wahn," in *Die Propagandaschau*, 11 January 2011, <https://propagandaschau.wordpress.com/2015/01/11/osterreich-burger-wehren-sich-gegen-politisch-und-medial-verordneten-gender-wahn/> (18 Nov. 2015).

16 "Der neue Erlass zur Sexualerziehung," "Unsere Kritik am Erlass," and "Gendertheorie," all available at <http://www.sexualerziehung.at/> in *Iniative Wertvolle Sexualerziehung*, n.d. (18 Nov. 2015).

17 Tracie Matysik, *Reforming the Moral Subject: Ethics and Sexuality in Central Europe 1890–1930* (Ithaca: Cornell University Press, 2008).

18 Britta McEwen, *Sexual Knowledge: Feeling, Fact, and Social Reform in Vienna, 1900–1934* (New York: Berghahn, 2012).

19 Kirsten Leng, *Sexual Knowledge/ Sexual Politics: Women and Sexology in Early-Twentieth-Century Germany*: forthcoming.

20 Sigmund Freud, *Gesamtausgabe* (Vols. I-IV), ed. Christfried Tögel with Urban Zerfaß (Giessen: Psychosozial-Verlag, 2015).

In the last decade, significant work has been done as well on the history of reproduction, including on the subjects of access to contraception and abortion. The renowned historian Maria Mesner—she, too, a contributor to the CAS special issue, but at the time with work focused on sex counseling in the first half of the twentieth century—has since completed a definitive book on struggles for reproductive self-determination, with fascinating comparisons between developments in Austria and other nations, especially the US.[21] This was a timely intervention, as May 2015 saw the forty-year anniversary in Austria of the decriminalization of abortion in the first trimester, with the MUVS museum in Vienna hosting distinguished activist professionals for a panel discussion on the call to remove Paragraph 144 from the criminal code entirely.[22]

But the history of reproduction involves yet further dimensions, among them the eugenics projects of the past (with their entanglement also in the thousandfold Nazi mass murder of the cognitively disabled and of those suffering from psychological illness) and the assisted reproductive technology developments of the present. The sense that there are unsheddable, profound burdens placed on the use of such technology in the present and future because of the hideousness of what was done, especially in the Austrian and German past, has lent a very specific tone of anxiety and ambivalence to the discussions around technological advance. "Because this is such a touchy subject…" begins the title of one recent contribution to the topic.[23] A significant collection concerned with Austrian eugenics is Gerhard Baader et al.'s *Eugenik in Österreich: Biopolitische Strukturen von 1900–1945* (2007).[24] Austria and eugenics were in the news as well of late in part because US journalist Steve Silberman's blockbuster history of autism, *NeuroTribes* (2015), contains a critical chapter on the work of Hans Asperger, and also because Swedish author Steve Sem-Sandberg

21 Maria Mesner, *Geburten/Kontrolle: Reproduktionspolitik im 20. Jahrhundert* (Vienna: Böhlau, 2010).

22 "Ungewollt schwanger: Wer soll entscheiden? 40 Jahre Fristenlösung und immer noch im Strafgesetz" (Podiumsdiskussion, MUVS, Vienna, 26 May 2015), <http://de.muvs.org/event/> (18 Nov. 2015).

23 Erich Griessler, "'Weil das so ein heißes Thema ist, rühren wir das besser nicht an.' Zur Regulierung kontroverser biomedizinischer Forschung in Österreich," in *ResearchGate*, January 2010, <http://www.researchgate.net/publication/270426852_Weil_das_so_ein_heies_Thema_ist_rhren_wir_das_besser_nicht_an._Zur_Regulierung_kontroverser_biomedizinischer_Forschung_in_sterreich> (19 Nov. 2015). See also Erwin Bernat, "Pränatale Diagnostik und Präimplantationsdiagnostik auf dem Prüfstand des österreichischen Rechts," in *Rechtsfragen der Präimplantationsdiagnostik*, eds. Christian Dierks et al. (Heidelberg: Springer, 2007).

24 Gerhard Baader, Veronika Hofer, and Thomas Mayer, ed., *Eugenik in Österreich: Biopolitische Strukturen von 1900–1945* (Vienna: Czernin Verlag, 2007), 66–139.

has written a novel on the Spiegelgrund murder facility.[25] Here too we see how unexpected developments in the present trigger the need for and the possibility for new original research in history.

* * *

Where do we need more work? Ironically, it's the specificities of the sexual revolution itself that remain understudied. Was there a revolution in Austria in the 1960s–1980s? What changed, and how much, and where? In 2008, in the pages of the Austrian newsmagazine *Profil*, frequent contributors Angelika Hager and Sebastian Hofer ruminated on what they saw as the main—depressing—attributes of the Austrian political and cultural climate in and around 1968: they wrote of "a republic permeated by anti-Semitism, parochialism, and deeply rooted misogyny." It was against this mustiness that the counterculture rebelled, but often with wholly ambiguous results.[26] An in-depth examination of the vicissitudes of the sexual revolution in Austria—in the cities and in the provinces—has yet to be attempted. But some interesting approaches have been made.

In conclusion, I want to call attention to two genuinely innovative projects, one just completed, and one still in its infancy but showing great promise. Detlef Siegfried's *Moderne Lüste: Ernest Borneman – Jazzkritiker, Filmemacher, Sexforscher* (2015) is a luminous biography of the paradoxical life of the gifted and hardworking con artist Ernest Borneman, who fled Nazi Berlin a few weeks before he was able to finish *Gymnasium* and spent the rest of his life inventing educational degrees he had never earned, while becoming spectacularly successful in the literary, music, and film worlds, ultimately also acquiring an academic post in Salzburg and in 1991 the Honor Cross First Class of the Republic of Austria. As an advice column writer, television talk-show guest, and indefatigable sex researcher and author, he shaped and defended the sexual revolution as much as he lived and studied it. Siegfried's final chapters ingeniously use the controversies in which Borneman was steeped as a way to recreate for the reader the most passionate debates about sexual freedom of the era.[27] In an utterly different register, but with similarly sensitive attention to complex nuances of emotion,

25 See in this context also Stanford University professor Edith Sheffer's linked projects on Asperger and on the interactions of Jewish and Nazi psychiatrists in 1930s Vienna and subsequent diaspora.

26 Angelika Hager and Sebastian Hofer, "Unsere 68er: Die gemütliche Revolution gegen Antisemitismus und Frauenfeindlichkeit," in *Profil*, 1 March 2008, <http://www.profil.at/home/unsere-68er-die-revolution-antisemitismus-frauenfeindlichkeit-198951> (18 Nov. 2015).

27 Detlef Siegfried, *Moderne Lüste: Ernest Borneman – Jazzkritiker, Filmemacher, Sexforscher* (Göttingen: Wallstein, 2015).

desire, sensation, and conflictedness, the young historian Sonja Matter's project on "'The Age of Consent': Sexuality, Law, and the Construction of Adolescence" has begun to mine a wealth of information out of Austrian court records and legal debates from 1950–1970. Here we can see the sexual revolution evolving, in all its confusing, contradictory, and unsettling facets, in the most poignant and mundane settings, among ordinary people at the grassroots. Matter reconstructs the all-too-often blurry mix of yearning and excitement and difficulty sorting out coercion from consent in adolescent encounters with sympathy and perceptiveness, and she is attuned both to the tone-deafness of the jurists and other authorities in charge, and to the telling moments when a change in sensibilities or a temporary disorientation that leads to insight become evident.[28] This is the kind of work we look forward to seeing more of in the future.

Select Bibliography

Baader, Gerhard, et al., eds. *Eugenik in Österreich: Biopolitische Strukturen von 1900–1945*. Vienna: Czernin, 2007.

Gehmacher, Johanna, and Gabriella Hauch, eds. *Frauen- und Geschlechtergeschichte des Nationalsozialismus: Fragestellungen, Perspektiven, neue Forschungen*. Vienna: Studienverlag, 2007.

Kurimay, Anita A. "Sex in the 'Pearl of the Danube': The History of Queer Life, Love, and its Regulation in Budapest, 1873–1941," PhD. diss., Rutgers University, 2012.

McEwen, Britta. *Sexual Knowledge: Feeling, Fact, and Social Reform in Vienna, 1900–1934*. New York: Berghahn, 2012.

Mesner, Maria. *Geburten/Kontrolle: Reproduktionspolitik im 20. Jahrhundert*. Vienna: Böhlau, 2010.

Siegfried, Detlef. *Moderne Lüste: Ernest Borneman – Jazzkritiker, Filmemacher, Sexforscher*. Göttingen: Wallstein, 2015.

Stauter-Halstead, Keely. "'A Generation of Monsters': Jews, Prostitution, and Racial Purity in the 1892 L'viv White Slavery Trial," *Austrian History Yearbook* 38 (2007): 25–35.

28 Sonja Matter, "'She doesn't look like a child': Girls and Age of Consent Regulations in Austria (1950–1970)," in *Journal for the History of Childhood and Youth*: forthcoming. The overall project—under supervision at the University of Bern—is entitled "'The Age of Consent': Sexualität, Recht und die Konstruktion von Adoleszenz."

Ash Wednesday.
FPÖ party chairman Heinz-Christian Strache at the FPÖ's traditional Ash Wednesday rally in Upper Austria.
Ried im Innkreis, Juerg Christandl, 02 10 2016
Credit: Kurier / APA PictureDesk

Volume 16: Günter Bischof/Fritz Plasser, eds. *The Changing Austrian Voter.* New Brunswick, NJ: Transaction 2008

The Changing Austrian Voter Today

Fritz Plasser

The Austrian electoral landscape is in a turbulent transitory phase. Had there been General Elections in the Fall of 2015, the right wing populist party Freiheitliche Partei Österreichs (FPÖ) would have become the strongest party with almost 30 percent. The Sozialdemokratische Partei Österreichs (SPÖ) would have occupied the second place with 25 percent, the Österreichische Volkspartei (ÖVP) would have been on the third place with only 23 percent. Of course these are projections of poll data, which should be interpreted very carefully. But the voting intentions of Austrian voters still point to dramatic changes in the relationships and attitudes toward political parties, obviously shaped by an issue agenda driven by pictures in the media of thousands of refugees from Syria, Afghanistan, and Iraq crossing Austrian borders daily, increased scepticism concerning the problem solving capacity of the European Union, rising unemployment rates and massive criticism of the performance of the ruling SPÖ/ÖVP-coalition government. Two factors, the dissolution of traditional party affiliations as well as polarizing issues, drive the ruling parties into the defensive.

While in 2006 still 55 percent of the electorate felt close to a certain political party, only 40 percent identify themselves with a particular party in 2015. 60 percent of the Austrian voters do not identify with any particular party. Even among voters of SPÖ and ÖVP only every second person identifies emotionally with his party. If at all, traditional party loyalties are only found among the older generations and senior voters of SPÖ and ÖVP. Consequently 55 percent of the core voters feel emotionally close to their party, while only 25 percent of swing voters and 15 percent of non-voters identify with a particular political party.

The erosion of traditional party affiliations accelerates the volatility of the electorate. At the General Elections 2008 and 2013 about every third person voted for a different party than at the previous election. There have also been considerable changes in the time of the final voting decision. In the General Election of 2006, only 15 percent of the voters made their final voting decision during the last weeks of the campaign. In the election of

2013, 38 percent had already decided on the party of their choice during the last weeks of the campaign. Never before had such a high share of "late deciders" existed in the history of Austrian elections.

The erosion of stable party affiliations has not only affected the rise of electoral volatility and the time of final voting decisions, but also the rate of voting participation. While thirty years ago voter turnout rates still remained constantly above 90 percent, in 2013 only 74.9 percent participated in the national election—the lowest turnout at national elections so far. The highest rate of participation was found among members of the older voter generation, of which 85 percent participated in the 2013 General Election. Among younger eligible voters, the participation only lay below 60 percent. Below average rates of participation could also be found among voters with lower educational background, blue collar voters and angry and alienated voters who were generally distant to politicians and political parties.

The erosion of traditional party allegiances, outspoken discontent concerning the performance of both government parties, SPÖ and ÖVP, and a growing group of voters who do not feel represented by any political party opened the electoral market for newly founded parties. One year before the 2013 National Election the Austro-Canadian entrepreneur and billionaire Frank Stronach founded the Team Stronach. The platform was completely based upon the personality of its founder and his success story. Stronach, who grew up in Styria, emigrated as a young man to Canada. After hard years of existential survival in a competitive business culture, he founded an enterprise that is one of the biggest automotive parts producers worldwide. Frank Stronach incorporates the Austrian version of the rags-to-riches myth and had, during his time as Chief Executive Officer of Magna also opened up production sites in Austria, creating thousands of positions for skilled workers. The central campaign message of Frank Stronach was simple and populist. He presented himself as anti-politician and anti-institutional candidate and mainly appealed to voters who were personally disappointed in the existing parties, felt their interests are not represented by any of the parliamentary parties, and projected their hopes and expectations in his image of economic success and entrepreneurship. Stronach invested about thirty-two million Euros in his campaign, completely taken from his private funds, and, prior to the election campaign for the 2013 General Election, motivated dissatisfied parliamentary members of the Bündnis Zukunft Österreich (BZÖ), who did not expect to have chances for a reelection on the BZÖ-ticket, to change to the party of Team Stronach. This way his party was already represented as a faction in Parliament before the General Election.

A series of highly unfortunate appearances on TV and the failure to articulate the real problems of his voters reduced the wave of public support for his party platform. While the Team Stronach still lay between 10 and 12 percent in the Spring 2013 surveys, it only just entered parliament with 5.7 percent at Election Day. Totally disappointed by the moderate results for his party, Stronach withdrew from Austrian politics. With his withdrawal, the fate of Team Stronach was also decided. Although still represented as a parliamentary faction, Team Stronach does not play an active role in the electoral arena anymore. Its voters largely changed over to the FPÖ or became non-voters in the meantime.

While Team Stronach as a flash party was only a temporary phenomenon, the second newcomer seems to remain a competitor in Austrian party politics. The Neos were founded in the fall of 2012 as a liberal party with topical emphasis on education, Europe, and direct democracy. The Neos mainly appeal to the younger, urban, educated, and skilled workers electorate and to those who are discontent with the performance of SPÖ and ÖVP. At the 2013 National Election the Neos were successful in entering Parliament with 5 percent.

Table 1: Austrian Parliamentary Elections 2006–2013 (in percent of valid votes)

Party	Austrian Parliamentary Elections			Poll Results (Projection)
	2006	2008	2013	Fall 2015
SPÖ	35.3	29.3	26.8	23.0-25.0
ÖVP	34.3	26.0	24.0	21.0-23.0
FPÖ	11.0	17.5	20.5	28.0-30.0
BZÖ	4.1	10.7	3.5	
Greens	11.0	10.4	12.4	13.0-14.0
Team Stronach			5.7	
Neos			5.0	6.0-7.0
Others	4.3	6.1	2.1	3.0-4.0

Source: Election Commission. Poll Data according to pooled surveys by GfK-Austria.

In the 2013 General Election, the weakening of both governing parties, SPÖ and ÖVP, continued remarkably. While in 2006 they still had gained combined 70 percent of valid votes, they only reached 50.8 percent together in 2013. Traditional core voter groups and retirees dominate both parties' electorates. The SPÖ gained above average percentages only among union members, blue-collar industrial workers, and members of the older voter generation. Similarly, based on their traditional electorate, the ÖVP only showed above average percentages among regularly Catholic churchgoers, self-employed, inhabitants of small rural communities and retirees. Both parties have increasing problems in appealing to younger, mobile, not party-affiliated, urban and suburban voters.

Among younger voters—especially younger men—the populist FPÖ reached its highest voting acceptance in 2013. Above average percentages were gained by the FPÖ also among blue-collar workers, middle-aged voters and those with a low professional qualification, as well as in the group of angry voters choosing the FPÖ out of protest. The Greens also reached above average percentages among younger voters—especially younger women—as well as members of the educated class and mobile, not party-affiliated urban voters. The profile of the Neos' electorate is similar to the profile of Green-voters. They reached above average percentages among those under thirty years of age, members of the higher educated class, urban professionals and persons discontented with both coalition parties.

Changes in voting behaviour also showed up during the European election in Spring 2014. The basic situation was thereby clearly different from the political situation at the European election of 2009. One difference was a substantially changed competitive environment: Hans Peter Martin for instance, whose list reached the third place with 17.7 percent of the votes in 2009, decided not to run for re-election. The BZÖ, on the other hand, was lacking organizational resources as well as attention in the mass media during the European campaign 2014.

The issue agenda had also changed dramatically. The consequences of the financial crisis of 2008/9, widespread Euro-scepticism, as well as unpopular measures for the consolidation of the state budget, increased discontent with politics and general protest motives.

On the eve of the election, in spite of a loss of 3 percent, the ÖVP held the first place with 27 percent of the vote. The SPÖ, who had already reached its European all time low at the election 2009, again was unable to increase its share and only reached 24.1 percent of the vote. The FPÖ clearly gained votes and reached 19.7 percent, doubled the number of its representatives, but had to accept place three. The Greens increased considerably in 2014 and reached with 14.5 percent of the vote, their so-far best result at a national election. The Neos got, with 8.1 percent of the vote, one seat in the European parliament. However, the results of the European Election of 2014 are overshadowed by the low voter participation of only 45.4 percent. More than 50 percent of eligible voters abstained from participation.

Although the sociodemographic profile of the voters at the European election is clearly different from the composition of voters at national elections, it still shows some well-known patterns: Male voters tended more often to vote for the ÖVP, while women preferred the SPÖ more often. More pronounced is the gender gap among FPÖ-voters.

While both governing parties were only elected by about one-third of voters below the age of thirty years, more than two-thirds of the above sixty-year-olds voted either for the ÖVP or SPÖ. Members of the youngest voter generation voted above average for the Greens and the Neos as well as the list "Europa Anders", while the FPÖ—different to the national elections—only reached below average votes among the under-thirty-year-olds.

However, the FPÖ again reached high percentages among blue-collar workers and voters with lower education, while the upper educational groups kept their distance from the FPÖ. Instead they voted over proportionally for the Greens and specifically the Neos, who reached the highest voter percentages in the top educational segment.

Despite the fact that European elections are defined as "second order elections," primarily driven by national issues, voting behaviour at European elections is shaped to a remarkable degree by attitudes toward the European Union and its politics. Voters and non-voters differ primarily in their attitudes and evaluation of the European Union. Views and evaluations concerning the European Union define the cardinal division between voters and non-voters; among voters at a European election, EU-critical views are popular, while among non-voters, positive attitudes toward the EU are often observed. This difference between voters and non-voters is not only visible in their different retrospective evaluations of joining the EU, but also in their individual evaluations of EU-membership and the introduction of the Euro. Among voters and non-voters, personal evaluations of advantages and disadvantages of EU-membership were considerably more positive among younger and better-qualified persons than among members of the older generation, retirees, and those coming from the blue collar milieu. Men tended to be more positive, while women—especially concerning the introduction of the Euro—were definitely more critical.

Different degrees of EU-scepticism are not only found between voters and non-voters, but also between the party electorates. By far the highest scepticism is found among FPÖ-voters. It exceeds in intensity the EU-scepticism among non-voters. Sceptical attitudes also characterize parts of the SPÖ-electorate, although they are clearly more moderate compared to the FPÖ-electorate. Compared to the voters of the SPÖ, critical attitudes toward the European Union are even weaker among voters of the ÖVP; the ÖVP-electorate is generally characterized by a more positive attitude to the EU than the SPÖ-electorate. Those who vote for the Neos only differ slightly from the ÖVP-electorate regarding their EU-critical attitudes. The comparatively lowest EU-scepticism is found among Green voters.

Eroding traditional party ties, increased volatility of voters, and electoral defeats of both governing coalitional parties are not confined to the federal level. Also the regional electoral landscape has entered a phase of transition; while in 2006, five of the nine regional parliaments dominant parties ruled with absolute majorities (Vorarlberg, Tyrol, Lower Austria, Vienna and Burgenland), in 2015 only one region—Lower Austria—is ruled by one party (ÖVP) with more than 50 percent of votes and representatives. In 2006 four of the nine Austrian regions were governed by the ÖVP (Vorarlberg, Tyrol, Upper Austria, Lower Austria), four by the SPÖ (Vienna, Styria, Salzburg, Burgenland) and one (Carinthia) by the BZÖ (former FPÖ). In 2015 the ÖVP had provincial governors in six of the nine regional areas. The SPÖ only leads in three regions (Vienna, Burgenland, Carinthia), and in Burgenland based on a coalition with the FPÖ. The coalition of the SPÖ-Burgenland with the FPÖ represents a remarkable break with the so-called "Vranitzky Doctrine," according to which the SPÖ was not to form a coalition with the FPÖ under any circumstances.

Table 2: Cycle of Regional Elections, 2013–2015: Gains and Losses of Regional Parties

Region	SPÖ	ÖVP	FPÖ	Greens
Lower Austria (March 2012)	- 3.9	- 3.6	- 2.3	+ 1.2
Carinthia (March 2013)	+ 8.4	- 2.4	- 28.0	+ 7.0
Tyrol (April 2013)	- 1.8	- 1.1	- 3.1	+ 1.9
Salzburg (May 2013)	- 15.6	- 7.6	+ 4.0	+ 12.8
Vorarlberg (Sept. 2014)	- 1.3	- 9.0	- 1.7	+ 6.6
Burgenland (May 2015)	- 5.5	- 6.3	+ 6.1	+ 2.3
Styria (May 2015)	- 9.0	- 8.7	+ 16.1	+ 1.1
Upper Austria (Sept. 2015)	- 6.6	- 10.4	+ 15.1	+ 1.1
Vienna (October 2015)	- 4.8	- 4.8	+ 5.0	- 0.8

Sources: Regional Election Commissions.

With the exception of the regional election in Carinthia, where the SPÖ had gained votes, the cycle of regional elections in 2013–2015 ended with general losses for ÖVP and SPÖ. The ÖVP suffered the heaviest losses at the regional elections in Upper Austria, Vorarlberg and Styria. Record losses for the SPÖ could be seen at the regional elections in Salzburg and Styria. Even the FPÖ was losing votes during the first half of the regional election cycle. Only when the masses of refugees from Syria reached the Austrian borders, and the attention of the public was almost totally focused upon the topic of refugees and asylum, was the FPÖ able to mobilize voters, who felt overtaxed by the sheer number of refugees and requested stronger measures from the government and more rigid border controls.

Around the regional elections in Burgenland, Styria, Upper Austria, and Vienna, the handling of the crisis of refugees was central topic in private conversations and discussions. The daily confrontation with thousands of exhausted refugees on the TV news, streaming across the Austrian border, over-occupied emergency quarters, with human tragedies and desperate hope of safety to be found in Germany, Sweden, or Austria, pushed other issues and problems into the background. At the same time, images in the daily news and in media reports produced insecurity and feelings of anxiety and helplessness in parts of the electorate, which were directly appealed to and reinforced by the FPÖ.

The issue of refugees and asylum polarized and divided the electorate in remarkable ways. While one half of the voters felt that Austria could accept even more asylum seekers, the other half saw the capacities as already exhausted. The question of refugees and asylum also divided the party electorates. Among Green-voters, 80 percent believed that Austria could take even more refugees, but 90 percent of the FPÖ-voters felt the Austria's capacity was exhausted. A similar polarization of the electorate also existed regarding the question how Austria should handle the security of her borders in the view of this rush. Half of the voters pleaded to keep the borders open for the refugees, the other half believed that Austria should try to reduce the incoming numbers by additional safety measures along the borders. Regarding this issue, too, the strongest polarization appeared between liberal Green-voters and FPÖ-voters, of whom 90 percent pleaded for a reinforcement of security along the borders. The position of the FPÖ in matters of asylum and immigration actually turned out to be the strongest motive to vote for the FPÖ. Every second voter at the regional elections in Styria, Upper Austria, and Vienna primarily gave their position in the issue of asylum and foreigners as reason to vote for the FPÖ.

When forming a compact sociocultural profile of the FPÖ-electorate, a remarkably homogenous picture appears regarding their attitudes and voting motives. Restrictive attitudes, closure and defence against further waves of migration, harder procedures of the executive forces at securing and controlling of borders, a pronounced scepticism toward the European Union and massive discontent with the performance of the SPÖ-ÖVP-coalition government reflect the picture of an electorate mobilized by anger, disappointments, different fears, resentment, and everyday cultural irritations as well as protest attitudes. Contrary to the cultural and social anxieties and resentments primarily defining the attitudes of the FPÖ-voters stands the electorate of the Greens and a majority of the SPÖ- and ÖVP-voters, although sociocultural cleavages and polarizations also can be found in the electorates of both governing parties.

There is no end of the refugee movement in sight for the near future, nor is there solidarity for a European solution regarding a fair distribution of asylum seekers among the twenty-eight members of the European Union. The sociocultural division of the electorate in questions of asylum and refugees will occupy the Austrian voters for a considerable time and thereby favour the electoral chances for profiling the right-populist FPÖ. In the view of more reduced expectations regarding economic growth and a record unemployment rate of almost 10 percent, the chances of the ruling parties regaining the confidence of the voters with economical success is limited in the near future. A volatile electorate without stable alignments, driven and polarized by highly contentious issues, will remain the characteristic feature of the Austrian voter today.

Select Bibliography

Hofer, Thomas, and Barbara Toth, eds. *Wahl 2008*. Vienna: Molden, 2009.

-----, eds., *Wahl 2013*. Vienna: Lit Verlag, 2014.

Kritzinger, Sylvia, Eva Zeglovits, Michael S. Lewis-Beck, and Richard Nadeau. *The Austrian Voter*. Vienna: Vienna University Press, 2013.

----------, Wolfgang C. Müller, and Klaus Schönbach, eds. *Die Nationalratswahl 2013*. Vienna: Böhlau, 2014.

Plasser, Fritz, ed. *Politik in der Medienarena*. Vienna: Facultas, 2009.

-------, ed. *Erfolgreich Wahlkämpfen*. Vienna: Facultas, 2012.

------- and Peter A. Ulram, eds. *Wechselwahlen*. Vienna: Facultas, 2007.

Russian Zone.
A Soviet military police officer is surrounded by Red Army soldiers in the the vicinity of Vienna.
Grünanger, Spring 1945
Credit: Archives of the Ludwig Boltzmann-Institute for the Study of the Consequences of War, Graz

Volume 17: Günter Bischof/Fritz Plasser/Barbara Stelzl-Marx, eds. *New Perspectives on Austrians and World War II.* New Brunswick: Transaction 2009

An Update on World War II Studies and Austria

Barbara Stelzl-Marx

"It is not surprising that in the vast literature on the European theater of World War II the material on Nazi Germany in English has paid relatively little attention to developments in Austria and how the war affected the way Austrians are portrayed." Thus Gerhard L. Weinberg described the status quo of World War II Studies and Austria in 2009.[1] In view of this, a key objective of Volume 17 in the *Contemporary Austrian Studies* series was to provide an overview of *New Perspectives on Austrians and World War II* (hence the title), tailored to an English-speaking audience. The work consists of a total of thirteen articles nearly all written by Austrian contemporary historians, addressing the following subjects: I. Soldiers, II. Social and Economic Life, III. War Crimes/Crimes Against Humanity, IV. The Aftermath: Occupation, Restitution, Memory. The following paper aims to give an update on research undertaken in these areas over the last six years, broadly following the four fields established in the volume in question.

Attempts have been made to improve the problem cited above: the relative dearth of publications in English both on Austrian contemporary history in general and on World War II Studies with particular reference to Austria. In pursuit of this, the Austrian Future Fund (ÖZF), established in 2005 by the Republic of Austria, has commissioned translations of several "standard" works on Austrian contemporary history to increase the international profile of the results of the research therein. Examples include *Austrian Resistance 1938–1945* by Wolfgang Neugebauer[2] and a volume

1 Gerhard L. Weinberg, "World War II Studies and Austria," in CAS 17, 1–4. I would like to thank Harald Knoll for valuable references and David Sinclair-Jones for the English version of this paper.

2 Wolfgang Neugebauer, *Austrian Resistance 1938–1945* (Vienna: Edition Steinbauer, 2014).

dealing with restitution and compensation during the era of *Bundeskanzler* Wolfgang Schüssel.[3] Translating these publications into English makes them more accessible to international researchers and other interested parties, an important goal also for both the Austrian Science Fund (FWF) and the Ludwig Boltzmann Society (LBG).

In this context, the growing importance of the Austrian Future Fund for research and publications, as well as exhibitions, commemorative and cultural projects, films, events, or educational activities should be mentioned. On behalf of *"Niemals wieder/Never Again!,"* so far more than 1,400 supported projects have united to commemorate the victims of the Nazi regime, in remembrance of the threat posed by totalitarian systems and in furtherance of mutual tolerance. Using its budget of 20 million euros, which was taken from residual funds of the Fund for Reconciliation, Peace and Cooperation (raised to compensate those forced to work for the Nazis in Austrian territory), the Austrian Future Fund has promoted research with particular emphasis on the field of Austrian WWII studies. A substantial portion of projects and publications described in this paper were supported by this important Austrian research institution.[4]

I. The End of the War in 1945: An Escalation of Violence

On 29 March 1945, the Red Army made its first incursion onto Austrian soil at Klostermarienberg in Burgenland. Thus began the Allied occupation of the country and its liberation from the NS terror regime, which was accompanied by an escalation of violence. Bombing, looting, and rape by Soviet soldiers still stand in the collective memory as one of the central images of the end of World War II. However, one aspect of this period is still largely hushed up even to this day: in the forty-one days remaining before the end of the war, on the 8 May 1945, about 30,000 more people fell victim in Austria to NS terror. Up to the last moment, Jews, opponents of the regime, shot-down Allied airmen, and war-weary soldiers condemned as "deserters" were hunted down and murdered. An exhibition shown in Vienna and Graz in 2015—entitled "41 Days"—showed the ambivalence of individual experiences and perceptions concerning the end of the Second

3 Stefan Karner and Walter M. Iber, eds., *Schweres Erbe und Wiedergutmachung. Restitution und Entschädigung in Österreich. Die Bilanz der Regierung Schüssel* (Innsbruck: StudienVerlag, 2015). The English version of this volume is due to come out in 2016.

4 An overview of the projects funded to mid-2015 can be found in: Günter Bischof, Barbara Stelzl-Marx, and Alexandra Kofler, *Zukunftsfonds der Republik Österreich: Entstehung, Entwicklung und Bedeutung* (Vienna: Böhlau, 2015). See also <http://www.zukunftsfonds-austria.at/> (25 Jan. 2016).

World War. Part of its approach was to draw on new research, which was also made available to the public via additional lectures.[5]

Graz historian Georg Hoffman's 2015 dissertation, *Fliegerlynchjustiz: Gewalt gegen abgeschossene alliierte Flugzeugbesatzungen 1943–1945*, highlights one of the main points at issue.[6] Drawing on source material from over 1,000 aircraft crashes and twenty-six detailed case studies Hoffmann highlighted an aspect of the bombing campaign against the "Third Reich" that had been largely ignored: the systematic abuse and murder of downed Allied airmen. This enabled him to correct the image of disgruntled civilians spontaneously taking revenge on enemy planes, put out by Nazi propagandists at the time and persisting to the present day. The real story that emerges relates rather to the *Fliegermorde*, a targeted lynching campaign ordered by Adolf Hitler in the summer of 1944, under which all enemy parachutists were to be killed on sight. This paved the way for an escalation of violence instigated by local Nazi functionaries, who detailed how "Gangsters of the Sky" and "Flying Terror Merchants" should be dealt with. Against the backdrop of the perceptions handed down by the citizenry through the years, Hoffmann looks closely at the question of "perpetrators and actors." When used in connection with the air war, these terms had a particular resonance: the aircrew who had been dropping bombs on Austrian territory were regarded as the "perpetrators," not the lynch mobs intent on *Fliegermorde*, or those who stood by and let it happen. Although these acts of intra-societal violence hinted at an extraordinary "break with civilization," many decades had to pass before such crimes could be re-examined.[7] This explains why, so far, there is only one monument in the whole of Austria relating to the murder of Allied airmen: an unassuming stone in Graz-Strassgang, set up in memory of the crimes carried out on 4 March 1945 against four US airmen in the presence of hundreds of people. The decades-long conflict over this stone shows how difficult it is to deal with the memory of the bombing campaign and to define an appropriate victim narrative even seventy years after the war.[8]

Another group of victims of violent crime by the Nazi regime, memorialized both in the exhibition and in several recent publications, is the Hungarian Jews. As slave laborers used during the construction of the *Süd-Ost-Wall* at the Burgenland-Hungarian border, they were evacuated in

5 See also the webpage for the exhibition *41 Tage* <www.oeaw.ac.at/41Tage> (25 Jan. 2016).

6 Georg Hoffmann, *Fliegerlynchjustiz: Gewalt gegen abgeschossene alliierte Flugzeugbesatzungen 1943–1945* (Paderborn: Ferdinand Schöningh, 2015).

7 Ibid., 298f.

8 Ibid., 373f.

the direction of the Mauthausen concentration camp at the approach of the Red Army in March 1945. During these "death marches," the guards had orders to shoot anyone who could not keep up. In addition to such "routine" assassinations there were several outright massacres, as at Präbichlpass, close to Eisenerz in Styria, where local SA men fired into the marching group, killing about 200 people. The most notorious case occurred in Rechnitz in the early hours of 25 March 1945: With the general retreat impending, a command was issued by guests at the Batthyány Castle Festival and relayed to the leaders of the *Süd-Ost-Wall*-fortifications, ordering the execution of about 200 Hungarian Jews who were no longer fit to march. Overall, the number of Hungarian Jews who died in Austria during this "final chapter of Holocaust" is estimated at some 23,000.[9]

An overview of the work, death marches and subsequent fate of Hungarian-Jewish forced laborers in Austria is given by Eleonore Lappin-Eppel in a monograph published in 2010.[10] Herein the historian distinguishes the different routes to Mauthausen followed by the evacuation marches.[11] There was, for instance, a stopover at camp Graz-Liebenau, where another of these last ditch crimes was perpetrated and subsequently ignored for decades: in April 1945, on command of the camp authorities, the exhausted Jewish forced laborers were compelled to spend the night in the open air, were given inadequate food and denied medical treatment. At least thirty-five were shot and buried in mass graves. In a war crimes trial in September 1947, four former members of the camp personnel were indicted, two of whom were condemned to death and executed. After this, the victims of the camp Liebenau were forgotten for decades—until the whole affair boiled over again in 2011, in connection with discussions about a planned hydroelectric power plant near the site of the former camp. This was taken up by the media and provoked much public debate. A scholarly review and a conference on the "Graz-Liebenau Camp in the NS Era" made this long uncharted segment of Graz Contemporary History available to the public.[12]

There is also some new research in the field of resistance to the Nazi regime and the persecution of its opponents, such as Florian

9 Walter Manoschek, ed., *Der Fall Rechnitz. Das Massaker an Juden im März 1945* (Vienna: New Academic Press, 2009).

10 Eleonore Lappin-Eppel, *Ungarisch-Jüdische Zwangsarbeiter und Zwangsarbeiterinnen in Österreich 1944/45: Arbeitseinsatz – Todesmärsche – Folgen* (Vienna: Lit Verlag 2010), 309 and 478.

11 Ibid.

12 Barbara Stelzl-Marx, *Das Lager Graz-Liebenau in der NS-Zeit. Zwangsarbeiter – Todesmärsche – Nachkriegsjustiz* (Graz: Leykam, 2012).

Traussnig's monography on Austrians in the US-Army.[13] This topic also takes center stage in the series *Nationalsozialismus in den österreichischen Bundesländern* (National Socialism in the Federal States), a reference book aimed especially at young readers, but which is also suitable for interested adults. Each of these volumes is devoted, as indicated in the titles, to the "victims —perpetrators—opponents" of Nazism. As is evident from, for example, the treatise dealing with Styria, the authors describe the organization and significance of the opposition in the final phase of the war with the help of several case histories.[14] Additionally, the part played by women in the resistance to Nazism is analyzed in a collection of essays edited in 2015.[15]

Amongst other works published in 2015 to mark the 70th anniversary of the end of World War II appeared a work by Heimo Halbrainer and Victoria Kumar *Kriegsende in der Steiermark 1945, Terror, Kapitulation, Besatzung, Neubeginn*, which also deals with "*Endphaseverbrechen*" (crimes in the final phase) in the back country: the murder of hundreds of political opponents, concentration camp prisoners, foreign workers, pilots, and Jews in the time immediately before the end of the Nazi regime. But alongside the terror perpetrated in these last weeks there was resistance to these crimes, where the local population not only showed courage, but also prevented the destruction planned by the Nazis, removing explosives from industrial plants and bridges. The anthology, which summarizes the contributions from a May 2015 conference in Graz, documents this final stage and also shows aspects of the liberation, the reappraisal and the new beginnings.[16] Moreover, several of these aspects can be found in Volume 9 of the *Geschichte der Steiermark*, which deals with, among other things, the NS ascendancy in Styria.[17]

In addition, mention should be made of the researches of Grazer historian Andrea Strutz into Austrian-Jewish emigrants to Canada. She

13 Florian Traussnig, *Militärischer Widerstand von außen. Österreicher in US-Armee und Kriegsgeheimdienst im Zweiten Weltkrieg* (Vienna: Böhlau, 2016).

14 Heimo Halbrainer and Gerald Lamprecht, *Nationalsozialismus in der Steiermark: Opfer – Täter – Gegner.* (Innsbruck: StudienVerlag, 2015); see also <www.erinnern.at> (25 Jan. 2016).

15 Christine Kanzler, Ilse Korotin, and Karin Nusko, eds., "*... den Vormarsch dieses Regimes einen Millimeter aufgehalten zu haben": Österreichische Frauen im Widerstand gegen den Nationalsozialismus* (Vienna: Praesens Verlag, 2015).

16 Heimo Halbrainer and Victoria Kumar, eds., *Kriegsende in der Steiermark 1945: Terror, Kapitulation, Besatzung, Neubeginn* (Graz: CLIO, 2015).

17 Alfred Ableitinger, ed., *Bundesland und Reichsgau: Demokratie, "Ständestaat" und NS-Herrschaft in der Steiermark 1918 bis 1945* (Geschichte der Steiermark, Vol. 9) (Vienna: Böhlau, 2015).

introduced the subject in Volume 17 of *Contemporary Austrian Studies* and has been able to carry out further extensive work on the subject in her 2015 postdoctoral thesis.[18]

II. The Aftermath: Occupation

Several key publications were released in 2005 on the occasion of the "great commemorative year" of the time from 1945 to 1955, illuminating the Soviet occupation of Austria and others for the first time on the basis of documents from Russian archives. One aspect of this, the contribution by Nikita Petrov, "The Internal Troops of the NKVD in the System of Soviet Organ of Repression in Austria, 1945–1946," found its way into the Volume 17 of *Contemporary Austrian Studies*. Further research into the occupation of Austria has taken place since then, of which the following two aspects in particular should be highlighted: Children of occupation, and the everyday life of Soviet soldiers in Austria. Furthermore, a work published in 2015 deals with the Moscow Declaration, which in April 1945 served the founding fathers' generation of the Second Republic as a basis for their development of the "victim doctrine": the idea of Austria as the "first victim of Nazism."[19]

By the end of the war and the occupation, several hundred thousand occupying Soviet nationals had come into direct contact with the capitalist West within the territory of Austria. For most of them it represented their first and often—for decades at least—their last look beyond the borders of the communist empire. For a number of the Soviet soldiers, that immediate insight into the life of their former enemy came as a profound cultural shock. The prevailing living conditions differed profoundly not only from those they had experienced in their youth in the Soviet Union, but also from the image that had been drummed into them for years by Stalin's propaganda machine. This discrepancy between the standard of living in Europe and what they had known at home was like a personal defeat for these conquerors, and at the same time raised doubts about the communist system per se.

This direct experience of life in Austria shaped the occupation soldiers' reaction to their own environment. At the same time, their first contacts with the population at the end of the War in 1945 put a great strain on the *portrait of the enemy* stamped into their consciousness by Soviet war propaganda. The postdoctoral thesis *Stalins Soldaten in Österreich*, published in 2012, made a systematic investigation of the Soviet

18 Andrea Strutz, "Studien zur österreichischen Migration nach Kanada unter besonderer Berücksichtigung der jüdischen Einwanderung. Auswanderung – Vertreibung – Erfahrung – Erinnerung," postdoctoral thesis, University of Graz, 2015.

19 Stefan Karner and Alexander O. Tschubarian, eds., *Die Moskauer Deklaration 1943: "Österreich wieder herstellen"* (Vienna: Böhlau, 2015).

occupation in Austria at a micro-historical level. Here one finds individual experiences of army personnel and officer's families: their mental state, their response to the strangers around them, their ideological training and the punishments they faced for committing criminal offences, their forbidden love affairs and children resulting from sexual relations with locals—all seen through the lens developed by the Red Army in Austria and taken with them back to their homeland.[20]

Based on this study, further research was carried out on children of Allied occupation soldiers and Austrian women, who came into the world after the Second World War as a result not only of love affairs, "survival prostitution," but also of rape. The first of these children of occupation came into the world around Christmas 1945; about nine months after the first Red Army soldiers had entered Austrian territory. They were regarded as "children of the enemy," even though their fathers were officially no longer enemies. Frequently they and their mothers were subjected to discrimination and stigmatization. For a long time the whole subject was taboo.

On this subject matter, the anthology *Besatzungkinder: Die Nachkommen alliierter Soldaten in Österreich und Deutschland* (*Children of Occupation: The Offspring of Allied Soldiers in Austria and Germany*) was published in 2015.[21] This book attempts, through the contributions of scholars concerned with aspects of the history, sociology, education, and psychology of children of occupation in Austria and Germany, to encapsulate the current status of research in this area. This was the first volume to give an overview of the situation faced by this particular group of war children, to analyze their socialization and their living conditions and to document the lifelong search many of them undertook to find their fathers. In autobiographical texts, occupation children are finally granted a voice of their own. Thus, a longstanding taboo has been brought into the public eye and a gap in contemporary history research has been closed at last.[22]

Whilst on this subject, it should be noted that several research projects centering on children of occupation are currently being undertaken in Austria. In "Lost in Administration," Philipp Rohrbach examines the biographies of children of Austro-Afro-American origin born between 1946 and 1956. Archival research and interviews shall not only establish the number of Afro-Austrian occupation children, but also provide insight into how the parties

20 Barbara Stelzl-Marx, *Stalins Soldaten in Österreich. Die Innensicht der sowjetischen Besatzung 1945–1955* (Vienna/Munich: Böhlau, 2012). Open Access: <http://www.boehlau-verlag.com/978-3-205-78700-6.html> (25 Jan. 2016).
21 Barbara Stelzl-Marx and Silke Satjukow, eds., *Besatzungskinder. Die Nachkommen alliierter Soldaten in Österreich und Deutschland* (Vienna: Böhlau, 2015).
22 Ibid.

concerned and their problems were handled by the authorities in Austria and in the United States.[23] Typical of the current interest in this long neglected—academically as well as socially and publicly—group is the presence of the feature film *Kleine Große Stimme* about the Vienna Boys Choir, which puts the destiny of a black child of occupation center stage.[24]

Rainer Gries directs a project in Vienna devoted to the "emotional legacies" left by occupation children to their own children. It examines the psychological as well as political dynamics of trans-generational passings on over four generations and examines how "European" the grandchildren see themsclves and are seen by others.[25]

Mention should also be made of the Marie Skłodowska-Curie Actions Training Network "Children Born of War—Past Present Future," which is financially supported by the European Union. The network will allow a young generation of researchers to explore the experiences of children of war in various conflict and post-conflict situations during the 20th century. Over the four-year period of the project (2015-2019), all together fifteen PhD students—working across several disciplinary boundaries—will combine to develop new perspectives on this theme. The interdisciplinary network is examining the impact of 20th century wars and armed conflicts on the lives of children born of sexual contact between local populations and (enemy) soldiers. It explores whether and how military authorities and governmental and nongovernmental organizations in their respective societies participated in the integration of these children and their mothers. At the same time, it points out the factors that influenced not just the psychosocial development of children and the collective memory of the War in general, but also societal norms and expectations. Altogether there are three projects that touch on Austrian children of occupation, including work by Lukas Schretter of the Ludwig Boltzmann Institute for War Consequences, who is carrying out research on children of British occupying soldiers in Austria, Germany and Great Britain, i.e. the offspring of so-called war brides.[26]

---

23 See Regina Fritz, Marion Krammer, Philipp Rohrbach, and Niko Wahl, "'Guter Dauerpflegeplatz gesucht': Kinder afro-amerikanischer GIS und österreichischer Frauen in der Besatzungszeit," in *Besatzungskinder*, ed. Stelzl-Marx/Satjukow, 207–217. For further information see <http://www.afroaustria.at> (25 Jan. 2016).

24 *Kleine Große Stimme*, Mona Film and Tivoli Film Produktion in cooperation with ORF et al., 2015.

25 For further information see the website of the research project "'Gefühlserbschaften' Von den Besatzungskindern zu den Besatzungsenkeln" at the University of Vienna, 2015 <http://franzvranitzkychair.univie.ac.at/forschung/gefuehlserbschaften/> (25 Jan. 2016).

26 For further information see CHIBOW <http://www.chibow.org> (25 Jan. 2016); Ludwig Boltzmann-Institut für Kriegsfolgenforschung <http://www.bik.ac.at> (25 Jan. 2016).

III. Soldiers

In connection with this new—international and interdisciplinary—research focus, several publications analyze sexual contacts between soldiers, whether during World War II or as members of the occupying forces, and indigenous women. Maren Roeger asks in her book *Kriegsbeziehungen* how new social hierarchies affected sexual encounters between Wehrmacht soldiers and Polish women in World War II. She portrays a wide range of sexual contact that broadly mirrors the experiences of occupation soldiers in postwar Austria: commercial, consensual, and coerced.[27] Regina Mühlhäuser in *Eroberungen* looks into sexual violence and intimate relationships indulged in by Wehrmacht soldiers in the Soviet Union. She provides a closer look at the sexual politics of Wehrmacht and the SS, emphasizing the close interweaving of masculinity, violence, and sexuality in time of war.[28] However, the focus in these two monographs is on the German Wehrmacht; the fact that Austrian men were serving in the ranks of the Wehrmacht and the SS is not addressed in detail.

By contrast, Bertrand Michael Buchmann, in his book *Österreicher in der Deutschen Wehrmacht*, focuses on Austrians in the Wehrmacht. He sets out their everyday experiences and lifestyles: their education and supervisors, their leisure and vacation, sickness and wounds on the same stage as war crimes, war propaganda, imprisonment, and coming home from the war. This volume takes a look at the highly personal reality of war as experienced by the soldiers. Against the background of the research mentioned above, it is somehow surprising that the sexual contacts made in the natural course of events by members of the Austrian armed forces with women in the different occupied areas are hardly addressed in Buchmann's monography.

Thomas R. Grischany, who published a section of his thesis "The Austrians in the German Wehrmacht, 1938–1945" in our CAS volume under review, deals with a similar subject. His dissertation on the integrations of Austrians in the *großdeutsche Wehrmacht* has now been published in German.[29]

27 Maren Roeger, *Kriegsbeziehungen, Intimität, Gewalt und Prostitution im besetzten Polen 1939 bis 1945* (Frankfurt am Main: S. Fischer Verlag, 2015).

28 Regina Mühlhäuser, *Eroberungen: Sexuelle Gewalttaten und intime Beziehungen deutscher Soldaten in der Sowjetunion 1941–1945* (Hamburg: Hamburger Edition, 2010).

29 Thomas R. Grischany, *Der Ostmark treue Alpensöhne. Die Integration der Österreicher in die großdeutsche Wehrmacht, 1938–1945* (Vienna: V&R Unipress, 2015).

IV. Prisoners of War and Forced Laborers

The broad topics of prisoners of war and forced laborers during the Nazi era were dealt with in two articles in Volume 17 of *Contemporary Austrian Studies*, which demonstrated the importance of this research area at the turn of the millennium. This was closely connected to the question of compensation for former forced laborers in Austria and the historical Commission appointed in 1998, as well as to the basic works published subsequently.[30]

More research in this context has been undertaken since 2009. With regard to Austria, one would cite Anna Maria Garcia's book: *Arbeitseinsatz für die Neuordnung Europas*, which focuses on the use of civil—and female—forced laborers from Yugoslavia in the "Eastern provinces."[31] In 2014, Oliver Rathkolb and Florian Freund put out an anthology entitled *NS-Zwangsarbeit in der Elektrizitätswirtschaft der 'Ostmark,'* in which monumental power stations such those in Kaprun or Ybbs-Persenbeug are described.[32] Irene Suchy examined the forced labor camp at Strasshof,[33] whilst Alois Nußbaumer has looked at forced labor in agriculture, using Pinzgau as an example.[34]

The repression suffered by forced laborers and prisoners of war is dealt with in the volume *Hitlers Sklaven – Stalins Verräter*, which focuses on the post-war fate of former Soviet forced laborers in their homeland and represents the results of the first project supported by the Austrian Future Fund.[35] This subject is studied in greater depth in the Volume *Zwangsarbeiter*

30 On the genesis of the Austrian Historians Commission, see Brigitte Bailer-Galanda and Eva Blimlinger, "The Austrian Historical Commission: International Background, Motives, Results, and Impact," in CAS 11, 212–218; the summary results of the Historians Commission can be found in Clemens Jabloner et al., *Schlussbericht der Historikerkommission der Republik Österreich. Vermögensentzug während der NS-Zeit sowie Rückstellungen und Entschädigungen seit 1945 in Österreich.* (Vienna/Munich: Oldenbourg, 2003); see also Karner/Iber, eds., *"Schweres Erbe."*

31 Anna Maria Grünfelder, *Arbeitseinsatz für die Neuordnung Europas. Zivil- und ZwangsarbeiterInnen aus Jugoslawien in der „Ostmark" 1938/41–1945* (Vienna/Cologne/Weimar: Böhlau, 2010).

32 Oliver Rathkolb and Florian Freund, eds., *NS-Zwangsarbeit in der Elektrizitätswirtschaft der "Ostmark," 1938–1945: Ennstalwerke – Kaprun – Draukraftwerke – Ybbs-Persenbeug – Ernsthofen* (2nd ed.) (Vienna: Böhlau, 2014).

33 Irene Suchy, *Strasshof an der Nordbahn. Die NS-Geschichte eines Ortes und ihre Aufarbeitung.* (Vienna: Metroverlag, 2012)

34 Alois Nußbaumer, *"Fremdarbeiter" im Pinzgau: Zwangsarbeit in der Landwirtschaft am Beispiel Pinzgau. Verarbeitungsstrategien von ZwangsarbeiterInnen, Zwangsarbeit im kollektiven Gedächtnis.* (Salzburg/Vienna: Ed. Tandem, 2011).

35 Peter Ruggenthaler and Walter M. Iber, eds., *Hitlers Sklaven – Stalins "Verräter." Aspekte der Repression an Zwangsarbeitern und Kriegsgefangenen* (Innsbruck: StudienVerlag, 2010).

in Österreich 1939–1945 und ihr Nachkriegsschicksal.[36] Moreover, Paul Schieder has published a book about the deployment of French forced labor in Austrian territory.[37]

Regarding Austrian prisoners of war in the Second World War and Allied prisoners of war detained in the *Ostmark*, several scholarly contributions expanding the research further have been published since 2009. Among them is Richard Germann's contribution: a study of intercepted conversations between "Austrian" Wehrmacht and Waffen-SS members in British and American POW camps,[38] as well as a comparison with life stories of Austrian POWs of World War II detained by the Soviets and the UK/US respectively.[39] There are also some in-depth essays by Stefan Karner about Austrians in Soviet custody.[40]

The POW camps in Austria also came in for repeated examination: particularly Stalag XVIII A/Oflag XVIII B Wolfsberg was made accessible to the public within the framework of a major exhibition in the Museum in Lavanthaus in Wolfsberg accompanied by a catalogue and several lectures.[41]

Résumé

"The situation of Austria has, however, not been neglected entirely," writes Gerhard L. Weinberg in the introduction to Volume 17 of *Contemporary Austrian Studies*. In the years since its release, significant works have been added that have filled more gaps in the research and/or

---

36 Dieter Bacher and Stefan Karner, eds., *Zwangsarbeiter in Österreich 1939–1945 und ihr Nachkriegsschicksal: Ergebnisse der Auswertung des Aktenbestandes des „Österreichischen Versöhnungsfonds." Ein Zwischenbericht* (Innsbruck: StudienVerlag, 2013).

37 Paul Schieder, *Französische Zwangsarbeiter im "Reichseinsatz" auf dem Gebiet der Republik Österreich* (Vienna: Böhlau, 2012).

38 Richard Germann, "Angezapftes Wissen: Abgehörte Gespräche 'österreichischer' Wehrmachts- und Waffen-SS-Angehöriger in britischer und amerikanischer Kriegsgefangenschaft," in *Terror und Geschichte*, ed. Helmut Konrad, Gerhard Botz, Stefan Karner, and Siegfried Mattl (Vienna: Böhlau, 2012).

39 Barbara Stelzl-Marx and Günter Bischof, "Hinter Stacheldraht: Parallele Lebensgeschichten österreichischer Kriegsgefangener des Zweiten Weltkrieges in sowjetischer und amerikanischer Hand," in *Wirtschaft. Macht. Geschichte: Brüche und Kontinuitäten im 20. Jahrhundert. Festschrift Stefan Karner*, ed. Gerald Schöpfer and Barbara Stelzl-Marx (Graz: Leykam, 2012), 291–320.

40 See for instance Stefan Karner, "Zur sowjetischen Umerziehung: Die 'Antifa' 1941–1949 und das 'antifaschistische Büro österreichischer Kriegsgefangener' in der Sowjetunion," in *Die Moskauer Deklaration 1943: "Österreich wieder herstellen,"* ed. Stefan Karner and Alexander O. Tschubarian (Vienna: Böhlau, 2015), 177–195.

41 Christian Klösch, *Lagerstadt Wolfsberg. Flüchtlinge – Gefangene – Internierte. Dokumentation zur Ausstellung* (Wolfsberg: Edition Museum im Lavanthaus, 2013).

opened up new topics. And yet—and there has been little change in this pattern since 2009—most of these works have appeared only in German. This makes this series all the more important, as it makes central issues of "Austrian Studies Today" available to an English-speaking audience.

Select Bibliography

Ableitinger, Alfred, ed. *Bundesland und Reichsgau. Demokratie, "Ständestaat" und NS-Herrschaft in der Steiermark 1918 bis 1945* (Geschichte der Steiermark vol. 9). Vienna: Böhlau, 2015.

Bacher, Dieter, and Stefan Karner, eds. *Zwangsarbeiter in Österreich 1939–1945 und ihr Nachkriegsschicksal: Ergebnisse der Auswertung des Aktenbestandes des "Österreichischen Versöhnungsfonds." Ein Zwischenbericht.* Innsbruck: StudienVerlag, 2013.

Bischof, Günter, Barbara Stelzl-Marx, and Alexandra Kofler. *Zukunftsfonds der Republik Österreich. Entstehung, Entwicklung und Bedeutung.* Vienna: Böhlau, 2015.

Grischany, Thomas R. *Der Ostmark treue Alpensöhne: Die Integration der Österreicher in die großdeutsche Wehrmacht, 1938–1945.* Vienna: Vienna University Press, 2015.

Grünfelder, Anna-Maria. *Arbeitseinsatz für die Neuordnung Europas: Zivil- und ZwangsarbeiterInnen aus Jugoslawien in der "Ostmark" 1938/41–1945.* Vienna: Böhlau, 2010.

Halbrainer, Heimo, and Gerald Lamprecht, *Nationalsozialismus in der Steiermark: Opfer – Täter – Gegner.* Innsbruck: StudienVerlag, 2015.

Hoffmann, Georg. *Fliegerlynchjustiz: Gewalt gegen abgeschossene alliierte Flugzeugbesatzungen 1943–1945.* Paderborn: Ferdinand Schöningh, 2015.

Karner, Stefan, and Walter M. Iber, eds. *Schweres Erbe und Wiedergutmachung: Restitution und Entschädigung in Österreich. Die Bilanz der Regierung Schüssel.* Innsbruck: StudienVerlag, 2015.

------, and Alexander O. Tschubarian, eds. *Die Moskauer Deklaration 1943:* "Österreich *wieder herstellen.*" Vienna: Böhlau, 2015.

Lappin-Eppel, Eleonore. *Ungarisch-Jüdische Zwangsarbeiter und Zwangsarbeiterinnen in Österreich 1944/45: Arbeitseinsatz – Todesmärsche – Folgen.* Vienna: Lit Verlag, 2010.

Neugebauer, Wolfgang. *Austrian Resistance 1938–1945.* Vienna: Edition Steinbauer, 2014.

Rathkolb, Oliver, and Florian Freund, eds. *NS-Zwangsarbeit in der Elektrizitätswirtschaft der "Ostmark," 1938–1945: Ennstalwerke – Kaprun – Draukraftwerke – Ybbs-Persenbeug – Ernsthofen.* 2. ed. Vienna: Böhlau, 2014.

Ruggenthaler, Peter, and Walter M. Iber, eds. *Hitlers Sklaven – Stalins "Verräter": Aspekte der Repression an Zwangsarbeitern und Kriegsgefangenen.* Innsbruck: StudienVerlag, 2010.

Schieder, Paul. *Französische Zwangsarbeiter im "Reichseinsatz" auf dem Gebiet der Republik Österreich.* Vienna: Böhlau, 2012.

Stelzl-Marx, Barbara. *Stalins Soldaten in Österreich: Die Innensicht der sowjetischen Besatzung 1945–1955.* Vienna: Böhlau, 2012.

Traussnig, Florian. *Militärischer Widerstand von außen. Österreicher in US-Armee und Kriegsgeheimdienst im Zweiten Weltkrieg.* Vienna: Böhlau, 2016.

Schüssel Haider Coalition.
Chancellor Wolfang Schüssel (r.) with Jörg Haider in a Porsche Cabriolet on their way to the traditional Kufenstechen in Feistritz im Gailtal.
Gert Eggenberger, 10 11 2008
Credit: APA PictureDesk

Volume 18: Günter Bischof/Fritz Plasser. *The Schüssel Era in Austria.* New Orleans/Innsbruck: University of New Orleans Press/*innsbruck* university press 2010

The Schüssel Era Today

David M. Wineroither

Fifteen years ago, the inauguration of Austria's disputed Wende government caused unprecedented political polarization at the domestic level, and the fourteen other EU member states to run sanctions against Austria. Turning right in terms of coalition-making was Wolfgang Schüssel's single most important decision. While he was far from taking it alone, it made him the first conservative chancellor since Josef Klaus, who was succeeded by social democrat Bruno Kreisky in 1970.

The ensuing uproar begs the question whether there was substance to the Wende. In this light, the essay addresses three questions: First, how much of a rupture did the absence of grand coalition government and the representation of right-wing populists in government mean in historical perspective? Second, has scholarly and public view of the Schüssel era changed over the last couple of years, and if so, in what regard and in which direction? Finally, what could today be identified as the legacy of the Wende and Schüssel's leadership?

The Wende: rupture and majoritarian turn with limitations

In contrast to its predecessor, the political system of the Second Republic operated in a power-sharing mode from the very beginning. In the Austrian polity, more than in other consociational democracies, effective division of power depended to large degree on grand coalition government, whether formalized in the executive arena or semi-formalized within the boundaries of neo-corporatist policy concertation, decision-making, and policy implementation.

Once the Wende was established in terms of government formation, the long shadow of majoritarian rule started looming over most other dimensions of consensual politics as well. In the legislative arena, "speed kills" (famously paraphrased by ÖVP party whip Andreas Khol) became the blueprint of a new conflictual style of governing that acted largely unconstrained by social partnership and other veto players in the political system's power structure.

The different style of politics helped the ÖVP to separate itself from the unwelcome images of the grand coalition era, and to effectively put all the blame for political deadlock on its former senior partner. In fact, the grand coalition had faced some kind of identity crisis following EU-accession.

It is important to recall, however, that this majoritarian turn did not prevail for long in some crucial arenas and domains of policy making. The government during Schüssel's second term faced much stronger opposition as the SPÖ had accepted its role as leading parliamentary opponent. The chancellor himself had a preference for a coalition agreement with the left-libertarian Greens following his convincing reelection in 2002, but ended up in a remake with a much weaker FPÖ in order to preserve his reform agenda. Jörg Haider lost his ability to act as undisputed leader and would finally split away in spring 2005.

Even more, the initially bypassed corporatist actors celebrated a partial comeback. In particular, the SPÖ dominated trade union demonstrated mobilization strength and organizational capacity in rallying against pension reform in 2003. Long before that, the government had started to shift away from its "speed kills" and balanced budget paradigm, now more and more closely following the electoral cycles. Policy-making became inspired by the "time of harvest" (Finance minister Karl-Heinz Grasser) rhetoric. Later, in the 2006 GE, the leftover cutbacks that were implemented credibly lost him re-election after the SPÖ had already won the presidential, European, and provincial elections in Salzburg (all in 2004), followed by a historical victory in Styria (2005).

In other instances, the ability of the federal government to push through large scale reforms proved to be simply nonexistent from the very beginning. Political and public resistance and organizational inertia could not be overcome in dealing with constitutional and armed forces reform, notwithstanding the fact that Schüssel had adopted a more inclusive approach of public deliberation during both processes. The *Länder* governments, and the provincial governors of ÖVP and FPÖ (Haider himself, extracting "pork" for Carinthia), continued to act as able veto players in federalist affairs.

Changing scholarly and public view: minor revisions, modest shifts

The formation of the Wende stirred immediate protest both at the international and domestic level. More precisely, the degree of polarization between supporters, defenders and critiques of the Schüssel-Haider pact was more pronounced at the elite level than at the mass level. Some elements of *Kulturkampf* could be found among intellectuals while many politicians, first of all those in the SPÖ, tended to overstate public discontent with the Wende government (e.g. by looking at the tireless "Thursday demonstrations"). Against this background, the bilateral sanctions at EU level imposed on the new government helped to consolidate its domestic electoral basis. While the SPÖ, now in opposition, would gain votes throughout regional and municipal elections for years, the dominant exchange happened within the government camp, thus preserving majorities of the entire political right in most elections, most importantly in the 2002 General Election.

With the years passing by, public perception has become more influenced by allegations of political corruption that have turned into adjudication and terms of imprisonment. Haider, who passed away in 2008, was involved in a number of machinations that translated into court trials, and the largest one, the Hypo Alpe Adria (HAAG) bank scandal, will continue to burden public finances both in Carinthia and at the federal level. Nevertheless, scholars should be cautious in subscribing to the by-now popular notion of a new era of political fraud established during the years of populist right executive representation. This readily underestimates the extent of corruption in prior decades of which one lacks valid and generalizable data (not to mention the prime examples of AKH scandal, BAWAG and NORICUM affairs).

Since the publishing of *The Schüssel Era in Austria* in 2009/10, few additional primary sources have been made available that contribute to a deeper understanding of the Wende. Most importantly, Schüssel himself went public in 2009. In a nutshell, he claimed to have preferred and actively sought to renew the grand coalition in 1999/2000 and until the very last moment of negotiations. In his view, this bargaining failure was solely caused by disunity within the SPÖ. While the erosion of chancellor Klima's leadership during these months has been apparent ever since, the proposals of ÖVP leaders did not simply target the SPÖ to commit to a modicum of innovative governing as a matter of style, but intended to arrive at greater policy control and steering capacity at the expense of the Social Democrats.

In the end, the ÖVP was simply well-equipped in the coalition poker game and was willing to play-off its trump with no restraint. This statement might serve as a lowest common denominator of a variety of assertive studies on this topic. Similarly, scholarly output on the question of Schüssel's motivation and role in meeting the challenge of right-wing populist ascendancy and Haider's charismatic leadership is characterized by ideological cleavages. In general, accounts of civic pundits dominate the stage. The emerging consensus would refuse to address the question of

Schüssel as either "dragon slayer" or coldhearted, ruthless power-politician, but point out that Haider's electoral rise would have been unstoppable had the grand coalition status quo politics been prolonged.

Altogether, more recent studies could add little to our understanding of the initial decision leading to the establishment of the Wende government. The same can be said about patterns of interparty relations and majority building in Parliament, where researchers have ably and early on detected relevant change towards conflict democracy. There have been just a few systematic accounts on evaluating the government's policy record and, to a lesser extent, attempts to change the country's polity, usually focusing on matters of style rather than performance. For most policy areas, authors have more or less clearly resumed predominance of business as usual, albeit less so for key portfolios of fiscal, economic and social policies, and reforms in the health care sector. Here both the performance evaluations and the attributed level of political conflict are more diverse and mixed. Put differently, the legislative imprint at the heart of redistributive efforts continues to be disputed.

Most fruitful are the handful of fresher studies that portray the starting point of the Wende by offering detailed accounts on past policy choices and bringing in the perspective of path dependency. Surprisingly rarely, the merits and pitfalls of the Schüssel cabinets (and the chancellor himself) is assessed against the benchmark of the performance of previous and following governments. This has been convincingly done, for example, in the domains of foreign and migration policy. The former became more conflicted during the Wende, indicated by Schüssel's famous dictum on neutrality on Austrian National Day (2001).[1] Again, however, the dominant party systemic feature is stability—continuation of foreign and security policy as overwhelmingly conditional on parties' domestic policy considerations. This includes double-talk on the compatibility of the country's neutrality with their (full) participation in the European Security and Defense Policy.

The highly salient issues of migration and integration followed a different pattern. The topic stayed controversial at both the elite and mass level throughout the last thirty years. Remarkably, the legislative output since the mid-1990s shows continuity instead of rupture. In fact, years ago Haider made the same claim, announcing the agenda of his notorious 1993 "Austria First" initiative had been cleared primarily during the years of grand coalition government before the birth of the Wende. In other words,

1 "The old templates—Lipizzaner, Mozartkugeln, or neutrality—do not cut it any more in the complex reality of the beginning of the 21st century."

the SPÖ during the 1990s already had to pay tribute to the structural majority of the political right.

Legacy of the Wende and Schüssel's leadership

What major consequences did the Schüssel era have for the country? Without a doubt, the ÖVP was the main profiteer of his leadership in party and government. First, he had sufficient authority to take key strategic decision that usually played out favorable: the opposition announcement in 1999, the call for early elections in 2002, the offer of the post of finance minister to Grasser during that campaign. Second, internally, Schüssel kept his party from the danger of breaking apart. Party leaders acted more coherently during his twelve years of chairman than before and after his term. In contrast to leadership continuity under Schüssel, the party has had four chairmen since 2007. Third, the experiences with the Wende deal established coalition building openness towards the FPÖ as ultima ratio within party leadership. The 'blue' option continued to translate into strong bargaining position vis-à-vis the SPÖ in 2007, 2008, and 2013. Fourth, not only did Schüssel secure a remarkable electoral rebound in the 2002 GE, but he achieved the first (and only) victory for the People's Party since the year 1966.

In terms of policy making, governing without the SPÖ and with the inexperienced FPÖ counterpart allowed for a lasting legislative imprint. Fiscal consolidation credibly enhanced Austria's maneuverability at the eve of the outbreak of the international financial crisis in September 2008. As for many other policies, the ongoing representation of the ÖVP in government allowed for effective policy insulation. This caused major frustration on the side of the SPÖ during the short-lived cabinet of Alfred Gusenbauer (2007/08). His predecessor actively managed affairs as leader of the ÖVP's caucus in the *Nationalrat*, which describes a rare scenario in following a failed re-election bid as head of government. Having said this, the SPÖ more recently could shift government policy closer to its ideal point on some crucial matters (integrated school, needs-based guaranteed minimum income).

The legacy of the Schüssel years has a European dimension as well. Coalescing with a right-wing populist party did break a taboo domestically, and it certainly became a trendsetter in international terms. It has not, however, affected the likelihood of inclusion of far rightist parties in government across Europe. This was national business in the year 2000, just as it is in 2016. In fact, right-wing populists have entered governments or backed minority governments of mainstream parties many times during this period simply due to its electoral strength.

The experience of the sanctions pulled against the Wende government nevertheless had a genuinely European dimension, an impact that can still be felt today. The European Commission and national governments of EU member countries have acted with much more restraint in similar scenarios ever since. They do so even in cases of severe threats to the functioning of liberal democracy. Whereas the Commission battles them on the grounds of treaty infringement processes, the European Council splits internally over party familial cleavages.

Sadly, it is here where Schüssel turns his back on his very own legacy of accomplished political leadership. He publicly defended grand coalition governing for having achieved accession to the EU during later years, continued the pro-integrationist policy developed under preceding party chairmen, and kept coalition partner FPÖ on a short leash when it came to European affairs (notably with regard to the EU's Eastern enlargement). Irritatingly, and inconsistently, Schüssel also repeatedly expressed his solidarity with conservative and right-wing populist political leaders in other countries that offended European and democratic values exhaustively, most prominently—and often—Italy's Silvio Berlusconi and Hungary's Viktor Orban, the latter who declares his country to be "at war" with the EU, calling Brussels the "new Moscow." At first sight, this is even more puzzling given that Schüssel describes the antipode to populist leadership; a sharp contrast in lifestyle, attitudes and actions. On this important matter, the "team player" credibly trumped the "ardent European" (Schüssel about himself).[2]

In many pivotal domains of democratic practice, the Schüssel years deferred trends or altered the status quo before the pendulum would swing back to its original position. Most notably, the Austrian political culture is still more consensual than in the majority of Western liberal democracies. Far-reaching interparty consensus characterizes governance of "grid and group" issues which are central to the structuring of party political space in many other countries, most prominently in the United States. This applies to the bulk of life issues (e.g. pro-life vs. pro-choice) and handling of nuclear power. In response to the outbreak of the international finance crisis in September 2009, citizens and political elites alike enjoyed a honeymoon of old-style corporatist policy concertation.

2 On his political personality see the elegant sketch provided by Peter Gerlich, "The Political Personality of Wolfgang Schüssel," in CAS 18, 7–20.

In sum, much speaks in favor of Anton Pelinka's earlier account of the Schüssel years as having reinforced trends rather than changed the course of Austrian history.[3] These trends can be summarized as de-Austrification and describe a consequence of democratic convergence. The event of the establishment of the 'Wende' government itself symbolized "late Westernization" (to borrow a term used during the 1990s).

Many reforms implemented by the Schüssel governments moved Austria closer to what can be labeled the European democratic average, such as steps towards academic autonomy (*Hochschulautonomie*), the temporary introduction of student fees, the ongoing process of welfare retrenchment, and (almost) full participation in Common European Security and Defense Policy (CDSP). Later grand coalition governments by and large followed this path: Electoral reforms made the formulas less party-centered and more personalist, and direct democracy has been strengthened to moderate degree. Policies and institutions point to more competitive settings, for example, by overcoming territorial boundaries, and in the educational sector, with the introduction of centralized school leaving examination and hiring and firing of personnel to the discretion of individual high schools' leadership.

By actively promoting, partially redefining, and managing this process of de-Austrification, Schüssel qualifies as one of the most influential and more successful chancellors since the end of the country's times of a veritable "happy island."

Select Bibliography

Gerlich, Peter. "The Political Personality of Wolfgang Schüssel," in CAS 18, 7–20.

Helms, Ludger, and David M. Wineroither, eds. *Die österreichische Demokratie im Vergleich*. Baden-Baden: Nomos, 2012 (2nd edition forthcoming).

Kriechbaumer, Robert, and Franz Schausberger, eds., *Die umstrittene Wende: Österreich 2000–2006*. Vienna: Böhlau, 2013.

Kriechbaumer, Robert. *"...ständiger Verdruss und viele Verletzungen." Die Regierung Klima/Schüssel und die Bildung der ÖVP-FPÖ-Regierung. Österreich 1997–2000.* Vienna: Böhlau, 2014.

Kritzinger, Sylvia, Wolfgang C. Müller, and Klaus Schönbach, eds. *Die Nationalratswahl 2013. Wie Parteien, Medien und Wählerschaft zusammenwirken*. Vienna: Böhlau, 2014.

3 Anton Pelinka, "Legacies of the Schüssel Years," in CAS 18, 320–338.

Pelinka, Anton. "Legacies of the Schüssel Years," in CAS 18, 320–338.
Schüssel, Wolfgang, and Alexander Purger. *Offengelegt*. Salzburg: Ecowin, 2009.
Wineroither, David M., and Gilg Seeber. "Die österreichische Nationalratswahl vom 29. September 2013: Das Ende Großer Koalitionen in Sicht," *Zeitschrift für Parlamentsfragen* 45, no. 1 (2014): 158–174.

Veterans reunion.
Start-up drive of the First Garrison of the Graz front fighter veterans to their gathering in Dobl near Graz.
Press Photography, 08 17 1924
Credit: Austrian National Library

Volume 19: Günter Bischof/Fritz Plasser/Peter Berger. *From Empire to Republic: Post-World War Austria*. New Orleans/Innsbruck: University of New Orleans Press/*innsbruck* university press 2010

Austria in the 1920s

John Deak

This is an exciting time for interwar Austrian history. After nearly two decades of a relative lull in publications, a wealth of conferences on the postwar order, new dissertations, and the push of transnational historical approaches are changing the field. This essay is thus a snapshot of a scholarship in motion. I will attempt to capture not the state-of-the-art, but rather where our scholarship is going and how, given the current trajectories of European history, the history of Austria will be rewritten.

When the nineteenth volume in *Contemporary Austrian Studies* appeared in late 2010, Tony Judt had just passed and his magnum opus, *Postwar*, could still be found on the front table of academic and popular bookstores.[1] Günter Bischof, inspired by Judt's book, as well as anticipating the surge of scholarly activity on the First World War, brought together with Fritz Plasser and Peter Berger a volume of essays on the aftermath of the First World War in Austria.[2] Our essays in that volume covered a number of areas from the fall of the Empire to the longer-term costs of war that the fledgling Austrian Republic inherited. What unified those essays was their sense of movement away from the standard political narratives that have often framed the story of the First Republic. Instead, the essays focused on many of the real issues that haunted Austria at the close of the First World War: broken economies, broken bodies, disillusioned minds, and the broken postwar order that Austria had to navigate.

Our volume was, in many ways, a harbinger of a new wave of scholarship. What we can now see emerging within the field of Central European history in general is a return to the themes of a common past and shared experiences. Austria shared a heritage and a common post-Habsburg fate with the other successor states of the Habsburg Empire,

1 Tony Judt, *Postwar: A History of Europe since 1945* (New York: Penguin Books, 2006).
2 CAS 19.

one that future scholarship must recapture.[3] In the following paragraphs, I will give an account of the standard narratives of postwar Austrian history, where they came from, and how they are currently being rewritten in a new and emerging scholarship.

The history of the First Austrian Republic has largely been told from the perspective of the Second. The Second Republic was an Austria that stood largely on its own, between East and West. Austria was separated from many of its neighbors after the Second World War by the Iron Curtain to the north and east. To the south, Austrian history was divided by language and the cementation of an ethnic identity from Italian national histories. To the west, the German-Austrian story has been dominated by lingering questions of ethnicity, language, identity, and the problem of coping and discussing the shared past of National Socialism, war, and genocide.

In many ways, traditional Austrian historiography has told the story of an Austria that stood on its own, both in distinction to Germany and to its neighbors to the north, east, and south, on the other side of the Iron Curtain. This story has been both narrow, more narrow than it should have been, and dominated by political history told through the perspective of its political parties.[4] We thus have tended to make sense of what happened and what people thought in terms of these party narratives. Moreover, the various narratives of Austrian history have followed a particular set of emplotments. In other words, narratives of the First Republic have largely revolved around the establishment of the Republic in 1918 and its subsequent failure. They begin with a *Stunde Null* in 1918, with Viktor Adler and Karl Renner proclaiming the foundation of the Austrian Republic on the steps of Parliament. The following plot points consist of Austria in transition: the initial years, when Austria had to establish its borders and the question of what was Austrian territory, followed by the punitive treaty with the Allies at St. Germain. As Austria settled into its small-state status, its politicians and scholars drafted a constitution in 1920, which featured political compromise, legal innovation, and postwar weariness. But that may have been the last high point; thereafter, Austria's political parties began a polarization process that pitted red Vienna against the black countryside. Violence in the streets between political factions increased as

3 Eric D. Weitz and Omer Bartov, *Shatterzone of Empires Coexistence and Violence in the German, Habsburg, Russian, and Ottoman Borderlands* (Bloomington: Indiana University Press, 2013).

4 See the brilliant and paradigm-forming 1954 essay by Adam Wandruszka, "Österreichs politische Struktur. Die Entwicklung der Parteien und politischen Bewegungen," in *Geschichte der Republik Österreich*, ed. Heinrich Benedikt (Vienna: Verlag für Geschichte und Politik, 1954).

the split between the Catholic countryside and the red city left Austria politically isolated. Socialists burned the Palace of Justice in the 1920s; Catholic conservatives increasingly turned away from democracy. At the end these narratives comes either the Civil War of 1934, complete with the military bombardment of the Karl Marx Hof socialist housing project, or the Anschluss of 1938, with Hitler's triumphal entry into Vienna.

The story of the failed First Republic has therefore been a story of politics and institutions. And no wonder; it is precisely the political history of Austria that makes sense to the post-1945 observer. These narratives have focused on the double failure of Austria in the 1930s: the failure of Austrian democracy with the rise of clerical, corporatist Austro-fascism in 1933–34, and the failure of Austria as a state identity in 1938. These events have framed in hardened steel a rigid emplotment for the First Republic and became a useable past for the Second Republic in the form of a cautionary tale to base the state in democratic principles and political cooperation. In this tale, Austria's common past, shared with its fellow post-Habsburg successor states, was subsequently hidden by other narratives, by Cold-War perspectives, and by official histories which privileged the nation state as the natural end of political development.

The historiography of post-WWI Austria is now much less internally focused and is beginning to be put in a larger context, one that interacts and is informed by the historiographic work being done in and about its neighbors and about the regions with which Austria shared a common Habsburg past. The last six years have brought massive changes in the scholarship of Central Europe, not least as the scholarship on the First World War has again brought increased attention to the region and forced a reappraisal of the individual national historiographies of the war. The greatest contribution that WWI scholarship is making to the history of postwar Austria is this larger, regional, even post-Habsburg perspective. What is now happening, then, is that historians are rediscovering this once lost, common past. The story of the First Republic will ultimately still be a story of failure, of succumbing to anti-democratic movements and the abandoning of the Austrian state, but that story will now reflect and engage with the stories of Austria's neighbors.

There are two main issues for historians dealing with the end of Empire and the beginning of the Austrian First Republic. Both issues consist of widening our perspective, taking more of the panorama of Central Europe after the First World War into our lens. Firstly, we should pay attention to the fall of the Empire beyond its constitutional terms, beyond the ready-made narratives of the parties themselves. The fall of the Habsburg Empire unleashed a discussion, by necessity, of what the postwar order would look like. Secondly, that discussion on the postwar order was by nature one that saw Austria interacting with its neighbors. The "near abroad"—those places that shared a common Habsburg past—were still relevant to how not only the Austrian government, but also Austrians (whoever they were) navigated a world of new nation states.[5]

Thus, what has traditionally been missing in such Austrian histories of the 1920s has been precisely the connections that remained with Austria's fellow successor states. It was as if the precious Austrian identity that has been cultivated after the Second World War needed to treat the turbulent society of the 1920s and the 1930s in a vacuum. That is now changing. Our view of Austria in the 1920s is now being challenged by exogenous pressures: a revision of the history of the Habsburg Monarchy's final decades and a concomitant revision of the histories of the individual successor states.

Take the period 1918 to 1920, for instance. Recent and compelling research has emphasized that the First World War, for much of Central and Eastern Europe, did not end on 11 November 1918.[6] For many, the war continued on and came closer to home as the old empires crumbled. Ethnic violence in border regions, pogroms, and the persistence of food and coal shortages united much of Central Europe. They were experienced directly, or in newspapers, working to create what one historian has called a "culture of defeat."[7] Uncertainty at the international situation, the shifting borders, and spaces of ethnic cleansing could only be deepened by a fear of Bolshevism, made very real in Austria by revolution across the borders in Bavaria and in Hungary.[8] At the same time, soldiers who abandoned their units or were returning from Bolshevik Russia formed green cadres that terrorized the countryside, regardless of where new state boundaries were drawn.[9]

5 Lisa Silverman, *Becoming Austrians: Jews and Culture between the World Wars* (Oxford/New York: Oxford University Press, 2012).

6 See, for instance, the evolving evolving, multivolume project on "Russia's Great War and Revolution, 1914–1923" at <http://russiasgreatwar.org/> (15 Jan. 2015). More generally, see Robert Gerwarth and Erez Manela, eds., *Empires at War: 1911–1923* (Oxford: Oxford University Press, 2014); Robert Gerwarth and John Horne, eds., *War in Peace: Paramilitary Violence in Europe after the Great War* (Oxford: Oxford University Press, 2012).

7 See "Tagungsbericht: Beyond Defeat and Victory. Physical Violence and the Reconstitution of East-Central Europe, 1914–1923, 17.09.2015 – 19.09.2015 Prague," in *H-Soz-Kult*, 25 November 2015, <http://www.hsozkult.de/conferencereport/id/tagungsberichte-6253> (15 Jan. 2015). "Culture of Defeat" is the term used by Robert Gerwarth in his keynote on 17 September 2015.

8 Paul Hanebrink, "Transnational Culture War: Christianity, Nation, and the Judeo-Bolshevik Myth in Hungary, 1890–1920," *The Journal of Modern History* 80, no. 1 (2008): 55–80, doi:10.1086/529077.

9 Jakub Beneš, "Zelené Kádry jako radikální alternative pro venkov na západním Slovensku a ve středovýchodní Evropě 1917–1920," *Forum Historiae* 9, no. 2 (2015): 20–34.

It was in this context of violence and uncertainty that Austria was created; it is such a multifaceted context that gave birth to Austria and what it meant to be an Austrian. Here, research on questions of citizenship are of utmost importance.[10] For who was an Austrian in 1919? This was unclear and had to be worked out, legally, and through international agreements, just as it had to be worked out in peoples' minds.[11] Moreover, this working out of identity and citizenship had to be done in a post-imperial space, one in which Austria's neighbors were having to create their own national histories, bind them to state institutions, and fix them into the postwar international system.[12]

Renewed recognition of international and transnational discourses on nation, citizenship, and the state has brought with it a new pressure to make our studies transnational, to see connections, networks and ideas which crossed boarders. Moreover, new studies which have focused on empires have had a lot to do with this. Global history and Empire studies, from C. A. Bayly to Jürgen Osterhammel, have focused on various kinds of networks that underpinned the power and the political and social cultures of empires.[13] We can debate whether the Habsburg Monarchy was truly an empire or not, but a multinational state it certainly was, with intellectual, cultural, political, religious, commercial, military, and legal networks that had been forged over and over again in the years since the War of Austrian Succession.[14] As the Empire collapsed after over four years of constant war, these connections did not disappear, nor were they forgotten.

What we find, therefore, is that the ground is shifting in the scholarship of interwar Europe. New scholarship, which is being produced in conference

10 Jane Caplan and John C. Torpey, *Documenting Individual Identity: The Development of State Practices in the Modern World* (Princeton N.J.: Princeton University Press, 2001).

11 Peter Thaler, *The Ambivalence of Identity: The Austrian Experience of Nation-Building in a Modern Society* (West Lafayette, Ind.: Purdue University Press, 2001); Ruth Wodak, *The Discursive Construction of National Identity* (Edinburgh: Edinburgh University Press, 2009); Friedrich Heer, *Der Kampf um die österreichische Identität* (Vienna: Böhlau, 1981).

12 For instance, see the recent work on Yugoslavian identity as a state project: Christian Axboe Nielsen, *Making Yugoslavs: Identity in King Aleksandar's Yugoslavia* (Toronto: University of Toronto Press, 2014); Igor Tchoukarine, "The Contested Adriatic Sea: The Adriatic Guard and Identity Politics in Interwar Yugoslavia," *Austrian History Yearbook* 42 (2011): 33–51, doi:10.1017/S0067237811000038.

13 Jürgen Osterhammel, *Die Verwandlung der Welt: eine Geschichte des 19. Jahrhunderts*, Historische Bibliothek der Gerda Henkel Stiftung (Munich: Beck, 2009); C. A. Bayly, *Empire and Information: Intelligence Gathering and Social Communication in India, 1780–1870* (Cambridge: Cambridge University Press, 1996).

14 Pieter M. Judson, "L'Austriche-Hongrie était-Elle Un Empire?," *Annales. Histoire, Sciences Sociales* 63, no. 3 (2008): 563–96; John Deak, *Forging a Multinational State: State Making in Imperial Austria from the Enlightenment to the First World War* (Stanford, Calif.: Stanford University Press, 2015).

volumes, dissertations, and articles, has not broken up the field yet, but it certainly will soon. Pulling out the continuities, how republican Austria emerged from the violence, hunger, and deprivations of the war in the midst of a "Wilsonian moment" that was both incredibly promising to its neighbors and incredibly disappointing to Austrians (as well as Hungarians, Italians, Ukrainians, and Slovenians) are the stories that need to be told.

For example, the work of Roberta Pergher on how Italy dealt with its new, non-Italian citizens has repercussions for a yet-to-be told story of how Austria dealt with its own, new unredeemed territories.[15] Borut Klabjan's work on the post-Habsburg Adriatic space sheds light on how the vestiges of the Habsburg Empire became ground for imperialist aims in the interwar period.[16] In a way, histories of postwar Austria have focused on what was being newly built: the constitutional and partisan institutions of a democratic republic. What the emerging scholarship of all the post Habsburg space calls us to do, however, is give equal attention to what was being dismantled, forgotten, and wiped away.

As First Republic Austrian history is increasingly situated in such a larger, post-Habsburg space, cultural and intellectual histories are shifting as well. Carl E. Schorske's *Fin-de-siècle Vienna* has long dominated our ideas about the cultural world of the Habsburg Monarchy. But the prevailing wisdom that emerged out of that work's preeminent position has meant that the 1920s are seen as a moment when the bright shining light of Vienna dimmed. But the revision of the last years of the Monarchy on the part of Habsburg historians, in so far as they have uprooted the once firmly implanted notions of the steady and advancing decline of the monarchy, force a reassessment of the 1920s as well. Work on economics, science, culture, medicine, has begun to look at the 1920s in Austria not as an era of cultural decline following state decline, but as a time when new national intellectual communities and ideas intersected with newly constructed global, European, and regional ones.

New studies have certainly shifted our thinking, and they have also challenged us to see Austrian culture as existing in a larger, Central European context. David S. Luft's recent work has demonstrated at once the larger zone of Austrian literature than just the present-day borders of the Republic, as well as how the intellectuals worked after the Second World War to create new meanings of what it meant to be Austria, erasing

15 Roberta Pergher, "Staging the Nation in Fascist Italy's 'New Provinces,'" *Austrian History Yearbook* 43 (April 2012): 98–115, doi:10.1017/S0067237811000610.

16 Borut Klabjan, "'Scramble for Adria': Discourses of Appropriation of the Adriatic Space Before and After World War I," *Austrian History Yearbook* 42 (2011): 16–32, doi:10.1017/S0067237811000026.

older ones in the process.[17] Out of this has come new work on Austria's Jews in the interwar period and the new meanings of what it meant to be an Austrian, as well as what it meant to be a human being.[18] Stefan Zweig has seen the greatest resurgence of scholarly interest with a new biography as well as a brilliantly assembled temporary exhibition at Vienna's Theatermuseum, appropriately titled "Abschied von Europa."[19] To this we can also add intellectual biographies of Joseph Roth, who had to navigate the narrowing of the Austrian mind and spirit after the fall of the Empire. It is through these studies that Austrian intellectual and cultural history has engaged in how a narrowing of what it could mean to be Austrian was part of a larger European discourse on race, nation, and citizenship, with disastrous consequences.[20]

Such a wider context is already working its way back into political histories of the First Republic, suggesting that the standard emplotment of Austria's First Republic is already changing. Janek Wasserman admirably demonstrates how Vienna's radical conservatives pushed Austrian political dialogue to the right, establishing both the feasibility and the desirability of an Austro-fascist state. Wasserman's account, revising our narrative of red Vienna versus the black countryside, focuses on how Austrians participated in the wider conflict between socialism, conservativism, and the growing acceptability of fascism.[21] Moreover, Erin Hochman's forthcoming book demonstrates how Austria fits into a wider, Central European network of discourses on nation and state in postwar Europe.[22] One of the consequences of the fall of the Habsburg Empire was the appearance and feasibility of new political constellations, including the argument for joining Germany. But though this topic, and the *Anschluss*, have always been hot button issues for Austrian history, what Hochman shows is that the discourse of

17 David S. Luft, "Austrian Intellectual History and Bohemia," *Austrian History Yearbook* 38 (2007): 108–21; David S. Luft, "Cultural Memory and Intellectual History: Locating Austrian Literature," *Studies in Twentieth and Twenty-First Century Literature* 31, no. 1 (2007): 25–45.

18 Silverman, *Becoming Austrians*.

19 Klemens Renoldner, *Stefan Zweig – Abschied von Europa* (Vienna: Brandstätter Verlag, 2014); George Prochnik, *The Impossible Exile: Stefan Zweig at the End of the World* (New York: Other Press, 2014).

20 Ilse Josepha Lazaroms, *The Grace of Misery Joseph Roth and the Politics of Exile, 1919–1939* (Leiden/Boston: Brill, 2013).

21 Janek Wasserman, *Black Vienna: The Radical Right in the Red City, 1918–1938* (Ithaca, NY: Cornell University Press, 2014).

22 Erin Hochman, *Imagining a Greater Germany: Republican Nationalism and the Idea of Anschluss* (Ithaca, NY: Cornell University Press, 2016); Erin R. Hochman, "Nationalism and Democratic Politics in the Weimar and First Austrian Republics," *German History* 32, no. 1 (2014): 29–52, doi:10.1093/gerhis/ght102.

Anschluss and by extension, the *großdeutsch* idea, was a fixture of republican politics in both Austria and Germany in the interwar period. By looking at the cross-border connections between German and Austrian republican politics and political discourse, Hochman finds that the *großdeutsch* idea circulated in both Germany and Austria as a part of a democratic, republic, state-building project.

Such seismic shifts in the state of Austrian history and Austrian studies should be celebrated, for it takes Austria out of its small-state and exceptional status and puts Austria right where it belongs: in the center of European history. How much of our telling of Austrian history will change is still unknown. What is certain is that new narratives are coming and they will prove to be interesting, multinational, integrative, and deepen our understanding of interwar Austria and interwar Europe.

Select Bibliography

Bayly, C. A. *Empire and Information: Intelligence Gathering and Social Communication in India, 1780–1870*. Cambridge: Cambridge University Press, 1996.

Beneš, Jakub. "Zelené Kádry jako radikální alternative pro venkov na západním Slovensku a ve středovýchodní Evropě 1917-1920," *Forum Historiae* 9, no. 2 (2015): 20–34.

Caplan, Jane, and John C. Torpey, *Documenting Individual Identity: The Development of State Practices in the Modern World*. Princeton N.J.: Princeton University Press, 2001.

Deak, John. *Forging a Multinational State: State Making in Imperial Austria from the Enlightenment to the First World War* (Stanford Studies on Central and Eastern Europe). Stanford, Calif.: Stanford University Press, 2015.

Gerwarth, Robert, and John Horne, eds. *War in Peace: Paramilitary Violence in Europe after the Great War*. Oxford: Oxford University Press, 2012.

Gerwarth, Robert, and Erez Manela, eds. *Empires at War: 1911–1923*. Oxford: Oxford University Press, 2014.

Hanebrink, Paul. "Transnational Culture War: Christianity, Nation, and the Judeo-Bolshevik Myth in Hungary, 1890–1920," *The Journal of Modern History* 80, no. 1 (2008): 55–80. doi:10.1086/529077.

Heer, Friedrich. *Der Kampf um die österreichische Identität*. Vienna: Böhlau, 1981.

Hochman, Erin. *Imagining a Greater Germany: Republican Nationalism and the Idea of Anschluss*. Ithaca, N.Y.: Cornell University Press, 2016.

-------. "Nationalism and Democratic Politics in the Weimar and First Austrian Republics," *German History* 32, no. 1 (2014): 29–52. doi:10.1093/gerhis/ght102.

Judson, Pieter M. "L'Austriche-Hongrie était-Elle Un Empire?" *Annales. Histoire, Sciences Sociales* 63, no. 3 (2008): 563–96.

Judt, Tony. *Postwar: A History of Europe since 1945*. New York: Penguin Books, 2006.

Klabjan, Borut. "'Scramble for Adria': Discourses of Appropriation of the Adriatic Space Before and After World War I," *Austrian History Yearbook* 42 (2011): 16–32. doi:10.1017/S0067237811000026.

Lazaroms, Ilse Josepha. *The Grace of Misery Joseph Roth and the Politics of Exile, 1919–1939* (Brill's Series in Jewish Studies, Vol. 47). Leiden/ Boston: Brill, 2013.

Luft, David S. "Austrian Intellectual History and Bohemia." *Austrian History Yearbook* 38 (2007): 108–21.

----. "Cultural Memory and Intellectual History: Locating Austrian Literature." *Studies in Twentieth and Twenty-First Century Literature* 31, no. 1 (2007): 25-45.

Nielsen, Christian Axboe. *Making Yugoslavs: Identity in King Aleksandar's Yugoslavia*. Toronto: University of Toronto Press, 2014.

Osterhammel, Jürgen. *Die Verwandlung der Welt: eine Geschichte des 19. Jahrhunderts* (Historische Bibliothek der Gerda Henkel Stiftung). Munich: Beck, 2009.

Pergher, Roberta. "Staging the Nation in Fascist Italy's 'New Provinces,'" *Austrian History Yearbook* 43 (April 2012): 98–115. doi:10.1017/ S0067237811000610.

Prochnik, George. *The Impossible Exile: Stefan Zweig at the End of the World*. New York: Other Press, 2014.

Renoldner, Klemens. *Stefan Zweig – Abschied von Europa*. Vienna: Brandstätter Verlag, 2014.

Silverman, Lisa. *Becoming Austrians: Jews and Culture between the World Wars*. Oxford/New York: Oxford University Press, 2012.

Tchoukarine, Igor. "The Contested Adriatic Sea: The Adriatic Guard and Identity Politics in Interwar Yugoslavia," *Austrian History Yearbook* 42 (2011): 33–51. doi:10.1017/S0067237811000038.

Thaler, Peter. *The Ambivalence of Identity: The Austrian Experience of Nation-Building in a Modern Society* (Central European Studies). West Lafayette, Ind.: Purdue University Press, 2001.

Wandruszka, Adam. "Österreichs politische Struktur. Die Entwicklung der Parteien und politischen Bewegungen," in *Geschichte der Republik Österreich*, ed. Heinrich Benedikt. Vienna: Verlag für Geschichte und Politik, 1954.

Wasserman, Janek. *Black Vienna: The Radical Right in the Red City, 1918–1938*. Ithaca, NY: Cornell University Press, 2014.

Weitz, Eric D., and Omer Bartov. *Shatterzone of Empires Coexistence and Violence in the German, Habsburg, Russian, and Ottoman Borderlands*. Bloomington: Indiana University Press, 2013.

Wodak, Ruth. *The Discursive Construction of National Identity*. Edinburgh: Edinburgh University Press, 2009.

Iran Talks in Vienna.
Dragan Tatic, 07 14 2015
Credit: Dragan Tatic / Austrian Federal Ministry for Europe, Integration and Foreign Affairs

Volume 20: Günter Bischof/Fritz Plasser/Anton Pelinka/Alexander Smith, eds. *Global Austria: Austria's Place in Europe and the World.* New Orleans/Innsbruck: University of New Orleans Press/*innsbruck* university press 2011

Austria's Global Position Today: Some Reflections on a Country in Decline

Alexander Smith

The twentieth anniversary issue of *Contemporary Austrian Studies* on *Global Austria* intended to assess both Austria's position in the global arena of the twentieth century and the impact of the globalizing world on the country. In a bid to get the full picture of Austria's global role, we chose to adopt a broad approach, encompassing the cultural and intellectual spheres of influence as well as the political and economic dimensions of Austrian significance in the world. To my knowledge, CAS Volume 20 is the only publication that provides a comprehensive examination of—as the subtitle of the book suggests—Austria's place in Europe and the world.

The first section of essays explores the global influence and significance of *fin-de-siècle* Vienna's culture of modernism (Steven Beller), Austro-Marxist and fascist thinking (Tim Kirk), and the Austrian School of Economics (Hansjoerg Klausinger). Further contributions address the Austrian capital's position as a financial center (Andreas Resch and Dieter Stiefel) and international conference site (Eric Frey). The second series of essays examines how the forces of globalization, the European integration process, and EU membership have impacted Austrian demography (Rainer Münz), political culture (Fritz Plasser and Gilg Seeber), the discourse on a Central European identity of Austria (Emil Brix), and Austria's stance on the EU (Sonja Puntscher-Riekmann).

Whereas CAS 20 looks at Austria's global position from different perspectives, the purpose of this essay is to critically outline the economic (and political) direction Austria has taken since the publication of *Global Austria* five years ago. It is argued that a country's economic condition has ramifications for its role on the world stage. I not only had the pleasure to serve as a guest editor—alongside Anton Pelinka—of CAS Volume 20, but also to contribute an article on the rise of the major Austrian oil and natural gas company OMV from a minor state-owned oil producer to a global player. My OMV article for the most part reads like a success story. The company's development prior to the early 2010s was, indeed, quite impressive. In recent years, however, OMV experienced some turbulences. The latter can be seen as symbolic of Austria's poor economic record in the last few years, which were largely characterized by political stagnation and economic decline. Austria, it seems, has fallen behind most of its European and international peers. This will negatively affect the country's global position in the future. However, remarkable success was achieved recently in bringing major political summits to Vienna. The Austrian capital was able to strengthen its position as a center of diplomacy and summitry.

Before elaborating on Vienna's role as an international meeting place and Austria's gradual economic downturn, let me briefly sketch what has not changed since the publication of CAS 20. In his introductory essay, Andreas Exenberger portrayed Austria as a highly globalized country that is well connected to the world. Various indices of globalization which Exenberger referred to in his article support this assessment. According to the renowned KOF Index of Globalization of ETH Zurich, Austria was the fourth most globalized country among 191 nations in 2015 (in 2011, it had even been second). The updated Maastricht Globalization Index (MGI) of 2012, another widely accepted measure that gives an impression of a country's global interconnectedness, ranks Austria fifth among 117 countries (in 2008, it had been sixth). Exenberger's statement that "these indices point to an extraordinary degree of globalization taking place in Austria" (29) still holds true.

Aside from that, Vienna succeeded in keeping its status as a leading international conference site. In his essay, Eric Frey made a reference to the worldwide ranking of cities that attract international meetings published by the International Congress and Convention Association (ICCA). The ICCA ranking had been led by Vienna since 2005 (147). Even though in 2010 the Austrian capital city lost its leading position and now ranks second by the number of international meetings (behind Paris), and fifth by the number of participants (behind Paris, Barcelona, Madrid, and London), Vienna still counts as one of the world's most popular conference sites.

Vienna: A Center of World Diplomacy

With the final round of the Iran nuclear negotiations in summer and the first Syrian peace talks in fall 2015, an important chapter can be added to Frey's article on the history of Vienna as a major international meeting place. The Austrian Foreign Ministry, under its committed young secretary

Sebastian Kurz of the People's Party (ÖVP), succeeded in bringing the Iran talks back from Geneva and Lausanne to Vienna. After more than a decade of deadlock, a historic agreement was reached in Vienna on 14 July 2015 between Iran and the five permanent members of the UN Security Council plus Germany and the High Representative of the EU for Foreign Affairs (the so-called "E3/EU+3") for Iran to limit its nuclear activities in return for the lifting of international sanctions. The Iran nuclear talks and the signing of a landmark deal that put an end to a major global dispute strengthened Vienna's role as a major center of world diplomacy. "For Austria, hosting the agreement has been something of a coup" according to a *Financial Times* report. "The country's foreign ministry went all out to secure the talks, in an effort to cement Vienna's place as Europe's principal diplomatic venue."[1]

The multinational negotiations to resolve the conflict in Syria that were held in October and November 2015 at the prestigious Hotel Imperial put the Austrian capital in the spotlight again. The so-called "Vienna Process" gained considerable attention as it brought the main players to the negotiating table, including the two regional arch-rivals Saudi Arabia and Iran. The Syrian peace talks provided another excellent opportunity for Vienna to position itself as a hub of international diplomacy and summitry, building on a long tradition that goes back to the Viennese Congress 1814–15 and the Kennedy-Khrushchev Vienna summit of 1961.

As pointed out by Exenberger and Frey in their contributions to CAS 20, Vienna has attracted a number of prominent international organizations, starting in 1957 with the International Atomic Energy Agency (IAEA). Then, in 1965, the Organization of the Petroleum Exporting Countries (OPEC) moved its headquarters from Geneva to the Austrian capital. One year later, the newly founded United Nations Industrial Organization (UNIDO) was located in Vienna. In the 1970s, Vienna became the third major United Nations office site alongside New York and Geneva. Several different UN agencies have a presence at the Vienna International Center ("UNO-City") that was constructed between 1973 and 1979. In the previous decades, further international organizations based their headquarters in the Austrian capital, including the Organization for Security and Cooperation in Europe (OSCE) and, most recently, the King Abdullah Bin Abdulaziz International Center for Interreligious and Intercultural Dialogue (KAICIID). The Saudi-funded religious center, named after the

1 Sam Jones, "A heady mix of diplomatic dining, spies and torte in Vienna," *Financial Times*, 20 October 2015, <www.ft.com/cms/s/2/edf2afd2-669a-11e5-97d0-1456a776a4f5.html#axzz3xLXJBNvZ> (5 Jan. 2016).

former Saudi monarch, was founded in October 2011 by the governments of Austria, Saudi Arabia, and Spain, with the Vatican being a founding observer.

In early 2015, a political controversy broke out in Austria over KAICIID when Chancellor Werner Faymann of the Social Democrats (SPÖ) criticized the Saudi-sponsored dialogue center for not speaking out against the public flogging of the Saudi human rights activist and blogger Raif Badawi, who was sentenced to a thousand lashes and ten years in prison for launching a liberal website and "insulting Islam." Faymann threatened to cancel the Austrian participation in KAICIID and to terminate the respective agreements if the center fails to distance itself from human rights violations in Saudi Arabia. The Green Party welcomed Faymann's uncompromising line of action against the Abdullah center whereas President Heinz Fischer, Vice-Chancellor Reinhold Mitterlehner (ÖVP), and Cardinal Christoph Schönborn, archbishop of Vienna, opposed the chancellor's undiplomatic approach that appeared somewhat populist to some observers. Saudi Arabia was certainly not amused by the Austrian chancellor's "campaign" against KAICIID. Riyadh reacted by threatening to relocate the permanent headquarters of OPEC or the OPEC Fund for International Development (OFID) away from the Austrian capital. Eventually, neither did Austria withdraw from the Abdullah center, nor did Saudi Arabia carry out its threat regarding OPEC. In any case, Faymann and parts of his government did a disservice to Vienna's position and reputation as a location of international organizations.

The Decline of Austrian Business

OMV's performance since the publication of CAS 20 was anything but successful. A series of unfavorable events has put the Austrian oil and gas company under pressure in recent years. By June 2013, it became clear that the OMV-led Nabucco pipeline project was moribund, because main natural gas suppliers in Azerbaijan chose the competing Trans Adriatic Pipeline (TAP) for the delivery of their gas to Europe. The aim of Nabucco had been to link the world's most prolific natural gas fields in the Caspian region and the Middle East to the Baumgarten natural gas junction in Lower Austria. With the failure of Nabucco, and the extension of the Nord Stream pipeline by a second underwater line across the Baltic Sea from Russia to Germany (OMV participates in the project), the Austrian transmission center is likely to become less important in European gas trade. Furthermore, OMV was hard hit by the civil wars in Libya and

Yemen, where it has sizable crude oil operations, and the recent oil price collapse, which forced petroleum companies to implement extensive cost-cutting measures. To make matters worse, OMV's chief executive, Gerhard Roiss, was ousted from office in October 2014. Rudolf Kemler, head of the company's supervisory board back then, was reportedly the driving force behind Roiss' inglorious removal. The circumstances under which Roiss was forced to leave OMV created some unease within the company. In light of this, it is not surprising that the OMV share price has dropped by around a third since early 2011.

The Austrian financial economy, which constitutes a major industry in the country, did not perform much better. The asset size of the Austrian banking sector amounts to more than three hundred percent of GDP[2] The banking business has been experiencing a difficult period following the world financial crisis of 2008–09. The Carinthian Hypo Group Alpe Adria, which was majority-owned by the Bayerische Landesbank from 2007 to 2009, was hardest hit among the Austrian banks. As outlined by Andreas Resch and Dieter Stiefel in their contribution to CAS 20, the credit institution received hundreds of millions of euros during the financial crisis from its Bavarian owners and the Austrian state (141). It soon became clear, however, that further capital was needed. In December 2009, Hypo Alpe Adria was taken over in a so-called "emergency nationalization" (*Notverstaatlichung*) by the Austrian state for a symbolic price of one euro. Prior to that, the Bavarians had threatened to send the Carinthian bank into a disorderly insolvency if the Austrian government refused to come to terms with them on this delicate issue. In the years that followed, Hypo Alpe Adria turned out to be a bottomless pit, resulting in a multibillion-euro loss to the Austrian taxpayer.

When a renowned auditing company found a capital gap of up to 7.6 billion euros in the course of an asset quality review, Finance Minister Hans Jörg Schelling (ÖVP) refused to inject further taxpayer money into the former Carinthian regional state bank. As a consequence of this bold move, in March 2015, Austria's Financial Market Authority (*Finanzmarktaufsicht*) imposed a moratorium on debt repayments by Heta Asset Resolution, the "bad bank" set up to wind down Hypo Alpe Adria's remaining assets. This decision by the Austrian authorities was a hard blow for the reputation of Austria's capital market, not least because some ten billion euros in Hypo debts have been guaranteed by the province of Carinthia. The imposition of the debt moratorium resulted in a loss of confidence in Austria as an international borrower. In German news reports, Austria was placed on

2 See European Central Bank, Banking Structures Report, October 2014, 9.

the same level as Greece. The Berlin daily *Die Welt* raised the question if Austria would turn into the "Greece of the Alps" and the *Süddeutsche Zeitung* featured the headline "Almost like Greece."[3] In any event, German and other international investors turned their back on the Austrian capital market, theretofore regarded as a safe haven for capital investments, in large numbers.

The "eventful history" of Vienna as a financial center, formidably portrayed by Resch and Stiefel in CAS 20, goes on. The Austrian banking industry is in a phase of economic disintegration at the moment. In late 2015, it became known that UniCredit, the Italian parent company of Bank Austria, plans to drastically restructure its retail business in Austria. Bank Austria announced the closing of eighty out of two hundred retail branches in Austria by 2018, reducing overall costs by around three hundred million euros. In addition, the UniCredit group's Central and Eastern European operations, which have been run by Bank Austria from its Vienna headquarters since 2006, will be moved to Milan. The decision to relocate Bank Austria's profitable Eastern European business away from Vienna constitutes a setback for the Austrian capital as a financial hub for Central, Eastern, and South-Eastern Europe.

Austria—the New Sick Man of Europe?

The Austrian economy has been weak ever since the global economic and financial crisis of 2008–09. Austria is losing ground as a business location. On the basis of various rankings and indicators that measure competitiveness, the country has performed poorly over the last few years. For instance, in the Global Competitiveness Index (GCI) of the World Economic Forum, Austria ranks in only twenty-third place among 140 countries. In 2012 and 2013, it had been sixteenth. In the international business site ranking of the renowned Institute for Management Development (IMD), Austria dropped from eleventh in 2007 to twenty-sixth in 2015 among sixty-one countries. The rapidity of Austria's economic decline is considered alarming by economists.[4] Christoph Leitl, President of the Austrian Federal Economic Chamber (*Wirtschaftskammer*) and one of the loudest voices criticizing the economic direction the country has taken, used the Austrian idiom "*absandeln*," which carries a decidedly negative connotation, in describing the poor development of the Austrian business location.

---

3 See Sebastian Jost, "Wird Österreich zum Griechenland der Alpen?," *Die Welt*, 10 April 2015; and "Fast wie die Griechen," *Süddeutsche Zeitung*, 13 March 2015.

4 Matthias Auer, "Das Schiff sinkt langsam, aber es sinkt," *Die Presse*, 28 May 2015, 13.

Due to its vibrant economy compared to most of Europe, Austria was labeled "the better Germany" in a *Stern* magazine article ten years ago. The splendor of past times has long since faded. For years, Austria had had the lowest unemployment rate in the EU. Now it's only fifth after Germany, the Czech Republic, Malta, and Great Britain. According to a recent study by the Vienna University of Economics and Business, the Austrian economy suffers from "a toxic mix of lacking reforms, high taxes, and weak productivity growth."[5] There is a fatal lack of leadership among the political elites. The current refugee crisis, the fifth wave of migration that adds an important chapter to Rainer Münz's essay in CAS Volume 20 on the history of migration from and to Austria, unveils the government's helplessness.

Austria is governed by an uninspired grand coalition government which, in truth, is not so grand anymore that restricts itself to the administration of the status quo. Short-term party political motives and the preservation of power largely dominate over the implementation of a future-oriented reform agenda. The SPÖ-ÖVP government did not make any progress with launching the structural reforms necessary for Austria to get back on the right path. With the economy, it seems, in long-term decline, Austria's political and economic impact in the world is likely to decrease in the years to come.

Select Bibliography

Austrian Federal Economic Chamber/Economic Policy Department. *Monitoring Report 2015: Austria in International Rankings*. Vienna: WKO, 2015.

Bischof, Günter, and Anton Pelinka, eds. *The Americanization/Westernization of Austria* (Contemporary Austrian Studies 12). New Brunswick, NJ: Transaction, 2004.

------- and Karlhofer, Ferdinand, eds. *Austria's International Position after the End of the Cold War* (Contemporary Austrian Studies 22). New Orleans/Innsbruck: University of New Orleans Press/ *innsbruck* university press, 2013.

Keuschnigg, Christian. *Standpunkte zur österreichischen Wirtschaftspolitik*. Vienna: Passagen Verlag, 2015.

Seidel, Hans. *Österreichs Wirtschaft und Wirtschaftspolitik nach dem Zweiten Weltkrieg*. Vienna: Manz, 2005.

Zotter, Christoph. *Österreich international: Die Bedeutung unseres Landes weltweit* (Reihe 1x1 der Politik 8). Vienna: Holzhausen, 2011.

5 See ORF <wien.orf.at/news/stories/2738101/> (21 Oct. 2015).

Eugenie Schwarzwald (1878–1940).
Berlin, Atelier Becker & Maas ca. 1920
Credit: Austrian National Library

Volume 21: Günter Bischof/Fritz Plasser/Eva Maltschnig, eds. *Austrian Lives*. New Orleans/Innsbruck: University of New Orleans Press/*innsbruck* university press, 2012

Biographical Contributions to Austrian Intellectual, Cultural and Political History[1]

Bernhard Fetz

The English novelist and politician Benjamin Disraeli recommended the following intellectual diet: "Rise early and regularly and read for three hours. ... Read no history, nothing but biography, for that is life without theory."[2] This citation suggests, like many others, the ambiguous character of biographical writings situated between scholarly study and the arts. It also suggests what is so fascinating about this genre of writing: both its abiding impact on many fields and its changing definition between various disciplines. Biography carries different meanings for sociologists, literary scholars, historians, philosophers, or anthropologists, depending on their respective methodological approaches and the inherent self-conception of the discipline. Ideal types of life trajectories derived from quantitative and qualitative surveys may be considered biographies just like literary lives. For philosophers, the issue of constructing the subject is the central question; for historians, how outstanding personalities have contributed to political and social developments, or whether this very focus on "great men"[3] is in dire need of correction. The philosopher Wilhelm Dilthey's contributions to biographical and autobiographical studies have greatly fertilized discourses on the subject matter; for him "great men" are worthy of biographical engagement because they are usually in the position of defining "the center."[4] Carlyle's and Dilthey's approach have been much improved on in recent biographical studies. In these days both "important" men (and more recently also women) as well as "common people" are worthy biographical

1 The text has been translated from German into English by Günter Bischof.

2 On the theory of biography, see Bernhard Fetz, "Die vielen Leben der Biographie. Interdisziplinäre Aspekte einer Theorie der Biographie," in *Die Biographie – Zur Grundlegung ihrer Theorie*, ed. Bernhard Fetz (Berlin: Walter de Gruyter, 2009), 3–66.

3 Thomas Carlyle, *On Heroes, Hero-Worship and the Heroic in History* (London, [1840]/1887), 43.

4 Wilhelm Dilthey, *Der Aufbau der geschichtlichen Welt in den Geisteswissenschaften* (Frankfurt am Main: Suhrkamp, 1981), 305 ff (here 309).

"subjects" and "objects," as are animals, cities[5] and even the titles of songs.[6] "Biography" today is not only the record of the distilled summary of a lived life, but exists in many different media formats. In fact, biography is in direct relationship to the history of media; it is fair to say that photography changed the genre at least as much as did the theory of biography. The same can be said about film and video recording. The possibility to record and conserve the human voice promised at least as compelling a re-bonding with lives lived in the past as did the portraiture of faces, gestures, and physiognomies in photography and film. Today's "social media," however, have changed the status of biography entirely. We have not developed yet a proper theory to fully understand the impact of these (auto)biographical representations on the Internet.

Volume 21 of *Contemporary Austrian Studies* mirrored a broad spectrum of biographical writing. *Austrian Lives* represented "political lives," "lives of the mind," "common lives," next to ordinary lives seen through the mirror of photography (i.e. "the photographic gaze"), and lives represented through "attitudinal" social science surveys. Taken together, the Volume presented a full spectrum of historically important "personalities" and biographical approaches, opening alternative gazes into Austria's history of the past 100 years. Looking back on the finished product of *Austrian Lives*, and on the biographies produced since the completion of the Volume, one cannot help but note that the "great man" approach is still dominant. Apart from Deborah Holmes' chapter on Eugenie Schwarzwald, the prominent educator, social reformer, and organizer of a Vienna salon, women were not present as historical subjects and/or artists.[7] Since then, Daniela Strigl has added a noteworthy biography of Marie von Ebner-Eschenbach, the great Austrian writer and pacifist.[8] Even the victims and perpetrators of the twentieth century history of violence historians are interested in, are usually men. The informative chapters on prisoners of war and war criminals during World War II, or the military personnel of the k.k. Army in World War I, are all focused on men. Women are clearly underrepresented in CAS 21. The individual chapters on Bruno Kreisky, Otto Bauer, and Ignaz Seipel, as well as the ones on Viktor Frankl, Wolfgang Kraus, and Günther Anders are dedicated to central figures of Austrian political and intellectual history.

5 Christopher Hibbert, *Florence: Biography of a City* (London: Penguin, 2004). Hibbert also wrote biographies of London and Rome.

6 A good example is the book of the American critics of popular music Greil Marcus, see *Like A Rolling Stone: Bob Dylan at the Crossroads* (New York: Public Affairs Press, 2005).

7 The chapter was based on Holmes full-fledged biography, see Deborah Holmes, *Langeweile ist Gift: Das Leben der Eugenie Schwarzwald* (St. Pölten: Residenz Verlag, 2012).

8 Daniela Strigl, *Berühmt sein ist nichts. Marie von Ebner-Eschenbach. Eine Biographie* (Salzburg: Residenz Verlag, 2016).

They reflect the broad spectrum of biographical research on "Austrian lives," yet they confirm the adage, "it's a man's world," when it comes to biographical representation.

Recent Biographical Studies on Austrian Cultural and Intellectual History

"Great men" are still dominating the biographical genre, as the following short survey of recent biographies demonstrates.[9] Biographers have focused on the lives of artists, namely Thomas Bernhard, Hugo von Hofmannsthal, Stefan Zweig—all leading luminaries of twentieth century Austrian literary life. The life of prominent *fin-de-siècle* Christian Social mayor of Vienna, Karl Lueger, has also attracted a major biography. The methodological approaches in recounting these lives could not have been more different. The exceptions, as suggested above, have been Deborah Holmes' biography of Eugenie Schwarzwald and Daniela Strigl's biography of the aristocrat Marie von Ebner-Eschenbach, whose writings concentrated on farmworkers and artisans and all aspects of modernization. Ebner-Eschenbach is of great interest as a writer because of her focus on the labor and social history of the late Habsburg Monarchy.

The biographies on Schwarzwald, Bernhard, and Hofmannsthal are the product of the Vienna-based Ludwig-Boltzmann Institute for the History and Theory of Biography. This is one of the few research centers in the German-speaking world that has been concentrating in great depth on the history and theory of biography. This center explicitly aims at developing new innovative models and templates for biographical production, next to writing "conventional" book-length biographies. It has produced biographical exhibitions, a multi-media DVD on the iconic poet Ernst Jandl, and biographies on the Internet. The Internet portal on the prolific Viennese writer and critic Karl Kraus is an example of the latter. It portrays the multiple personae of the writer Kraus based on his central role in the literary life of the Austrian capital: "the reader," "the legal subject," and "the editor." The online biography is based on thousands of documents from his personal papers, including audio tracks and visual records.[10]

---

9 In this short essay is impossible to present a full-fledged survey of the proliferating international biographical production. Instead, I will comment on recent biographies that either deal with Austrian subjects or are interesting from the methodological perspective.

10 See Ludwig Boltzmann Institut für Geschichte und Theorie der Biografie <http://gtb.lbg.ac.at/> (18 Feb. 2016), and Katharina Prager, "Karl Kraus Online," in *Wienbibliothek im Rathaus/Ludwig Boltzmann Institut für Geschichte und Theorie der Biografie*, 2015 <www.kraus.wienbibliothek.at> (18 Feb. 2016).

Traditional biographies present a chronological development of someone's life story and reproduce the ideology of a consistent and organic life trajectory, interrupted by personal crises that the subject mastered. *Hugo von Hofmannsthal: Orte* presents an alternative biographical model and focuses on the venues frequented by the Austrian poet Hugo von Hofmannsthal, venues which defined his life.[11] While it is not a collection of edited essays, collective authorship defines this book-biography.

The multiple authors focus on the numerous relationships between the locations Hofmannsthal favored in the course of his life. They are interested in the "mutability" of their biographical "object" and the places that molded him. This is not the straightforward narration of a conventional life trajectory. In the course of his life, Hofmannsthal came into contact with numerous people and movements. The defining "characteristics" of his life were, the collective biographers argue, "to extract his very own nature from the amalgamation of foreign influences and to develop what is new based upon tradition." This creates a challenge to define Hofmannsthal's "very nature and to give his life's story a clear signature."[12] Based on these convictions, the authors decided to tie Hofmannsthal's life to twenty places that shaped him, starting with the classical loci that shape any life such as parental home/family life, schools, namely his high school (the Akademisches Gymnasium) and the University in Vienna; the authors then follow the budding playwright to the world famous court theater, Burgtheater, and the literary café Griensteidl; they pursue him all the way to Switzerland (his "asylum far away yet so close"), and to the summer resort Aussee (the locus of "the poetry of life"), where the emperor and the aristocracy also took holidays. The book tries to do justice to Hofmannsthal's "continuous self-inventions by way of strategically chosen changes of places." This biography, then, "is about feeling out one's own ego, a life lived in full, an individual fully blossoming only in certain situations and places."[13]

The life trajectory of a poet, one would have to assume, is fundamentally different from that of a homo politicus such as Karl Lueger's, who engendered an entirely different biography. The two were contemporaries. In the case of Hofmannsthal's life, the focus is on "the poetry of life" and a rich literary oeuvre that deals with perceptions. The "spirit" of his poetry derives both from his very productive imbibing of a classical education—what the Germans call "*Bildung*"—and the concrete-sensual observance of everyday life.

11 Wilhelm Hemecker and Konrad Heumann, eds., *Hugo von Hofmannsthal: Orte* (Vienna: Paul Zsolnay Verlag, 2014).
12 Ibid., 9.
13 Ibid., 11.

Every biography is full of biographical projections. This is also true for quasi-"objective" biographical forms such as a legal warrant or a court arraignment, or a regular "bio" such as a resumé or curriculum vitae. In the case of the many contributors to the Hofmannsthal biography, the various locations become biographical projections presenting the poet as a sensuous medium of perceptions. Whereas in the case of another famous author of Viennese modernism in the beginning of the twentieth century, the logic is a template for literally disrobing the subject; the publisher calls Ulrich Weinzierl's biographical treatise of Stefan Zweig an "intimate character portrait." Zweig probably is the most popular Austrian author who is still perused around the world. The blurb on the back cover of the book even calls Stefan Zweig "the foremost European in German literature."[14] If we consider Zweig as the foremost proponent of the "European idea," this is a correct assessment. Zweig's devotion to "the idea of Europe" was embedded out of necessity in his global citizenship (Weltbürgertum) and was a reaction to the catastrophe of World War I, when Europeans sadly eviscerated themselves. In 1942, together with his second wife Charlotte Altmann, Zweig committed suicide in his Brazilian exile. In his famous memoirs *Die Welt von Gestern* (*The World of Yesteryear*), Zweig's initially ambiguous stance on the "Great War" and his work for the Viennese War- and Press Headquarters, which generated the k.u.k. war propaganda, appears in a more opaque light retrospectively. There can be no doubt, however, that Zweig became a pacifist in late 1917 and turned towards the promotion of European mutual understanding. Zweig's first wife has shaped our image of Zweig as a suffering European and great moralist and, in fact, created the prototype of the intellectual conscience of Europe.

Yet Weinzierl's book also presents another Zweig persona: a bourgeois man driven by his sexual obsessions, whose easy successes with both women and men were pervasive. The "burning secret" of Zweig's life, according to Weinzierl, was his exhibitionism, which he habitually practiced in public places such as Vienna's parks. This sex drive almost doomed Zweig. The sensitive reader surely will ask: what biographical truth lies in such a "burning secret"? Will a minute reconstruction of Zweig's sexual appetites help us better understand his personae? The three individual chapters of Weinzierl's biography separate his life into "Scenes from a Marriage," his complex relationship with his first wife, the divorcée Friderike Winternitz; "Disorientation of Feelings," an allusion to one of his best novellas dealing with his homoerotic feelings; and finally the chapter "Burning Secret"

14 Ulrich Weinzierl, *Stefan Zweigs brennendes Geheimnis* (Vienna: Paul Zsolnay Verlag, 2015).

unveils Weinzierl's persuasive case of "Zweig the exhibitionist" based on many references from his rich diaries and letters. Weinzierl anticipates and meets the possible charge of his critics head on, namely that he is engaging in a "peeping Tom" perspective. Towards the end of the book, he refers to Zweig's essay on Casanova, one of the subjects of the great writer's many biographical studies. Zweig concludes that Casanova has become immortal since immortality was beyond good and evil, which is to say beyond any ethical or moral judgment. Ulrich Weinzierl relates this character trait back to the author of the biographical essay in order to validate Zweig's oeuvre beyond the author's questionable moral standards: "For this very reason, too, we still read Stefan Zweig today; all over the world."[15] Zweig's questionable private demeanor in this case relates not only to his exhibitionism vis-à-vis girls and young women, but also a total lack of being conscious of what is wrong when it comes to sexual exploitation, which is to say sexual contact with minors. Ulrich Weinzierl pursued no lesser goal than dismantling a literary saint. His major biographical essay nicely illustrates the juxtaposition between an individual and its personae. He hereby shows the strength of biographical writing over purely scholarly representations, on the one hand, and purely literary approaches on the other hand.

Concentrating on the body, its ailments and sexual mores, is not a privilege reserved for writing the lives of artists. Joachim Radkau's book of the iconic sociologist Max Weber is one of the most ambitious, expansive, and critically acclaimed biographies of a scholarly life in recent years. In this biography, the analysis of Weber's scholarly oeuvre, the impact and legacy of his work, and his (dys)functioning body are all related to each other.[16] Radkau reconstructs in minute detail Weber's impotence, his incurable insomnia and anxieties, all based on the deep immersion in the enormous collection of Weber's personal papers. Radkau was also criticized for aligning Weber's sexual and scholarly productivity, considering that he devotes 100 pages to his impotence, but only thirty pages each to his principal scholarly contributions, "The Protestant Ethic and the Spirit of Capitalism" (1904/5), and "Economy and Society" (1915).[17] Observers may differ about the utility of such prioritizations, yet we might agree that including the "scandalizing" gaze of the human body signals unmistakable progress in recent scholarly biographical writings. A human life can summarily be reconstructed only with the interplay of gazing at the individual body, the educational and professional lives that rarely are linear, as well as the inclusion of institutional, political, and social contexts.

15 Ibid., 227.

16 Joachim Radkau, *Max Weber: Die Leidenschaft des Denkens* (Munich: Carl Hanser Verlag, 2005).

17 See Gustav Seibt's review in the *Süddeutsche Zeitung*, 10 Dec. 2005.

Biographical production also mirrors a full spectrum of different methodological approaches. We have on the one hand Ulrich Weinzierl's Zweig essay, and on the other hand John Boyer's voluminous biography of Karl Lueger.[18] Boyer concentrates on an almost endless number of dry details—especially for those of us who are not historians. Beginning in the mid-nineteenth century, the Chicago-based historian narrates the prehistory of the Christian Social Party and its breakdown into many different political groupings (the subject of two previous books by the author). This approach is dramatically different from the artist-biographies mentioned above. In this account, Lueger-the-private-person almost falls by the wayside. Boyer ventures a general assessment for the first time on page 75: "Wealth had no meaning for him. His only goal was the professional exercise of political power."[19] To map out the long path to political power by way of party formations and social stratification, Boyer devotes an extensive microanalysis to the radicalization and demise of the Viennese artisans' movement. Boyer devotes only a few poignant sentences to covering Lueger's public persona, his success as a tribune of the masses: "Lueger was not the first politician in Vienna who exhausted the explosiveness of an exaggerated political rhetoric full of hyperbole. What made him so wildly successful was his brilliance in reducing complex problems in the public arena to a basic comprehensible level. Such simplicity quickened the public-political imagination of his voters, most of whom approached the world full of anger."[20] Boyer's ascetic biographical approach when it comes to the analysis and interpretation of Lueger the private man is governed by the ethos of the historian steeped in the archives. His heuristic interest, then, is different from Radkau's Max Weber biography, whose important lecture "Politik als Beruf" (politics as a calling) serves Boyer to deliver the subtitle and the thesis of his biography "Christlichsoziale Politik as Beruf" (Christian Social politics as a calling). Boyer is mainly interested in Lueger's political persona, not his physical persona. Lueger's individual traits, such as his ability to assert himself and his relentless will to power, are contextualized both in the higher k.u.k. administrative apparatus and in the social and political movements in turn-of-the-century Vienna. Interestingly, the subtext of Boyer's characterization of Lueger's rhetorical skills and his impact on inhomogeneous audiences serves as an analysis of contemporary populist politics. Boyer concludes his book with a citation from the contemporary author Felix Salten, who characterized Lueger as a

18 John W. Boyer, *Karl Lueger (1844–1910): Christlichsoziale Politik als Beruf* (= Studien zu Politik und Verwaltung, vol. 93) (Vienna: Böhlau Verlag, 2010).
19 Ibid., 75.
20 Ibid., 92.

monarchical figure who ruled over "an army of servants, workers, officials, teachers, doctors and professors."[21] This characterization squares well with the public image of Lueger's powers of integration, namely his political skills in shaping a homogenous political movement out of a great variety of political interests. In his 1926 text "Remembering Lueger," Salten hones his earlier assessment by devoting more attention to the populist: "The ideals of Vienna's petit bourgeoisie became his ideals, their personal comforts were his. [...] He sat next to them, the small people, he was one of them, out of their midst he looked for the most talented, promoted them to serve as his chiefs of staff and could have cared less whether they were educated. The less education they had, the more he appreciated them. All they needed to bring to the table was a keen intelligence and a big mouth. When he mingled with the petit bourgeois and the people from the outer districts, he became one of them; then he repudiated the rest of mankind, ranted and railed against those who were not part of them, namely the professors and physicians, the scholars and intellectuals. Nothing else seemed to exist, nobody was worth their existence but the petit bourgeois and the denizens of the outer districts, and they kept their faith in him."[22]

The biographical imagination of the feuilleton-writer impresses with its clear vision of the man; he situates Lueger's notorious anti-Semitic populism in the grey areas between the public and private personae. This is the decisive advantage of the biographical imagination vis-à-vis the matter-of-fact historian. It sharpens the details beyond the over-determination of historical source material and out of the respective contemporary contexts suggests what biographers call "habitus," "personality," or "character," without ever fully catching its meaning.

Deborah Holmes' biography of Eugenie Schwarzwald sits between straightforward biography and a life of the times. Unlike male biographers, she addresses the problem of imagining a person no longer alive early in her introduction. In the case of Eugenie Schwarzwald the problem begins with how to address her biographical subject properly. During her lifetime, Schwarzwald "was known under many different names."[23] Given her graduation as the first female PhD in German Studies from the University of Zurich, addressing her as "Fraudoktor" became proverbial. The familiar "Du" became common for her many acquaintances, friends and pupils at the legendary Schwarzwald-Schools. She was "Genka" to her husband, and

21 Ibid., 456, referencing Felix Salten, *Das österreichische Antlitz* (Berlin: S. Fischer Verlag, 1909), 137f.

22 Felix Salten, "Erinnerung an Lueger," *Neue Freie Presse*, 19 Sep. 1926.

23 Holmes, *Schwarzwald*, 7.

"Genia" to her admirers. The Nazis, who forced her to emigrate, renamed her "Eugenie Sara Schwarzwald." The biographer concludes: "Whatever name one ends up choosing for her does not make it easier in maintaining a professional distance from Eugenie Schwarzwald. Her overpowering personality and her nigh-unceasing energy produced frequently severe responses from her contemporaries."[24]

To a certain extent, the biographies of Eugenie Schwarzwald and Karl Lueger complement each other. They can be compared in their biographical approaches and in their historical complementarity of two crucial figures for Viennese and Austrian history, who were yet so different. Her "unceasing energy" was directed towards her many projects, above all her schools. Lueger's ambition pursued first and foremost acquiring and maintaining political power. He found a way to instrumentalize both the legal norms of the Habsburg state and the specific conditions of Vienna towards attaining his ambition. Schwarzwald labored very hard over many years establishing a high school for girls equal to the boys' *Gymnasium*. This ambition put her into a perpetual clinch with the authorities, not only the school boards of Vienna and Lower Austria, but also the Education Ministry.[25] By the eve of World War I, she had succeeded in implementing her school, largely due to her tenacity and her ruses in dealing with the complex state bureaucracy. In her work, she was second to none in establishing in Austria equal access to schooling for boys and girls. Deborah Holmes, however, does not hero-worship her subject, but ventures into analyzing into the darker sides of the reform movements in the 1910s as well: "Unconsciously and under the guise of internationalism, the reform movement—and Schwarzwald was part of it—had contributed to preparations for war."[26] The chapter on World War I is a highlight of this important biography. In approaching their subjects so differently, we can learn a great deal from a synoptic reading of the biographies of the historian Boyer, the literary scholar Holmes, and the journalist Weinzierl—in seeing these lives together we learn to understand an era from different perspectives. Their overlapping and crosscurrents produce that rich picture of an era that complements the historical, structural, social, and mental studies.

In the end, we want to look at a biography that deals with the core elements of Austrian post-World War II history. It raises controversial topics, such as Austrian repression and amnesia of Austrians' involvement

24 Ibid., 7f.
25 Ibid., 120.
26 Ibid., 173.

with National Socialism during World War II, the legacies of National Socialist ideas and structures in the Second Austrian Republic, and the continued authoritarianism in Austrian rural society. Manfred Mittermayer's biography of the writer Thomas Bernhard had also been developed as part of the Ludwig Boltzmann Institute for the History and Theory of Biography. While he lived, people hated Bernhard passionately, but since his death the prolific author has enjoyed cult status.[27] The premier of the play *Heldenplatz* (the central Viennese "heroes square"), commissioned for the "year of memory" in 1988 by Claus Peymann, then the director of the Burgtheater, turned into a scandalous event elevating its author to the status of protagonist in contemporary history. The play became much more than a mere literary text; it became the centerpiece of Austria's struggle with mastering its World War II past. Ever since the controversial World War II veteran Kurt Waldheim became a candidate for the presidency in 1986, Austria's most recognizable writers, such as Elfriede Jelinek, the later Nobel Prize winner in literature, Thomas Bernhard, Doron Rabinovici, Christoph Ransmayr, Peter Henisch, Elisabeth Reichart, and Josef Haslinger, made dealing with the past the focal point of Austrian literature in the 1980s and 1990s. Mittermayer's biography recounts the *Heldenplatz* scandal in minute detail, along with all the other controversies swirling around Bernhard's persona and oeuvre. The biographer's claim is to collect all the crucial facts in the life of Bernhard. Yet every reader of Bernhard's (auto)biography knows that these very facts touch on many of the central and controversial topics of Austrian contemporary history. Additionally, the biographer also aims at explaining how out of very difficult life circumstances a literary oeuvre grew that is now considered part of world literature.[28]

Raimund Fellinger, who served as Thomas Bernhard's long-time editor and today is the chief editor of the Suhrkamp publishing house, tore the book apart in a highly polemical review. He charges that the biographer failed to produce new insights into the famous author's life story. Worse, he reproached the biographer for hiding behind the larger-than-life figure of Bernhard by recounting only factual information without analysis and providing his own judgments for the reader.[29] Fellinger's is an unfair hatchet job with a hidden agenda. Mittermayr's biography provides "the facts" of Bernhard's life for a broad public; he does so in scrupulously detailed fashion within the context of the author's life and times. Fellinger,

27 Manfred Mittermayer, *Thomas Bernhard: Eine Biografie* (Vienna: Residenz Verlag, 2015).

28 Ibid., 9f.

29 Raimund Fellinger, "Ungenierte Tertiärbiografie," *Volltext: Zeitschrift für Literatur*, no. 4 (2015): 30f.

however, touches on the Achilles heel of all biographical work: what is the relationship between facts and the narrative style, expounded upon in a rich discourse ever since Hayden White's path-breaking theories? Furthermore, how far must the biographer go to approximate the "biographical truth"? This is the place where the body comes into play once again. Manfred Mittermayer refused to reference in his book Alfred Pfabigan's Bernhard biography, which was driven by the thesis that all of Bernhard's writing revolved around his homosexuality.[30] The book alludes to this persona but does not further delve into it.[31] It seems that the biographers simply could not agree on the role Bernhard's homosexuality played in his writings.

We may conclude that the work of biographers has become a central factor in locating the distinctiveness of Austrian contemporary and intellectual history. Intellectual discourses in Austria are richer than people living outside of the country are wont to admit. Moreover, political processes are closely related to the "human factor." This is not only visible in the leading figures who make history, but also in the anonymous "common lives." The chapters in Volume 21 of *Contemporary Austrian Studies* continue to be timely, both content-wise and methodologically.

Select Bibliography

Dausien, Bettina. *Sozialisation – Geschlecht – Biographie: Theoretische und methodologische Untersuchungen eines Zusammenhangs.* Wiesbaden: Verlag für Sozialwissenschaften, 2011.

Fetz, Bernhard, ed. *Die Biographie – Zur Grundlegung ihrer Theorie.* Berlin: Walter de Gruyter, 2009.

----, and Wilhelm Hemecker, eds. *Theorie der Biographie: Grundlagentexte und Kommentar.* Berlin: Walter de Gruyter, 2011 [English version to be published].

----, and Hannes Schweiger, eds. *Spiegel und Maske: Konstruktionen biographischer Wahrheit* (Profile, vol. 13). Vienna: Paul Zsolnay Verlag, 2006.

Hemecker, Wilhelm, ed. *Die Biographie – Beiträge zu ihrer Geschichte.* Berlin: Walter de Gruyter, 2009.

Klein, Christian, ed. *Handbuch Biographie.* Stuttgart: Verlag J.B.Metzler,

30 Alfred Pfabigan, *Thomas Bernhard: Ein österreichisches Weltexperiment* (Vienna: Zsolnay Verlag, 1999).

31 Mittermayer mentions the fact that Bernhard did an apprenticeship in the store of the homosexual Salzburg merchant Podlaha, see Mittermayer, *Bernhard*, 69.

2009.

Unseld, Melanie, and Christian von Zimmermann, eds. *Anekdote – Biographie – Kanon: Zur Geschichtsschreibung in den schönen Künsten.* Cologne: Böhlau Verlag, 2013.

Zimmermann, Christian von. *Biographische Anthropologie: Menschenbilder in lebensgeschichtlicher Darstellung (1830–1940)* (Quellen und Forschungen zur Literatur- und Kulturgeschichte 41). Berlin: Walter de Gruyter, 2006.

Zimmermann, Nina von, and Christian von Zimmermann, eds. *Frauenbiographik: Lebensbeschreibungen und Porträts* (Mannheimer Beiträge zur Sprach- und Literaturwissenschaft, vol. 63). Tübingen: Narr, 2005.

Fall of the Iron Curtain.
Austrian Minister of Foreign Affairs Alois Mock and his Hungarian colleague cutting the Iron Curtain at the Austrian-Hungarian Border.
Robert Jäger, 06 27 1989
Credit: APA PictureDesk

Volume 22: Günter Bischof/Ferdinand Karlhofer. *Austria's International Position after the End of the Cold War.* New Orleans/Innsbruck: University of New Orleans Press/*innsbruck* university press, 2013

The State of Austrian Foreign and Security Policy in Times of Geopolitical Change

Emil Brix

Twenty years after the end of the Cold War, Stanford University and the University of Vienna convened a conference about Austria's international position after the end of the Cold War. The conference papers were then published (with additional essays by Ursula Plassnik, Andreas Resch, and the author of this essay) in 2013 as Volume 22 of *Contemporary Austrian Studies* to present the state of Austrian foreign and security policy a quarter century after the seminal changes of 1989. At the time of publication, the picture of the post-Cold War world order seemed to be quite unambiguous and for analysts the only still-open intellectual question was the famous question from 1989 whether the world was now moving towards Francis Fukuyama's "end of history" or towards Samuel Huntington's "clash of civilizations." The last few years have shown that both these paths are not only possible but have been happening concurrently.

We have experienced developments towards a more liberal—in essence unified—world in places like Myanmar, Cuba or Iran. But we have also seen the rise of a radical Islamic state-like entity, an old-school military conflict in the Ukraine and the illegal annexation of the Crimea and Sevastopol by an assertive Russia, new Cold War rhetoric between the US and Russia, and a strengthening of right-wing populism in quite a few of the European countries. In fact, the European theater has become highly contested again. Election wins for left-wing protest parties in Southern Europe are in stark contrast to gains for EU-skeptic, nationalistic parties in countries as diverse as the UK, France, Austria, Sweden, Poland, Hungary, and others. The UK tries to negotiate for less EU-integration. The Greek financial crisis questions the ability of the common currency zone to cope with economic diversity. At the same time, the European welfare states have to cope with an unexpected surge of refugees and other migrants from the conflict areas in the Middle East and in Afghanistan, which adds to the discussion of burden sharing and solidarity within the EU, as well as to the already difficult issue of relations with Turkey. You may add to this mix the consequences of the Arab Spring for countries such as Syria, Yemen, Egypt, or Libya, and the volatility of world economy due to the rapid decline of prices for energy, and a less clear picture for the future development of the economy in China, to understand that the speed of geopolitical change has definitely increased during the last few years. What are the consequences of these developments for the Austrian foreign and security policy?

In my opinion, one can still agree with the confident criticism Ursula Plassnik formulated in her essay in 2013 against the position of the historian Michael Gehler who had claimed that "the autonomy and independence of Austrian foreign politics, within the EU framework, is a thing of the past."[1] The practical options for a distinct Austrian profile within the EU and worldwide have actually increased. But is her overall assessment from only two years ago still adequate that "during the last twenty-five years, Austrian politicians and diplomats, together with their European partners, had the truly unique privilege to write the script by which we want to live. Step by step, this process has made Austria freer, more committed to solidarity and more self-confident"? Do we really have "the privilege to write the script by which we want to live"?

When assessing Austria's international position since the end of the Cold War one has to take into account a series of major paradigm shifts in the international arena as well as in Austria itself. Since 1989 it has become obvious that the post-Cold War era is a long transitional period with no clear geopolitical balance of power. The unilateral dominance of the United States is challenged by the economic prowess of China and the renewed political and military assertiveness of Russia. The European integration project moved from enlargement euphoria to crisis management. Islamist ideologies feed international terrorism. Today it is anyone's guess what the role of old and new superpowers, of supranational integration processes, the fragmentation of foreign policy actors and the rise of fundamentalist ideologies, will be.

European and global consequences of a more fragmented world order with a growing number of non-state actors did not fundamentally change Austrian foreign and security priorities, which are still based on the consequences of the end of the "Iron Curtain" in 1989 and on becoming a member state of the EU in 1995. Both developments worked in favor of a strong position of Austria

1 Ursula Plassnik, "On the Road to a Modern Identity: Austrian Foreign Policy from the Cold War to the European Union," in CAS 22, 56, cites Michael Gehler, Österreichs *Außenpolitik der Zweiten Republik: Von der alliierten Besatzung bis zum Europa des 21. Jahrhunderts* (Innsbruck: StudienVerlag, 2005), 1021.

in Central Europe and increased Austria's potential to formulate its national interest within Europe. The transfer of parts of state sovereignty to the EU level was compensated by chances to influence the European integration process and EU policies, to profit from the European Single Market, and to contribute to the Common Foreign and Security Policy (CFSP). Priorities had to be adapted accordingly, but there have remained obvious continuities until today. These continuities include an active neighborhood policy, a strong commitment to help stabilize the Western Balkans, to foster cultural dialogue, to strengthen the authority of international law, a commitment to protect human rights and to support multilateral diplomacy (UN, OSCE), including international peacekeeping missions, and an active neutrality policy. Most of these core elements of present day Austrian foreign and security policy are typical priorities of smaller countries. Only the continued interest in active neutrality, the strong interest in the future of the Balkan countries, and the objective to foster the dialogue between cultures and religions makes the Austrian case special. Are these priorities still good enough "unique selling propositions" for Austria?

An Active Neutrality Policy

In 2013, Günter Bischof wrote in the preface to Volume 22 of *Contemporary Austrian Studies*: "The country lost its exposed Cold War geopolitical location on the margins of Western Europe along the Iron Curtain. Austria moved back into its central location in Europe and rebuilt her long-standing traditional relations with neighbors to the East and South. Austria joined the European Union in 1995 and thus further 'Westernized.' Its policy of neutrality—so central to its foreign policy during the Cold War—largely eroded during the past quarter century, even though *pro forma* and reasons of identity, the country holds on to its neutral position. Austria failed to join NATO and gained the reputation of a 'security free rider.'" Similar critical statements about the security side of Austrian foreign policy all refer to the fact that Austria belongs to the small group of neutral countries in the European Union that did not join NATO, and where state expenditure for defense is neither popular nor great. In the Austrian case, "neutrality" was a successful child of the "Cold War," which lost much of its meaning (and substance) after the end of the ideological East-West confrontation and with Austria joining the EU. But it is interesting to note that the Austrian version of this concept is flexible enough not only to be seen as a positive form of identification and security element in a Cold War scenario, but also for times of a much more fragmented world order. Austria can and does offer valuable resources as a widely respected place for dialogue (cf. OSCE secretariat in Vienna, recent Iran and Syrian talks in Vienna) and as a country with excellent human resources for international mediation and diplomacy (cf. Austrian diplomats in international functions in Bosnia-Herzegovina and in Ukraine). It forms an essential part of its new national Security Strategy of 2013 that Austria also promises a continued strong participation in foreign deployments for peacekeeping and crisis management operations of the United Nations and also EU, NATO and OSCE. Since 1960, more than 80,000 Austrians have served in international operations. The sudden withdrawal of Austrian UN-Peacekeepers (UNDOF) from the Golan Heights in 2013 because of the civil war in Syria created some doubts about Austria's sustained commitment to international missions, but it was generally correctly interpreted as an exception to the rule of an active Austrian engagement caused by domestic policy.

In the essay of Erwin Schmidl in Volume 22 of *Contemporary Austrian Studies* one can find the laconic comment, "The social acceptance of the military in Austria is not very high." In principle this is still very true, although some recent developments have helped to increase the standing of the military in Austrian public opinion. The principle of obligatory national service was approved by a large majority in a (consultative) referendum in 2013. Because of security concerns of the public in the eastern provinces of Austria, the military controlled the borders ("*Grenzraumüberwachung*") to the former Warsaw Pact countries from 1990 to 2011(!). And since the beginning of the arrival of large numbers of Syrian and Afghan refugees at the Austrian borders towards Hungary and Slovenia in the second half of 2015, Austrian soldiers have been commissioned to secure the border and to help managing the influx and transfer of migrants.

Altogether the flexible Austrian interpretation of neutrality seems to serve a purpose again. In times of fundamental geopolitical changes, it may be the best strategy for a smaller European country to stick to proven instruments and objectives. Still most foreign policy analysts believe when the dust settles Austria will have to make decisions in order to secure a respected and reliable position in the international community. In their recently published book about Austria's foreign policy, the retired top diplomats Franz Cede and Christian Prosl underline this challenge by quoting the former Austrian president Rudolf Kirchschläger: "Whoever is without a function in the international community, his existence is permanently in danger." The author of this essay is willing to admit that after 1989 he saw little reason for Austria to stick to an outdated concept of permanent neutrality, which supported the Austrian self-illusion that we are an "island of the blessed," and that he saw some good reasons for showing European solidarity by also joining NATO. But in hindsight, it was the much better option to incrementally adjust and reformulate the principle of neutrality, because we still do not know if and when the dust will settle. As a neutral country, Austria has at the moment more options to fulfill a constructive role for the international community than would be the case as the full member of a military alliance.

A Credible Partner of the Balkan Region

Austria's self-declared role as a "Balkan Activist" (a wording used by Hanspeter Neuhold in his essay in Volume 22 of *Contemporary Austrian Studies)* started in 1989 and the soon following dissolution of Yugoslavia. Since that time, this role has increased with every step of European integration, from Austria's membership in the EU, to the so-called Eastern enlargement of the EU in 2004 and 2007, to Croatia joining the EU in 2013, and to the ongoing accession talks with the countries in the "Western Balkans." Due to Austria's long-standing manifold interests in the Balkans, (historic ties, concerns about political stability in a volatile neighboring region, economic opportunities, migrant populations from the region), Austrian foreign policy has consistently supported the efforts of the international community to end violent conflict and foster political reform and, among EU member states, Austrian foreign policy is the most outspoken supporter of full EU-integration. To stay committed to a foreign policy priority for more than twenty-five years is no mean achievement in times of geopolitical change. In the Balkans, Austria has acquired a distinct reputation as a credible and valuable partner, which is also due to the fact that—among EU partners—Austria enjoys a remarkable reputation for expertise and practical knowledge with regard to the region. Austria's commitment to the European future of the Balkans is the most striking example of a foreign and security priority that serves the national interest, lies in the interest of our partner countries, and provides for a distinctive positive role within the international community.

Soft Power Revisited

When discussing specific Austrian traditions in international relations, one has to mention yet another continuity which has played a central role in positioning Austria since the end of the Second World War and continues to do so. In my essay in Volume 22 of *Contemporary Austrian Studies*, I presented the rationale for this type of foreign and security policy in a small country with big cultural resources. Austrian diplomacy puts great efforts in communicating its culture and heritage internationally. For Austrian public diplomacy cultural cooperation is the main instrument to project internationally the image of a country that can build trust by using its worldwide reputation as a "cultural superpower." Cultural cooperation and cultural relations with foreign publics are seen as crucial for the image and perception of Austria abroad. The thin line which separates narrating your own cultural narrative from outright propaganda has lately become very obvious when terrorist organizations, but also some states, have started to complement their geopolitical ambitions and their international positioning with aggressive and exclusive stories of a cultural or recivilizing mission ("exceptionalism"). Some of these developments come in the disguise of being a reaction to centuries of Western dominance, which might be discredited by its very success: Cultural dominance tends to corrupt and absolute cultural dominance tends to corrupt absolutely. Thus Austria should continue putting its eggs into the basket of "dialogue" between cultures and religions based on its own lessons from history (including the fact that Austria was the first European country which recognized Islam as an official religion in 1912 but also the fact that it took this country almost fifty years to fully accept responsibility for the participation of Austrians in the "Third Reich," and that there are moral consequences for Austria that have followed from this).

In times of geopolitical change, it does not come as a surprise that propaganda and hard power, which try to tell people that the world is best organized in black and white by an unavoidable battle between good guys and bad guys, are back in play. Power struggles are a constant in human history, but it is the task of diplomacy to manage them peacefully. This is the reason why we promote Austria more than ever as a leading venue for international dialogue and as a host country for international organizations. And this is also the reason why active cultural diplomacy is a most valuable asset for our international position. Cultural exchange—when it is promoted but not controlled in its contents by governments—provides access to civil societies and is a chance for high credibility and the creation of trust, which are ever more valuable commodities in international relations. Austria should and shall stick to cultural diplomacy that respects and furthers the two-way-relationship which is pertinent for modern communication.

The Relationship between Domestic and Foreign Policy

There has been a long tradition of bipartisan "grand coalition" foreign and security policy with a quarter century of Foreign Ministers coming from the conservative Austrian People's Party. But the Austrian political system is in a flux. There is a growing frustration with the perceived lack of reform in the substance and structure of the political system, which results in a seemingly constant decrease in the support for the two traditional center parties, a strong increase for the populist right-wing Freedom Party, and a much strengthened influence of civil society. The relevance of these developments became obvious with the so-called EU-sanctions against Austria in 2000, when the Freedom Party joined the government. Also the specifically strong influence of a few Austrian media on politics and politicians results in a concentration on the domestic agenda. All this bears significance for Austrian foreign and security policy because further EU-integration, a liberal migration policy, a good-neighborhood policy, and other core elements of Austria's current foreign policy have become highly contested topics in domestic politics, which can decide the outcome of regional and national elections. The success of the Austrian economy depends heavily on its competitiveness in international markets. The strong and still growing export orientation of the Austrian economy is a further indication of how important the link between domestic and foreign policy has become in times of volatile European and global markets. There are no signs that the significance of how a country manages to interlink domestic and foreign policy interests will decrease. On the contrary, in all imaginable post-Cold War scenarios, this interdependence will further gain momentum. When the Austrian political system is in a flux, the challenges for a national coordination of international policies may even get bigger.

Knowing that the re-naming of state institutions very often follows a party-political logic rather than a change of direction or nature, it is nevertheless significant that the Austrian Foreign Ministry was twice re-named during the last quarter century. In 2007 the official name of the Ministry was changed to "Ministry for European and International Affairs" in order to also symbolically underline that for an EU member European politics ceases to be "foreign affairs." Only seven years later the Ministry was re-named again. Its present name, "Ministry for Europe, Integration and Foreign Affairs," is a consequence of its new additional competence for integration policy, but it signifies at the same time that there is a growing understanding of how much domestic and foreign policy has become interrelated. Foreign policy decisions such as the current EU-sanctions against Russia or the close coordination with Germany about managing the Syrian refugee crisis have immediate effect on domestic policy. And domestic policies such as decisions about the Austrian banking sector and energy infrastructure or about immigration laws directly affect our international standing.

A Realistic View of the Chances and Limits of European Integration

An essay about Austria's present-day foreign and security policy cannot end without a short evaluation of the most important factor for its success or failure: our relationship within the European Union. The geopolitical upturn of 1989 opened for Austria the way towards EU-membership and then (since 1995) full participation in the European integration project. Two thirds of the Austrian population voted in a referendum in 1993 for joining the European Community (EC), later the European Union. EU-membership was indeed vital for necessary structural changes and for opening the minds after decades of "a seemingly protected marginal existence at the intersection of two irreconcilable political rivals, courted by both for its neutrality" (Ursula Plassnik). The economic advantages were and are still visible (including the common currency and free movement in the Schengen area). EU membership meant also less economic dependence on Germany, and it meant a return to the never totally forgotten Central European identity.[2] Austria is by now fully integrated in the intricate decision-making processes on the EU-level. But Austrian foreign policy failed on one truly essential front: in spite of a courageous good neighborhood policy across the Iron Curtain before 1989, we did not manage to become part of an effective Central European regional grouping within the EU. It is in the Austrian national interest that we should sincerely try to make amends.

So far all Austrian governments have agreed that the price to be paid for EU-membership, in the form of reduced national sovereignty, financial contributions to the EU-budget, and common initiatives as well as a re-formulated design of neutrality, is not too high. The further deepening and enlarging of the Union seemed to be only a question of time. But today the European Union is in crisis mode. The euro zone area needs more integrated economic policies and some member countries need a real "transfer union." The Schengen area is threatened by an unsatisfactory response to the Syrian refugee crisis and the lack of solidarity by quite a few of its member countries. In many member countries, EU-skeptical parties are on the

2 See my essay: Emil Brix, "Austria and Central Europe," in CAS 20, 200–211.

rise and the UK, as one of the economically strongest EU-countries, has organized a referendum to decide whether it shall remain within the EU. In some member countries, governments openly demand some redistribution of powers back to the national level. The Common Foreign and Security Policy and even more so the project of a Common Security and Defense Policy still show the EU's limited capacity to act in situations of crisis, as became painfully manifest during the Yugoslav wars and also currently in the Syrian crisis. The Russian Foreign Minister Sergei Lavrov was recently asked whether he was optimistic about the possible success in a specific negotiation process. His answer was that he is not paid to be an optimist. The same holds true for Austrian foreign policy. It is not there to be an optimist about the future of the EU. Only a critical analysis and an open discussion with our twenty-seven partners about perspectives and limits of European integration serve the Austrian national interest best.

Select Bibliography

Beller, Steven. *A Concise History of Austria*. New York: Cambridge University Press, 2006.

Cede, Franz, and Christian Prosl. *Anspruch und Wirklichkeit Österreichs Außenpolitik seit 1945*. Innsbruck: StudienVerlag, 2015.

Gehler, Michael. *Österreichs Außenpolitik der Zweiten Republik: Von der alliierten Besatzung bis zum Europa des 21. Jahrhunderts*. Innsbruck: StudienVerlag, 2005.

------. *Vom Marshall Plan zur EU: Österreich und die europäische Integration von 1945 bis zur Gegenwart*. Innsbruck: StudienVerlag, 2006.

Jandl, Gerhard. "Zur Bedeutung des Balkans für die österreichische Außenpolitik," *Wiener Blätter zur Friedensforschung* 160, no. 3 (2014).

Kramer, Helmut. "Strukturentwicklung der Aussenpolitik (1945–2005)," in *Politik in Österreich: Das Handbuch*, ed. Herbert Dachs et al. Vienna: Manz Verlag, 2006, 807–837.

Luif, Paul, Elisabeth Vyslonzil, and Michael Gehler, eds. *Die Dimension Mitteleuropa in der Europäischen Union: Geschichte und Gegenwart*. Hildesheim: Georg Olms AG, 2015.

Nye, Joseph S. Jr. *Soft Power: The Means to Success in World Politics*. New York: Public Affairs, 2004.

Schmidl, Erwin A. "Wien als internationales Zentrum," in *Wien: Die Metamorphose einer Stadt*, ed. Michael Dippelreiter. Vienna: Böhlau, 2013, 703–730.

First World War.
Austrian Defence Minister Gerald Klug in front of the "Sarajevo-car" at the Heeresgeschichtliches Museum in Vienna. Guided tour with journalists for the Exhibition "The First World War."
Vienna, Herbert Neubauer, 06 27 2014
Credit: APA PictureDesk

Volume 23: Günter Bischof/Ferdinand Karlhofer/Samuel R. Williamson, Jr. *1914: Austria-Hungary, the Origins, and the First Year of World War I.* New Orleans/Innsbruck: University of New Orleans Press/*innsbruck* university press, 2014

The State of World War I Scholarship

Hannes Leidinger

Preconditions

It is not an Austrian peculiarity that the history of World War I has been written since the beginning of the fighting in 1914. In the connection between the outbreak of the Great War and the start of its commemoration, the immediate beginning of commemorative work was not so much initiated by private circles; on the contrary, writing the history of World War I became the responsibility of officials, in particular of the military administration. The consequences for the following decades seem to be manifold. First, the final military campaigns of Austria-Hungary were expected to be historicized exclusively within the scope of former officers and propagandists in the "spirit of 1914." Past elites of the lost empire created an atmosphere of a kind of backward reason of state that prevailed until the 1930s, especially after the Social Democrats were ousted from power and later on from legal existence. The Austrofascist regime promoted a kind of Austrian ideology, a historical engineering that favored pro-Habsburg commemorations, exhibitions, consecrations of memorials as well as celebrations of the "glorious" imperial armed forces and their military operations from 1914 to 1918. These pro-Habsburg interpretations turned into the opposite under National Socialist rule, though the military and even martial aspect of World War I remained the crucial point of expert studies before and after 1938.

A more fundamental caesura marked the end of World War II and Nazi tyranny. The following Allied occupation and the establishment of the Second Austrian Republic resulted in a break with pro-German and martial feelings. Parallel to that, the "era of catastrophe" was wiped out of collective memories on different levels, while Austrian historians outside the sphere of military competence applied new methods and went over a historiography of officers since the 1960s. But contemporary history in Austria from the 1980s onwards was generally employed to overcome the taboo of Austrian guilt during the National Socialist terror. Thus, the role of the Habsburg Empire in the "European catastrophe" at the beginning of the 20th century was doomed to disappear in an "antique shop's dim corner of the forgotten history," according to Manfried Rauchensteiner's opus *Der Tod des Doppeladlers* (*The Death of the Double-Headed Eagle*) about Austria-Hungary in World War I.[1]

The last two decades

In retrospect, Rauchensteiner's book refers to a turning point in Austria's WWI historiography due to the attention paid to the topic since the 1990s. Apart from outline histories of the First World War written by Austrian scholars, specific studies about the Dual Monarchy and some of its regions, as well as the combat zones of the Habsburg army, have been published especially since 2000. For example, the Tyrolean School has done some outstanding scholarly work on the fighting in the Alps. Besides the traditional researches on weapons or single regiments supported by the Museum of Military History in Vienna, the regional scholarly centers have also stressed theoretical and thematic innovations. Hence, members of a special research group dealing with aspects of modernity (*Sonderforschungsbereich Moderne* in Graz) have carried out important work on discourses on the war before and after 1918.

Together with Viennese and international historians, these pressure groups turned to many different matters, such as experiences of Austrian-Hungarian POWs in Russia, the problem of captivity within the boundaries of the Habsburg Empire, studies on causes and consequences of the refugee problem, military justice and deserters, mass executions in Galicia in 1914/15, and the internment of enemy aliens as well as Austrian-Hungarian citizens. Other focal points were studies about the domestic policy, the decisions of elites, the government, the court and the ruling Habsburg dynasty, war economy, works on gender aspects, biographical approaches, and analyses of social, religious and ethnic groups.

Thus, the events from 1914 to 1918 were increasingly examined as a civilian topic in Austria. While some representatives of a traditional military history started to fear that classical themes of battles, strategies, and so forth could be thrust aside completely, other scholars welcomed

1 Manfried Rauchensteiner, *Der Tod des Doppeladlers. Österreich-Ungarn und der Erste Weltkrieg* (Graz: Styria, 1994).

the recent trends. Correctly, the latter realized that the new approaches are closely linked to the actual interests and debates of the international scholarly communities and institutions. Older deficiencies were therefore surmounted by approaches not only to the topics mentioned above but also to other fields of research like the role of media, literature and theatre, science, and above all medical services and medicine during the Great War, as well as cultures of memory after 1918.

2014

From the perspective of a more broad interest in WWI history, the richness of activities presented during the commemorative year of 2014 in Austria was based on impressive preliminary studies. Compared with analyses being presented until 2013, several commentators even questioned the value of a historiography in the wake of the WWI anniversaries at all. Some other critics were very skeptical about the quantity of 2014 publications and exhibitions, wondering whether new insights could be found and scholarly progress in the field could be made altogether. The Austrian weekly *Profil* noted in August 2014 that during this "dizzying memory blitz no one has mentioned the numerous war crimes committed by the Habsburg armies in Galicia and Serbia."[2]

Yet the *Profil* statement was too early. Two months later a book was published which focused exactly on such war atrocities, as well as Austro-Hungarian violations of international conventions in regard to the laws and customs of war, on cruelties, exploitation and failed occupation policies in the Balkans and in the Ukraine, or on the tragedy of refugees and prisoners of war. But even in and before August many other articles, books and conferences presented critical descriptions of Habsburg's last war. Manfried Rauchensteiner reissued an extended version of his *Death of the Double-Headed Eagle*—based on current expert studies—pointing at, among others, new details about the fate of refugees, internees and POWs as well as at the problematic management of the July Crisis of 1914 by the Viennese court and government. Rauchensteiner was not reluctant to blame Franz Joseph personally for unleashing the war, while some authors concentrated on the role of military leaders like Franz Conrad von Hötzendorf, who certainly also has to take his share of the blame.

Nevertheless, resuming this sort of narratives, exponents of a critical historiography of the Habsburg empire agree upon the necessity to avoid—

2 *Profil*, 18 Aug. 2014, 32–35.

after long periods of endeavors to play down or idealize the role of Dual Monarchy—an extreme counter-representation as defined by a sort of a *leyenda negra*, a "black legend." It is important to reject the use of unreliable figures of victims of the Austro-Hungarian conduct of war—as it happened in the past and still happens sometimes—as well as false comparisons with the genocide of the Armenians from 1915 to 1918, with the dimension of totalitarian violence in the 1930s and 1940s, or worst of all the Holocaust.

Apart from this moral and, of course, crucial debate about whether or how a (regular) military conflict can or should be carried out, quite a few scholars are convinced that the commemorative year brought about many activities which resulted in scholarly progress. Apart from the fact that the wider public profited immensely from the impulse for "public history" objects, new approaches to the World War I studies in Austria have come into existence on several fields of research. In this regard, collections of hitherto unknown sources have been presented, and innovative methodical and theoretical approaches, new topics, narratives and interpretations have been brought into focus. Current results have shed new light on front lines and combat zones that were mostly neglected by older studies. For instance, the scholarly community has learned more about the events and developments on the Eastern and the Balkan fronts.

Some experts have focused on the role of the First World War in the history of media and the emergence of various cultures of memory. In many ways, omnibus volumes resembled a scientific industrial fair, if one looks at the catalogues of conferences held and exhibitions organized in Austria. Apart from publications connected with the massive exhibition "Jubel & Elend. Leben mit dem Großen Krieg 1914–1918" at the Schallaburg in Lower Austria,[3] it was Alfred Pfoser's and Andreas Weigl's task to collect roughly sixty innovative contributions dealing with a great variety of WWI themes and including above all home front aspects in a omnibus book about Vienna as the "epicenter of power."[4]

Additionally, there is good reason to assume that "new wine" was filled in "new skins"—to refer the metaphor used at a conference in Graz in the fall of 2014—as the audience was confronted with research trends on two

3 Peter Fritz and Christian Rapp, eds., *Jubel & Elend: Leben mit dem Großen Krieg 1914–1918: Katalog zur Schallaburg-Ausstellung 2014* (Schallaburg: Schallaburg KulturbetriebsgesembH, 2014). Notwithstanding the extensive catalogue of the exhibition see also: Stefan Karner and Philipp Lesiak, eds., *Erster Weltkrieg. Globaler Konflikt – lokale Folgen. Neue Perspektiven* (Innsbruck/Vienna/Bozen: StudienVerlag, 2014).

4 Alfred Pfoser and Andreas Weigl, eds., *Im Epizentrum des Zusammenbruchs: Wien im Ersten Weltkrieg* (Vienna: Metroverlag, 2013).

different levels. First, a younger generation of scholars opposed the remnants of the Habsburg myth against the backdrop of the seminal catastrophe of 1914 to 1918. Second, academic circles and initiators or curators of exhibitions encouraged the population to take part in a widespread quest for sources in private property.

The Schallaburg team made a call for the public to send in personal records, with the result that masses of photos, letters, diaries, mementos and so forth were sent and therefore became available for the exhibition(s). These collections not only represent new sources for different themes, they also help us to reconstruct a more intimate life during the Great War, facing individual and family experiences, even on a global scale. Unlike comparable activities in Great Britain and the United States of America, for example, with its longer tradition to turn to a "history of the ordinary (wo)men," a "history from below," Austria's commemorative year is therefore also a landmark on the way to alternative historical narrations based on a new foundation of recently discovered sources.

Besides, developments in the realm of Digital Humanities paved the way for virtual exhibitions and archives. For instance, Schloß Schönbrunn, together with members of the University of Vienna, worked on a website focusing on World War I.[5]

Many other activities saw Austrian institutions as collaborators when, for example, moving images of various European countries and its archives were united in the "European Film Gateway," encompassing 5,600 newsreels, documentations, features, propaganda and pacifist films, amounting to more than 650 hours of footage. Yet, it should be noted that the vast majority of the Austrian film sources are not integrated in the "European Film Gateway" up to now. Fortunately, there is a collection of three DVDs with a lot of additional footage, edited by the Austrian Film Archives in 2014.[6]

In addition, the national libraries of ten European countries, including Austria, made more than 400,000 objects—books, letters, posters, photos, newspapers, maps, leaflets, medals, coins, propaganda materials and many more—accessible with the digitalization project "Europeana Collections 1914–1918."[7]

---

5 Website *Der Erste Weltkrieg und das Ende der Habsburgermonarchie*, published by Schloß Schönbrunn Kultur- und Betriebsgesellschaft m.b.H.: <http: www.habsburger.net/ersterweltkrieg>

6 Thomas Ballhausen et al., eds., *Krieg der Bilder. Filmdokumente zur Habsburgermonarchie im Ersten Weltkrieg*, three-part DVD edition (Vienna: Filmarchiv Austria, 2014).

7 <http: www.europeana-collections-1914-1918.eu>

Conclusions and suppositions

The conclusion of all these different projects is easy to draw: New wine—metaphorically speaking—came into being in the course of the commemorative year. Apart from innovative interpretations and fields of research, 2014 brought about major impulses for Digital Humanities and Public History in Austria, as well as the accessibility and linkage of hitherto unknown and important sources beyond boundaries. On the one hand, the Alpine Republic is a good example for a concentrated European and global network strengthening historical research and cultures of memory. On the other hand, the enormous number of activities and the intensified commemoration of "Habsburg's final war" is—considering other and above all neighboring countries and successor states of the Dual Monarchy—an Austrian peculiarity without doubt.

This phenomenon requires further deliberations and explanations, perhaps as follows: After 1918, the monarchy as a constitutional system or as a power factor in the form of a monarchist party has not represented a real threat to the republic for many decades. However, it has also been true since the interwar period that Austria's mentality and culture can be described as "monarchical" in many ways and sometimes up to the present. Thence, to look back at a more remote past and not into the dark chapters of civil war, authoritarian and totalitarian rule between 1933 and 1945, even nowadays for many Austrians means to turn into a "world of yesterday" permeated at least to some degree by a traditional "Habsburg myth."The trauma due to the loss of the empire maybe still exists in a transformed manner. Of course not as a fresh wound, causing deep mourning, but as a significant standpoint, to say the (old) (German-)Austria's outlook on the other nations, cultures and countries, as well as the widely unspoken understanding that the important caesura of 1914 with its multitude of implications had many repercussions on further developments—particularly of the Alpine Republic.

Annotation and Select Bibliography

This article is based on the author's presentations, "Old wine in new skins? World War One in Austrian Historiography around the Commemorative Year 2014," held at the International Conference *Histories of 1914. Debates and Use of the Origins of World War One in South Eastern Europe* in Graz, November 2014; "The Memory of World War I after One Hundred Years—The Austrian Perspective," held at the *39th Annual Conference of the German Studies Association* in Washington, D.C., October

2015, and the international conference *Gedenken und (k)ein Ende – Was bleibt vom Jahr 2014? Das Gedenkjahr 1914/2014 und sein historiografisches Vermächtnis* in Vienna, 10–12 Dec 2014 (2nd Biennial Conference of the Forum Österreich-Ungarn im Ersten Weltkrieg in cooperation with the Österreichisches Staatsarchiv and the Österreichische Akademie der Wissenschaften) as well as—among many other publications—on the following selected bibliography:

Allmayer-Beck, Christoph, Peter Broucek, and Manfried Rauchensteiner. "Der Erste Weltkrieg in der Österreichischen Geschichtsschreibung zwischen 1914 und 1984," in *Neue Forschungen zum Ersten Weltkrieg: Literaturberichte und Bibliographien von 30 Mitgliedsstaaten der "Commission internationale d'histoire militaire compare,"* ed. Jürgen Rohwer. Koblenz: Bernard und Graefe, 1985, 267–286.

Bischof, Günter. "Austria's World War I 'Memory Blitz.' The Summer of 2014 was all about 1914," *Austrian Studies Newsmagazine* 26, no. 2 (2014): 14–15.

Eichtinger, Martin. "Austria's Commemoration of World War I," in *Austrian Federalism in Comparative Perspective*, ed. Günter Bischof and Ferdinand Karlhofer (CAS 24). New Orleans/Innsbruck: University of New Orleans Press/*innsbruck* university press, 2014, 214–226.

Jerabek, Rudolf. "Die österreichische Weltkriegsforschung," in *Der Erste Weltkrieg. Wirkung, Wahrnehmung, Analyse*, ed. Wolfgang Michalka. Munich: Piper, 1994, 957–958.

Leidinger, Hannes. "Der Erste Weltkrieg in der Forschung. Entwicklung und Standortbestimmung," in *Jubel & Elend: Leben mit dem Großen Krieg 1914–1918: Katalog zur Schallaburg-Ausstellung 2014*, eds. Peter Fritz and Christian Rapp. Schallaburg: Schallaburg KulturbetriebsgesembH, 2014, 188–193.

Peball, Kurt. "Österreichische Militärhistorische Forschung zum Ersten Weltkrieg zwischen 1918 und 1968," in *Die Auflösung des Habsburgerreiches. Zusammenbruch und Neuorientierung im Donauraum*, eds. Richard Georg Plaschka and Karlheinz Mack. Munich: R. Oldenbourg, 1970, 312–313.

Rauchensteiner, Manfried. "Die Militärgeschichtsschreibung in Österreich nach 1945," in *Militärgeschichte in Deutschland und Österreich vom 18. Jahrhundert bis in die Gegenwart*, ed. Militärgeschichtliches Forschungsamt. Herford/Bonn, 1985, 134–161.

Suppanz, Werner. *Österreichische Geschichtsbilder. Historische Legitimationen in Ständestaat und Zweiter Republik.* Vienna: Böhlau, 1998.

Überegger, Oswald, ed. *Zwischen Nation und Region. Weltkriegsforschung im internationalen Vergleich. Ergebnisse und Perspektiven.* Innsbruck: Wagner, 2004.

---------. *Erinnerungskriege. Der Erste Weltkrieg, Österreich und die Tiroler Kriegserinnerung in der Zwischenkriegszeit.* Innsbruck: Wagner, 2011.

Williamson, Samuel R., Jr. "New Literature on Austria-Hungary and the First World War," in *Austrian Federalism in Comparative Perspective*, ed. Günter Bischof and Ferdinand Karlhofer (CAS 24). New Orleans/Innsbruck: University of New Orleans Press/*innsbruck* university press, 2014, 201–213.

The Eternal Emperor.
Title page of "Viribus unitis. The Book of the Emperor" by Max Herzig (ed.), published on occasion of the 50 year's anniversary of Francis Joseph's accession to the throne.
Design by Kolo Moser.
Chromolithography 1898
Credit: Austrian National Library

Vienna 1900: a world of yesterday, today—and tomorrow?

Steven Beller

In my previous CAS essay of five years ago, I wondered if Vienna 1900 studies could survive the decline of *fin-de-siècle* Vienna as a topic, and find a new explanatory model to rally and bring together the many different approaches to the subject; so far, I do not see one. Instead, I sense a prevailing mood of drift.

The very centrality and significance of Vienna 1900 to modern culture is no longer so evident. One of the best historical books published in the last few years, Jürgen Osterhammel's compendious *Die Verwandlung der Welt: Eine Geschichte des 19. Jahrhunderts* (2009, in English 2014) barely mentions Vienna 1900 at all, treating the Habsburg Monarchy only in passing, as a type of imperial problematic. Another recently published, and well-received, book in which one would have thought Vienna 1900 would be central, Florian Illies's *1913: The Year before the Storm* (2013), does include Vienna, but Vienna is not especially central. It is as though the revolutionary changes in historiography that put Vienna front and center as a capital of modernity in the 1980s have run their course, and things have returned to "normal." The death of Carl E. Schorske in September of this year led to a flurry of laudatory pieces on the doyen of *fin-de-siècle* Vienna's scholarly achievement, as was his due, but this ebbed, and his passing has only added to the sense of his topic's decline.

The sense of nostalgia extends to the silver screen. *Woman in Gold* (2015) was admittedly all about the history of a painting that had been a central icon of the Schorskean world, Gustav Klimt's *Portrait of Adele Bloch-Bauer*, but in the film the painting's story was about the Jewish patroness it depicted, the persecution of her husband and their heirs by the Nazis, and the successful struggle of the surviving heir, Maria Altmann, to reclaim her property despite the resistance of official Austria. This was not about the birth of modernism so much as a backward-looking account of the crimes and injustices of the past against a specific ethnic group, Jews, being put right.

The second major film with a Vienna/Central European-1900 theme was *Grand Budapest Hotel* (2014). Wes Anderson's almost fairy-tale *homage* to a bygone world of Central European sophistication and cultivation, before the horrors of totalitarianism smashed it, did not mention the ethnicity of its protagonists. What was striking about the film from the perspective of Vienna 1900, however, was its completely nostalgic approach, with the action being separated from the modern present by two or even three stages of looking back. This again has nothing much to do with the birth of modernity. Even more discouraging from the point of view of the academic subject, the model on which this historical fantasy was based was not Vienna 1900, or Central Europe 1900, or *fin-de-siècle* Vienna, but rather Zweig's nostalgic and self-deceiving *World of Yesterday*. This was a step backward, not forward, in the popular-cultural understanding of Vienna 1900.

There has been major change in the historiographical context *around* Vienna 1900. The centenary of the First World War's beginning brought forth many reevaluations of the war's origins. The strong implication by Christopher Clark in his *The Sleepwalkers: How Europe went to War in 1914* (2014) that Germany was not primarily responsible for starting the war, but rather that all the great powers in some way were, has had a particularly radical impact. The context of the war's origins now has a much more Southeast and Central European orientation, in which what happened in and around the Habsburg Monarchy is of much more significance than it was when Germany was "to blame" for its efforts to realize its "place in the sun." Political tensions in the Monarchy and between the Monarchy and Serbia have returned to center stage and, although not directly related to the *cultural* history of Vienna 1900, there is definitely an indirect relationship. There is a large paradox to answer: if the Habsburg Monarchy was such a successful engine of pluralist cultural innovation, why was it that its monarch formally started the war that destroyed that very pluralist culture? This additional question should return the spotlight onto the political *and* cultural context of Vienna/Central Europe 1900, but it is yet another question awaiting a good answer.[1]

I might be asking just too much; it is not as if there have not been many good books published in the last few years on aspects of the subject. A certain consolidation, even, of the received opinion is demonstrated in the republication of Christian Brandstätter's stately volume, *Vienna 1900: Art, Life and Culture* (2011). There have also been attempts to bring new perspectives. The two London-based projects I mentioned five years ago, on

1 Pieter Judson, *The Habsburg Empire* (Cambridge, Mass.: Belknap, 2016) was not available at the time of writing.

madness and the coffeehouse respectively (not entirely separate concepts), have both come to fruition as very informative, insightful books: Gemma Blackshaw and Sabine Wieber's *Journeys into Madness* (2012) along with Charlotte Ashby et al.'s *The Viennese Café and Fin-de-siècle Culture* (2013). There was, further, a major exhibit on portraiture in Vienna 1900 in London's National Gallery in 2013–14, with an accompanying publication: Gemma Blackshaw's *Facing the Modern* (2013).

Extending the portraiture theme, one of the more high-profile recent attempts at a new approach has been Eric Kandel's *The Age of Insight* (2012). This explication of the development of modern brain science and its relation to the aesthetics of Vienna 1900 has the merit of reclaiming for Vienna 1900 a prominence in the history of the natural sciences that, as I explained five years ago, was obscured by the concept of *fin-de-siècle* Vienna. It also brings together the culture of Vienna's School of Medicine with that of its School of Art History (especially through the figure of Ernst Kris) in an interesting way. Its treatment of many of the individual figures of Vienna 1900 and the larger cultural context remains somewhat reductive, but then Kandel himself asserts that reductionism is what he is after, in delineating one particular narrative—the origins of brain science—out of the many of which Vienna 1900 is comprised. His synthesis of the aesthetics of the Secession and of the Expressionists with psychoanalysis, art history and brain science is quite impressive, with some Central European polymathic flair, but the book does not in itself provide much more than an interesting sidelight on the main concerns of Vienna 1900.

Some of the most interesting work in the field continues to be done on the Jewish part of the story. Two themes in particular have been prominent. Behind the *Woman in Gold* film was a whole literature about the wealthy Jewish families who were dispossessed and decimated by the Holocaust. Anne-Marie O'Connor's *The Lady in Gold* (2012) details the story on which the film was based, building on the really pioneering work of Hubertus Czernin's *Die Fälschung* (1999). But this is just one of many such tales of a gilded age for Jewish financial and mercantile dynasties cut short by Nazi rapacity: Alexander Waugh's *The House of Wittgenstein* (2009) was among the first of these, and has now been joined by Tim Bonyhady's *Good Living Street* (2011). Perhaps the best of these is Edmund de Waal's *The Hare with the Amber Eyes* (2010), a veritable saga of the Ephrussi clan that takes the reader from dusty Odessa to Renoir's Parisian *Boating Party*, Vienna's *Ringstrasse*, New York, Tokyo, and back to Odessa.

Backing up all of this is the continuing working out of Austria's restitution process, and the ever-remarkable extent to which Viennese modern culture was indeed financed and owned by Jewish families, as detailed by the work of Tina Walzer and Stephan Templ, *Unser Wien* (2001); Sophie Lillie, *Was einmal war* (2003); Melissa Müller and Monika Tatzkow, *Lost Lives, Lost Art* (2010); and the as yet incomplete work of Georg Gaugusch, *Wer einmal war: Das jüdische Großbürgertum Wiens 1800–1938 A–K* (2011) (the second volume's publication is imminent). The restitution meme is unlikely to die down anytime soon, given the controversial fact that the only person imprisoned in recent years regarding the restitution scandal has been, by the strange workings of the Austrian legal system, one of the historians who did most to broach the topic in the first place, Stephan Templ.

There has also been substantial work done on the more creative and intellectual side of Jewish participation in Vienna 1900. Julie M. Johnson's *The Memory Factory* (2012) has reminded us of the significant role of Jewish women artists as pioneers of modern art in Vienna 1900. Hillary Hope Herzog's *Vienna is Different* (2011) and Lisa Silverman's *Becoming Austrians* (2012) both contribute greatly to our understanding of the complex, dialectical role played by Jewish "difference" in forming both Jewish *and* "Austrian" identity. This is a theme well worth comparing with other centers; Mary Gluck's forthcoming *The Invisible Jewish Budapest* will provide just this comparison, a complementary and very stimulating analysis of the analogous Hungarian/Jewish relationship as it formed Budapestian modern culture.

The theme of the complex dialectics of Jewish identity also picks up on themes that Paul Reitter explored in his 2008 work on Karl Kraus, *The Anti-Journalist*. Then again, whatever his Jewish identity, Karl Kraus as a critic of language and the media remains one of the most central figures in Vienna 1900. The fact that his *Fackel* and associated texts have been given a lavish electronic rebooting by Katharina Prager in "Karl Kraus Online" attests (rightly) to Kraus's continued significance to our modern culture. One of the more intriguing new developments in and around Vienna 1900 studies has been the involvement of the author Jonathan Franzen in reintroducing Kraus to contemporary American readers in his *The Kraus Project* (2013)—as a critic of modern media whose insights still bear validity.

This is despite the many ways in which Kraus has been attacked and criticized in recent years as a Jewish anti-Semite, whose so-called campaign for truthful language was just as rhetorical as the literary culture of Young Vienna (and its Jewish writers) that he criticized for their abuse and of the German language—just as Adolf Loos attacked the Secession for its reliance on superficial ornament instead of getting to the truth that lay beneath, in the structures of modern architecture or the expressionist, "x-ray" portraits of his protégé Oskar Kokoschka. One of the stronger versions of this sort of argument against the main protagonists in Allan Janik and Stephen Toulmin's *Wittgenstein's Vienna* (published in 1973), was made by Claude Cernuschi in *Re/Casting Kokoschka: Ethics and Aesthetics, Epistemology and Politics in Fin-De-Siècle Vienna* (2002). Cernuschi details how Wittgenstein's later philosophy contradicts and undermines many of the claims to truth, and hence ethical superiority, of the Schopenhauerian Kraus-Loos-Kokoschka circle that provided Wittgenstein with so many of the aspects of his first philosophy, of the *Tractatus Logico-Philosophicus*.

Questioning the epistemological basis of Kraus's critique of Viennese society and culture, as though that would invalidate Kraus's insights, seems to me, however, a little simplistic and naïve. The same goes for questioning the epistemological basis of Loos's critique of the facades and masks by which Vienna re/presented itself, as though Vienna was not in fact liable to this habit of dissemblance, and had been for centuries. Quoting Wittgenstein 2 to suggest that Loos and Kraus were mistaken in their understanding of truth is an entertaining exercise, but means not very much if we can still show that Kraus and Loos were indeed onto something. In this respect it is amusing to see Kandel take what Cernuschi has to say about the concept of the truth being "inside" rather than on the surface, then completely ignoring Cernuschi's epistemological critique, and blithely seeing this rather as an *insight* that allowed great advances, eventually, in his field of brain science. Cernuschi might have a good point, but it is largely irrelevant to the *history* of Viennese and Central European modern culture.

In his new major work, *Zur Kulturgeschichte Österreichs und Ungarns 1890–1938: Auf der Suche nach verborgenen Gemeinsamkeiten* (2015), William M. Johnston seeks to use Cernuschi's views as a rhetorical scourge of the naysayers of what he sees as the inclusive, pluralist world of the Habsburg (Dual) Monarchy. Yet I am not sure it works. Johnston certainly has much to contribute to creating a new pluralistic, marginocentrist, and Central-European-wide explanatory model to replace *fin-de-siècle* Vienna. His book also brings us all up to speed on a whole mountain of tertiary literature on the subject: essays, think-pieces, articles, reviews, as well as more substantial literature from the more obscure Central European language-cultures, especially Magyar. Consequently, there is a strong emphasis on giving the Hungarian half of the Monarchy its cultural, intellectual and literary due, which is in many regards welcome. Yet the large idiosyncrasies that Johnston's book also displays mean that I doubt that it will be very effective in providing a coherent new direction to the subject.

Johnston is fairly clear, and very well-informed, in laying out the idea of the Monarchy as a space that allowed for all kinds of fruitful cultural interactions because of its remarkable diversity, and the first half of the book is fairly unobjectionable in laying out this pluralist, marginocentrist argument. Where Johnston begins to lose me is in the second half, when he tries to come to his own conclusions about how we should evaluate and explain Central Europe 1900's fecundity and the nature of its cultural achievement. I do not follow his argument about the Central European specialty in "unclassifiable creative figures," nor do I think he deals with the Monarchy's critics (then and now) any better than Cernuschi. If one is attempting to create a new, inclusive paradigm, as Johnston claims, it would seem to mc wiser and more consequential to include the critics along with the proponents, rather than try to disprove, and hence exclude, them. As a meta-theory of Central Europe 1900, Johnston appears to be onto something, but when it gets to the details, it all gets too messy and confusing to be effective. Could this be, perhaps, because a Central-Europe-wide theory that seeks to explain everything in so complex and diverse a region is always bound to be verging on incoherent?

As a new explanatory model, Johnston's paradigm seems to me to fall short, so Vienna (Central Europe) 1900's condition today remains problematic. What of future prospects? There are at least two books and three projects that encourage optimism. Pieter Judson's history of a pluralist Habsburg Empire might provide a more coherent interpretation of the cultural as well as political development of the region; and Mary Gluck's work on Jewish Budapest promises to reintegrate the histories of Vienna and Budapest, and hence Central Europe, by looking, perhaps unsurprisingly, at the Jewish side of Budapestian *popular* culture.

In Vienna itself, Matti Bunzl's appointment as Director of the Vienna Museum promises a renewal of that museum's Viennese identity that should help revivify Vienna 1900 as a concept. Also in Vienna, the forthcoming creation of a "House of History Austria" that concentrates on Austrian history in the last century and a half, from the first modernity to the second, as it were, should also bring new thinking about Vienna 1900's place in history. The framework of the two modernities—from 1850 and from 1980—suggests that Vienna 1900 will not have its former primacy, as modernity is seen as coming from elsewhere (à la Osterhammel), but that still leaves Vienna 1900 in a significant place between modernities, and the project's prospectus gives Vienna 1900 a large place in the museum's purview. Interestingly enough, it calls for all the major concepts of Vienna 1900 to be included in the museum's treatment: the Schorskean emphasis on generations, the Czakian emphasis on plurality and multi-ethnicity, and the Beller/LeRider emphasis on the Jewish aspect. We should keep an eye on how that develops.

It is a third, related project that holds out the best hope for a fruitful reevaluation or revitalization of our understanding of Vienna 1900. Radmila Schweitzer has been promoting a project, The Wittgenstein Initiative, for several years, with the advice of Allan Janik and Ray Monk among others, and it is now gaining some momentum in Vienna. It sometimes appears as a fool's errand, but I think there is a brilliant idea in here. Building off the version of Vienna 1900 outlined in *Wittgenstein's Vienna*, Schweitzer's idea is to reintroduce to Vienna the memory, and one hopes the spirit, of intellectual inquiry and cultural innovation that marked Vienna 1900, and reached its apotheosis in the philosophy of Ludwig Wittgenstein, versions 1 *and* 2. It is a hard sell in today's Vienna, where Wittgenstein never quite had the aura that he has elsewhere. Yet who could be a better symbol for Vienna 1900? A scion of a Protestant father and a Catholic mother, both of Jewish descent, who were great patrons of the arts and music, as well as the father being one of the great industrialists of the age, Ludwig Wittgenstein created one philosophy that was at least partly inspired by the critical modernists of Vienna 1900 around Kraus and Loos, and then created another that, in its multifaceted approach to interpretation and its emphasis on the derivation of meaning from language *use*, was about as Central European, even Austrian, a philosophy as one could wish for. This strikes me as the proper symbol, and the proper context, to bring forward our understanding of Vienna 1900.

The Wittgensteinian perspective suggests that, ultimately, the inclusive pluralism of the Monarchy, its diversity as well as its cross-fertilization, was not in opposition to its critical side, rather the inclusive and the critical sides were two sides of the same marginocentric phenomenon, and at the center of that phenomenon was the region's most prominent marginal group, whether in Austria or Hungary, Vienna 1900 or Budapest 1900: Central European Jewry. If the Wittgenstein Initiative can build on that insight, then there may be a tomorrow for Vienna 1900 after all.

Select Bibliography

Ashby, C., T. Gronberg and S. Shaw-Miller, eds. *The Viennese Café and Fin-de-siècle Culture*. New York: Berghahn, 2013.

Blackshaw, G., and S. Wieber, eds. *Journeys into Madness: Mapping Mental Illness in the Austro-Hungarian Empire*. New York: Berghahn, 2012.

Blackshaw, G., ed. *Facing the Modern: The Portrait in Vienna 1900*. London: National Gallery, 2013.

Bonyhady, T. *Good Living Street: Portrait of a Patron Family, Vienna 1900.* Crow's Nest: Allen and Unwin, 2011.

Brandstätter, C., ed. *Vienna 1900: Art, Life and Culture.* New York: Vendome, 2011.

Cernuschi, C. *Re/Casting Kokoschka: Ethics and Aesthetics, Epistemology and Politics in Fin-De-Siècle Vienna.* Madison: Fairleigh Dickinson UP, 2002.

Clark, C. *The Sleepwalkers: How Europe went to War in 1914.* New York: Harper, 2014.

Czernin, H. *Die Fälschung.* Vienna: Czernin, 1999.

Franzen, J. *The Kraus Project.* New York: Farrar, Straus and Giroux, 2013.

Gaugusch, G. *Wer einmal war: Das jüdische Großbürgertum Wiens 1800–1938 A–K.* Vienna: Amalthea, 2011.

Gluck, M. *The Invisible Jewish Budapest Metropolitan Culture at the Fin de* Siècle. Madison: Univ. of Wisconsin, forthcoming.

Herzog, H. H. *Vienna is Different: Jewish Writers in Austria from the Fin de Siècle to the Present.* New York: Berghahn, 2011.

Illies, F. *1913: The Year before the* Storm. Brooklyn: Melville House, 2013.

Johnson, J.M. *The Memory Factory: The Forgotten Women Artists of Vienna 1900.* West Lafayette: Purdue UP, 2012.

-------. *Zur Kulturgeschichte Österreichs und Ungarns 1890-1938: Auf der Suche nach verborgenen* Gemeinsamkeiten. Vienna: Böhlau, 2015.

Judson, P. *The Habsburg Empire.* Cambridge, Mass.: Belknap, 2016.

Kandel, E. *The Age of Insight: The Quest to Understand the Unconscious in Art, Mind, and Brain, from Vienna 1900 to the Present.* New York: Random House, 2012.

Lillie, S. *Was einmal war. Die enteigneten Kunstsammlungen Wiens.* Vienna: Czernin, 2003.

Müller, M., and M. Tatzkow. *Lost Lives, Lost Art: Jewish Collectors, Nazi Art Theft, and the Quest for Justice.* New York: Vendome, 2010.

O'Connor, Anne-Marie. *The Lady in Gold: The Extraordinary Tale of Klimt's Masterpiece, Portrait of Adèle Bloch-Bauer.* New York: Knopf, 2012.

Osterhammel, J. *Die Verwandlung der Welt: Eine Geschichte des 19. Jahrhunderts.* Munich: Beck, 2009 (in English 2014).

Prager, K. "Karl Kraus Online," October 2015 <http:www.kraus. wienbibliothek.at>.

Reitter, P. *The Anti-Journalist: Karl Kraus and Jewish Self-Fashioning in Fin-de-Siècle Europe.* Chicago: University of Chicago, 2008.

Silverman, L. *Becoming Austrians: Jews and Culture between the World Wars.* Oxford: Oxford UP, 2012.

de Waal, E. *The Hare with the Amber Eyes*. New York: Farrar, Straus and Giroux, 2010.

Walzer, T., and S. Templ, *Unser Wien. 'Arisierung' auf österreichisch*. Berlin: Aufbau, 2001.

Waugh, A. *The House of Wittgenstein: A Family at War*. New York: Doubleday, 2009.

New Government.
Minister Sebastian Kurz, Vice Chancellor Michael Spindelegger, Chancellor Werner Faymann, Minister Johanna Mikl-Leitner, and Minister Rudolf Hundstorfer before the Meeting of the Council of Ministers on occasion of the inauguration of the SPÖ-ÖVP government at the Office of the Austrian Federal President.
Vienna, Roland Schlager, 12 16 2013
Credit: APA PictureDesk

Political Culture in Austria

Peter A. Ulram

By political culture we understand systematic patterns of orientations, which are important for the behavior of the members of a polity and their attitudes towards the political system. These patterns of orientations can be consonant with (the functional prerequisites of) a given or developing political system, which then contribute to the system's stability. If not, they can be a source of political instability.[1]

Postwar Austria: Building a New Consensus

After 1945 the reborn Austrian republic was faced with political culture legacies that posed considerable problems for the consolidation of a small democratic nation state. The first was the question of national identity. While most Austrians favored independent statehood (not only due to the occupation by the Allied Powers, but also due to their negative experiences in the German Third Reich), it was not clear whether they considered themselves to be a part of the German nation or a proper nation. In 1956, opinions were divided on this issue and as late as 1980 about one third—mostly those born and socialized between 1938 and 1945—still thought that the *Anschluss* had brought "a natural connection with the German people."[2] The second problem was tensions stemming from the mutual aversion and mistrust between the two (social-democratic and Christian-conservative)

1 Oscar W. Gabriel, "Citizens Politics: Das Konzept und seine wissenschaftliche Bedeutung," in *Deutschland, Österreich und die Schweiz im neuen Europa. Bürger und Politik*, ed. Oscar W. Gabriel and Fritz Plasser (Baden-Baden: Nomos, 2010). For the concept of political culture see the seminal works by Gabriel A. Almond and Sidney Verba, eds., *The Civic Culture: Political Attitudes and Democracy in Five Nations* (Newbury Park/London/New Delhi: Sage, 1989); and Gabriel A. Almond and Sidney Verba, eds., *The Civic Culture Revisited* (Newbury Park/London/New Delhi: Sage, 1989). Central to this article is the notion that political culture is not static but subject to change and influenced by political action.

2 Peter A. Ulram and Svila Tributsch, "Das österreichische Geschichtsbewusstsein und seine Geschichte," in *Geschichte und Identität*, ed. Franz Schausberger (Vienna: Böhlau, 2008), 41–43.

socio-political subcultures or camps ("*Lager*"),[3] which had led to constant conflicts, civil war, and dictatorship in the First Republic. The third problem was authoritarian orientations, not only an inheritance from the NS-era, but often reaching back to Habsburg and interwar times (antiparliamentarism, subject culture or *Untertanenmentalität*, a view of democracy as a mere means to reach political goals, rather than a value and end in itself).

The dominating parties (ÖVP and SPÖ) responded to these challenges with cooperation and power sharing in the fields of government, labor relations, public administration and the vast state-owned sector of the economy, as well as a policy of political, social and organizational integration, at the same time marginalizing other political forces (Communists and German National VdU/FPÖ). Austria became a party state including a vast and deep-reaching spoils system, involving the distribution of material benefits to party adherents and a political penetration of the state apparatus and the media. After the first turbulent years, political participation was highly formalized and routinized, concentrating on voting and party-centered activities[4] (turnout in national elections amounted to over ninety percent, about one quarter of the adult population were party members) leaving little space for unconventional activities. Not surprisingly, the sense of both internal (subjective competence) and external (responsiveness of institutions and public functionaries) political efficacy was low. But politicians were regarded as trying hard for their voters and doing a good job. Austrians felt that "officials and politicians ignore them but can be trusted to do what is right and care for a common collective good."[5]

Together with strong economic growth, rising standards of living and the expansion of the welfare state, this strategy proved successful: the fringe parties lost much of their initial electoral support, tensions between the camps lessened, allowing later for a smooth transition from great coalition to single party governments, and national consciousness consolidated.[6]

A Civic Culture with Some Flaws

Success often comes with a price, and some features of the first decades of the Austrian Republic brought new problems for a civic culture in

3 Gerhard Lehmbruch, *Proporzdemokratie: Politisches System und Politische Kultur in der Schweiz und in Österreich* (Tübingen: Mohr, 1967); Bingham Powell Jr., *Social Fragmentation and Political Hostility: An Austrian Case Study* (Stanford: Stanford University Press, 1979).

4 Sidney Verba, et. al., *Participation and Equality. A Seven Nations Comparison* (Cambridge: Cambridge University Press, 1978).

5 Alan Marsh, *Political Action in Europa and the USA*, abridged edition of *Political Action* (Houndmills/London: Palgrave Macmillan, 1990), 167.

6 Peter A. Ulram and Svila Tributsch, *Kleine Nation mit Eigenschaften. Das Verhältnis der Österreicher zu sich selbst und zu ihren Nachbarn* (Vienna: Molden, 2004).

the years to come. The established structures of the parties and the big professional organizations (like trade unions and chambers with compulsory membership) and the entrenched behavioral patterns of the political elite, e.g. paternalism and frozen routines, were not well-suited to new values and aspirations of an increasing number of people. In the 1980s, old emotional political bonds began to loosen and wither away, and political interest and feelings of civic competence began to grow. New issues (environmentalism, discontent about bureaucracy, tax burden, the spoils system, and later immigration) entered the political arena. One finds a widening gap between perceived internal and external political efficacy.[7] In the years between 1974 and 2005, whereas citizens become more self-confident and want to have more say in political matters, they also consider the political system closed, unresponsive to their demands, and fossilized (see Table 1). The consequences are twofold: on the one hand, conventional participation like voting and engagement, as well as membership in parties and professional organizations, declines (see Table 2); on the other, anger and dissatisfaction increase. This gap becomes reinforced by the return of great coalition governments which—undeniable achievements notwithstanding—provide a fertile ground for resentments and oppositional movements of various inspirations.[8] Populist appeals against the "political class," more often than not in accordance with and driven by media and newsroom-populism,[9] are on the upswing. The image of politics and politicians—mostly associated with the two incumbent parties—has worsened considerably: the former appear less capable of handling and resolving important problems, and the latter are seen remote from their constituencies and less productive (see Table 3).[10]

Deficits in process culture and a lower level of political trust have no visible effects on the identification with the political community. National consciousness and national pride become even stronger, sometimes accompanied with introspective and isolationist tendencies. Although

7 Fritz Plasser and Peter A. Ulram, "Bürger und Politik in Österreich," in *Deutschland, Österreich und die Schweiz*, ed. Gabriel and Plasser.

8 Peter A. Ulram, *Hegemonie und Erosion. Politische Kultur und Politischer Wandel in* Österreich (Vienna: Böhlau, 1990).

9 Fritz Plasser and Peter A. Ulram, "Striking a Responsive Chord: Mass Media and Right-Wing Populism in Austria," in *The Media and Neo-Populism: A Contemporary Analysis*, ed. Gianpietro Mazzoleni, Julianne Stewart, and Bruce Horsefield (Westport/London: Praeger, 2003).

10 Note that the image of politicians was always ambiguous. They were seen as striving for personal benefits, often open to corruption, and distant from the "common people." However, the idea of a "political class" did not gain a footing in Austria until their substantive performance was questioned.

Austrians voted by a large majority for the country's EU-accession, they did not develop an emotional attachment to the EU, but rather combined a pragmatic view with mental reservation.[11] More important, dissatisfaction in some areas has not challenged the core values of a democratic political culture. Civil rights, democratic procedures and political tolerance are values shared by a vast majority.[12] Compared to the postwar years, Austrians also seem to be more ready to take personal risks to defend these principles should they be endangered (see Table 4). There is quite a lot of support for more direct democracy and unconventional participation (mostly referenda and grass-root activities), but authoritarian alternatives do not strike a responsive chord.

Table 1: Political Interest and Political Efficacy (1974–2005)

in percent	1974	1981	1984/5	1989	1996	2001	2005
I am very much or rather much interested in politics			24	27	31	33	32
I think that I am able to fulfill a political function as well as other people (a)				38	43	44	46
Sometimes politics are so complicated that people like me can't understand what's going on (a)	26	23		30	42	40	33
People like me have no influence on what the government does (b)	18		26	24	32	25	33
Parties are only interested in votes, they don't care about what voters think (b)	24		25	26	21	22	18
Politicians don't care much about what people like me think (b)	27		26	23	26	23	18

(a): internal efficacy: percent agreeing with (able to)/rejecting (can't understand) the statement.

b): external efficacy: percent rejecting the statement.

Source: POLITICAL ACTION (1974); GfK-AUSTRIA, Political Indicators (representative surveys 1981–2005)

11 Fritz Plasser and Peter A. Ulram, "Ungeliebt aber unverzichtbar. Die Österreicher und die EU," in *Europa als Prozess, 15 Jahre Europäische Union und Österreich*, ed. Roman Pfefferle, Nadja Schmidt, and Gerd Walchers (Vienna/Berlin: LIT, 2010). But emotional distance and dissatisfaction notwithstanding, there was never a majority of Austrians for leaving the EU or the EURO.

12 Plasser and Ulram, "Bürger und Politik in Österreich," in *Die österreichische Demokratie im Vergleich*, eds. Ludger Helms and David Wineroither (Baden-Baden: Nomos, 2012).

Table 2: Conventional Participation (1945/1966–2006/2013)

average percent per period	1945-66	1970-86	1990-2002	2006-2013
Voting turnout (national parliamentary elections)	95	92.1	85.7	77.1
Party membership (survey data)	38	23	15	10

Table 3: Politicians and Politics: Capacity and Care (1981–2011)

in percent	1981	1989	1996	2005	2010	2011
Politicians are trying hard for their voters (rejection of the statement)	37				52	
By and large politicians are doing a good job (rejection of the statement)	30	55			50	
Austrian politics are failing always or often in crucial matters	33	43	45	42	56	71

Source: IFES (1981), GfK-AUSTRIA (1989–2005), MMO (2010, 2011), Representative Surveys

Table 4: What Is Worth Fighting For (1955 and 2004)

in percent	would rather fight to preserve		would rather live in peace and risk to lose	
	1955	2004	1955	2004
Personal freedom of Austrians	56	88	36	9
Human dignity and respect for the individual	46	85	43	11
Democracy	40	83	48	13
National independence of Austria	50	71	41	24
Freedom of religion	33	55	55	40
Independence of other West European countries	17	35	74	58

Source: INSTITUT FÜR MARKTFORSCHUNG (DR. FESSEL INSTITUT), USIS Barometer Study (1955), GfK-AUSTRIA, Österreichische Identität (2004)

Democracy, the Only Game in Town

"Attitudinally a democratic regime is consolidated when a strong majority of public opinion holds the belief that democratic procedures and institutions are the most appropriate way to govern the collective life in a society such as theirs ... democracy becomes the only game in town ... even in the face of a severe political and economic crisis."[13] If the proof of the pudding is in the eating, the financial and economic crisis labeled "the great contraction" by Reinhard and Rogoff[14] can serve as a yardstick. In 2009, Austria suffered from the worst recession since 1945, bringing a decline of the gross national product and a concomitant rise of unemployment. Furthermore, both the assessment of the economic situation and the outlook for economic and labor market development were the gloomiest seen in recent decades.[15] Not so the development of satisfaction with democracy. In the same year, twenty-five percent of Austrians complained about the way democracy worked in their country, the number of dissatisfied persons lay well below the prior level (thirty-four percent on the average between 1995 and 2005) (See Table 5). The same holds true for the evaluation of democratic efficacy: thirteen percent expressed doubts about the capability of democracy to solve the problems the country was facing, less than in the late 1990s. Most of all, doubts or discontent did not prejudice the principle preference for democracy as a form of government. In every year between 1987 and 2009, about nine out of ten Austrians considered democracy to be preferable to authoritarianism in any case ("democrats" following the typology of Linz and Stepan).[16] Five percent thought that dictatorship might be better under certain circumstances ("authoritarians"), and the same percentage said that for people like them it made no difference whether they lived under a democratic or an authoritarian regime ("alienated"). Among the unemployed and persons who were afraid to lose their jobs or showed pessimism about the economic perspectives, one finds more "worried" and "dissatisfied" democrats (i.e. people who prefer democracy but doubt its capability to solve problems or are not satisfied with the way it is working) as well as an above-the-average share of the "alienated" type, but not more "authoritarians" (See Table 6).

---

13 Juan J. Linz and Alfred Stepan, *Problems of Democratic Transition and Consolidation. Southern Europa, South America and Post-Communist Europe* (Baltimore/London: John Hopkins University Press, 1996), 5.

14 Carmen M. Reinhart and Kenneth Rogoff, *This Time is Different. Eight Centuries of Financial Folly* (Princeton: Princeton University Press, 2009).

15 *Consumer Confidence Barometer* (Brussels: European Commission, since 1995) and *Wirtschaftsbarometer* (Linz: Spectra, since 1995) for long-reaching time-series data on economic sentiments.

16 Linz and Stepan, *Problems of Democratic Transition and Consolidation.*

According to conventional wisdom, an economic crisis should trigger political extremism or radicalism. Due to the lack of a sizeable number of left-wing extremists, the main suspect(s) in Austria would be the FPÖ (and its later break-away, the BZÖ). Although these parties are rather more Nativist right-wing populists[17] than outspoken extremists, they are located on the very right of the political spectrum, and in the 1990s nearly four out of ten Austrians described the position of the FPÖ as "very right" too.[18] FPÖ and BZÖ had their hitherto best results in national parliamentary elections in 1999, a year without grave economic problems, and in 2008, when economic pessimism started to rise but had not reached its later peak. In 2009, they gained votes in the European parliamentary elections, but remained well below their former top results. Furthermore, exit polls conducted on both election days showed that economic or employment issues played practically no role as voting motives for them. In these, as in previous elections, the FPÖ/BZÖ-vote was mainly motivated by a general rejection of the incumbents, a hope for political change, discontent with the EU, corruption and featherbedding, the immigration issue, and a positive view of the top candidates.[19]

To gain a deeper insight in the political impact of the crisis, Ulram and Kalinowski[20] conducted a multivariate analysis of factors determining voting

---

17 Hannes Betz, *Right-Wing Populism in Western Europe* (New York: Palgrave, 1994); Herbert Kitschelt, *The Radical Right in Western Europe. A Comparative Analysis* (Ann Arbor: Palgrave, 1995); Plasser and Ulram, "Striking a Responsive Chord"; Reinhard Heinisch, "The Austrian Freedom Party: A Phenomenon in International Comparison—Success and Failure of Identitarian Populism," in *Österreichische Zeitschrift für Politikwissenschaft* 33, no. 3 (2004): 247–61. A different view is offered by Sonja Puntscher-Riekmann, "The Politics of *Ausgrenzung*, the Nazi-Past and the European Dimension of the New Right in Austria," in CAS 7, 78–105.

18 For representative surveys see *Political Indicators* (Vienna: GfK Austria, 1976–2009). Percent giving the FPÖ the value 5 on a 5-point-scale reaching from 1=very left to 5=very right.

19 An analysis of economic growth, economic sentiments and the FPÖ-vote in national parliamentary elections from 1975 to 2013 shows no correlation between FPÖ-results and economic conditions and sentiments. This runs contrary to the findings of Markus Brückner and Hans Peter Grüner, "Economic Growth and the Rise of Political Extremism: Theory and Evidence," *CEPR Discussion Paper* No.7723 (2010): four for sixteen OECD-countries between 1970 and 2002: "Our main finding is a negative and significant effect of per capita GDP growth on the support for extreme political parties. ... There is a clear effect on the support for extreme right-wing parties." However, the results are only on aggregate (sixteen countries) level and the effects of the economic and financial crisis 2008–2009 are not included.

20 Peter A. Ulram and Gerd Kalinowski, "Determinanten des Wahlverhaltens II" (unpublished paper, Vienna 2010). The analysis is based on representative telephone surveys in the years 2007–2009 (18,000 respondents for every year) using multinominal logistic regression. Explaining variables were sociodemographics (age, gender, education), periods (pre-crisis, crisis, post-crisis), economic pessimism and the combined variable period and economic pessimism. The explained variable was voting preferences for FPÖ, SPÖ, ÖVP and GREENS, more precisely the probabilities ("odds") for the respective preferences. Prospective economic pessimism was selected among various economic climate indicators as the factor having the strongest impact.

preferences. Generally, the explanatory power of economic sentiments was rather low, especially in case of the FPÖ-vote. But there was an important difference between the period of economic stability before the crisis and the peak of the crisis. In the pre-crisis period, when an optimistic outlook prevailed in the country, those worried about the economic situation showed a higher probability to cast a vote for the FPÖ. During the crisis and to a lesser degree when economic tensions eased off again (post-crisis), the worried ones showed a significantly lower probability to vote for the FPÖ and a higher probability to favor the traditional parties (ÖVP and SPÖ).

Table 5: Democratic Consciousness (1987–2013)

Critical or negative attitudes in percent	1987	1995	1996	1997	1998
Not satisfied with the way democracy works in Austria		36	29	39	35
Democracy is not able to solve the problems our country is facing				25	
For people like me it makes no difference whether they live in a democracy or a dictatorship	3		6		
A dictatorship can be better than a democracy under certain circumstances	5		5		

Critical or negative attitudes in percent	1999	2001	2005	2009	2013
Not satisfied with the way democracy works in Austria	23	28	30	25	26
Democracy is not able to solve the problems our country is facing	23	15		13	
For people like me it makes no difference whether they live in a democracy or a dictatorship	3	3		5	
A dictatorship can be better than a democracy under certain circumstances	5	3		5	

Source: GfK-AUSTRIA and EUROBAROMETER, Representative Surveys (1987–2013)

Table 6: Democracy Typology and Crisis Indicators (2009)

in percent*	Confident Democrats	Worried Democrats	Satisfied Democrats	Dissatisfied Democrats	(all) Democrats
Total Austria	80	9	70	20	90
Actually or recently unemployed	77	13	64	28	92
Afraid to lose their job	65	18	46	38	84
Unemployment will rise	80	10	70	20	90
Economic situation will get worse	75	14	69	21	90

in percent*	Alienated	Authoritarians
Total Austria	5	5
Actually or recently unemployed	8	1
Afraid to lose their job	13	4
Unemployment will rise	5	5
Economic situation will get worse	7	5

* Difference to 100% = no response or rounding difference

Confident/Worried Democrats: Prefer democracy and believe/do not believe that democracy can solve problems. Satisfied/Dissatisfied Democrats: Prefer democracy and are satisfied/dissatisfied about the way democracy works. “Democrat”: Agree with the statement: “Democracy is better than dictatorship in any case.”

Source: GfK-AUSTRIA, Bevölkerungsbarometer (2009)

Summing up the empirical evidence, one finds that the FPÖ feeds mainly on resentments and discontent of various kinds, among them economic dissatisfaction, especially under conditions of a stable or improving economic situation. But in a real crisis, when the general level of economic anxiety is very high, those who are most preoccupied with the economy are especially looking for more reliable actors. During the only grave economic crisis in recent times, right wing populism did not flourish, and even more important, democratic consciousness did not weaken, which is the central attitudinal characteristic of a consolidated democracy.

Conclusion

Within Austria's political culture is a civic culture with merits and flaws. Many problematic legacies from the past, which were still present in the first postwar decades, have been overcome or at least significantly reduced. Most of all, antidemocratic orientations are confined to small minorities while the overwhelming majority strongly supports democracy, its rules and basic values, and there are functioning barriers against succumbing to authoritarian solutions even in difficult economic times. Citizens now feel better-informed and more competent than in former years, and at the same time, they have become more critical about perceived shortcomings of traditional politics and politicians. On the other hand, conventional participation has decreased, the gap between internal and external efficacy has widened, and populist appeals sometimes obtain a sympathetic hearing. In this Austria is no exceptional case. Many other European countries, both long-standing and new, post-authoritarian democracies, display similar traits, ranging from a lack of trust in political elites, to a decrease of traditional alignments and participation, to thriving negative voting.

List of Authors

Steven Beller is a historian who resides in Washington, D.C.

Günter Bischof is the Marshall Plan Professor of History and the Director of Center Austria: Austrian Marshall Plan Center for European Studies at the University of New Orleans (UNO).

Emil Brix is the Austrian Ambassador in the Russian Federation and deputy chairman of the Institute for the Danube Region and Central Europe in Vienna.

John Deak is an assistant professor in the Department of History as well as a Fellow of the Nanovic Institute for European Studies at the University of Notre Dame.

Gerda Falkner is Director of the Institute for European Integration Research at the University of Vienna.

Bernhard Fetz is Director of the Literary Archives of the Austrian National Library and also the Founding Director of the Austrian Literature Museum.

Dagmar Herzog is Distinguished Professor of History and Daniel Rose Faculty Scholar at the Graduate Center, City University of New York.

Ferdinand Karlhofer is an associate professor and chair in the Department of Political Science at the University of Innsbruck.

Tim Kirk is a professor of European history at Newcastle University.

Hannes Leidinger is teaching history at Universities of Berne, Budapest, Salzburg, and particularly Vienna.

Paul Luif was research fellow at the Austrian Institute for International Affairs 1980–2013. He is Lecturer at the Department of Political Science, University of Vienna.

Charles Maier is the Leverett Saltonstall Professor of History at Harvard University.

Anton Pelinka is a professor of political science and nationalism studies at the Central European University in Budapest.

Fritz Plasser is a retired professor of political science at the University of Innsbruck.

Oliver Rathkolb is Professor of history in the Department of Contemporary History at the University of Vienna.

Peter Ruggenthaler is a senior researcher at the Ludwig Boltzmann Institute for Research on Consequences of War in Graz.

Alexander Smith is a doctoral candidate in economic history and political science at the University of Innsbruck.

Barbara Stelzl-Marx is Deputy Director at the Ludwig Boltzmann Institute for Research on Consequences of War (BIK) in Graz and vice president of the Austrian UNESCO-Commission.

Peter A. Ulram is a political and social scientist who worked for many years as a public opinion and market researcher with Fessel GfK, GfK Austria, and ecoquest.

Reinhold Wagnleitner is an amateur musician and retired Professor of modern history at the University of Salzburg.

David M. Wineroither is Austrian Visiting Professor in the Department of Political Science at the University of Alberta.

Paul M. Zulehner is a retired professor of sociology at the Theological Faculty at the University of Vienna. He was teaching in Bamberg, Passau, Bonn and Salzburg. Member of the Austrian and the European Academy of Science.

Contemporary Austrian Studies

Günter Bischof, Anton Pelinka/Fritz Plasser/Ferdinand Karlhofer, Editors

Volume 1 (1992)
Austria in the New Europe

Volume 2 (1993)
The Kreisky Era in Austria
Oliver Rathkolb, Guest Editor

Volume 3 (1994)
Austria in the Nineteen Fifties
Rolf Steininger, Guest Editor

Volume 4 (1995)
Austro-Corporatism: Past—Present—Future

Volume 5 (1996)
Austrian Historical Memory & National Identity

Volume 6 (1997)
Women in Austria
Erika Thurner, Guest Editor

Volume 7 (1998)
The Vranitzky Era in Austria
Ferdinand Karlhofer, Guest Editor

Volume 8 (1999)
The Marshall Plan in Austria
Dieter Stiefel, Guest Editor

Volume 9 (2000)
Neutrality in Austria
Ruth Wodak, Guest Editor

Volume 10 (2001)
Austria and the EU
Michael Gehler, Guest Editor

Volume 11 (2002)
The Dollfuss/Schuschnigg Era in Austria: A Reassessment
Alexander Lassner, Guest Editor

Volume 12 (2003)
The Americanization/ Westernization of Austria

Volume 13 (2004)
Religion in Austria
Hermann Denz, Guest Editor

Volume 14 (2005)
Austrian Foreign Policy in Historical Perspective
Michael Gehler, Guest Editor

Volume 15 (2006)
Sexuality in Austria
Dagmar Herzog, Guest Editor

Volume 16 (2007)
The Changing Austrian Voter

Volume 17 (2008)
New Perspectives on Austrians and World War II
Barbara Stelzl-Marx, Guest Editor

Volume 18 (2009)
The Schüssel Era in Austria

Volume 19 (2010)
From Empire to Republic: Post-World War I Austria

Volume 20 (2011)
Global Austria: Austria's Place in Europe and the World
Alexander Smith, Guest Editor

Volume 21 (2012)
Austrian Lives
Eva Maltschnig, Guest Editor

Volume 22 (2013)
Austria's International Position after the End of the Cold War

Volume 23 (2014)
1914: Austria-Hungary, the Origins, and the First Year of World War I
Samuel R. Williamson, Jr., Guest Editor

Volume 24 (2015)
Austrian Federalism in Comparative Perspective